THE ANGELIC
Assassin

ANOTHER LUKE TREMAYNE ADVENTURE

THE ANGELIC Assassin

CRIMINALS AND CONSPIRATORS
LONDON 1652

GEOFF QUAIFE

ARPress

ARPress
45 Dan Road Suite 36
Canton MA 02021

Hotline: 1(800) 220-7660
Fax: 1(855) 752-6001

Ordering Information:
Quantity sales. Special discounts are available on quantity purchases by corporations, associations, and others. For details, contact the publisher at the address above.

Printed in the United States of America.

ISBN-13:   Softcover   979-8-89356-769-4
                 eBook   979-8-89356-770-0
                 Hardback   979-8-89389-395-3

Library of Congress Control Number: 2024916231

THE LUKE TREMAYNE ADVENTURES

(In chronological order of the events portrayed)

SOME LEADING CHARACTERS

The English Army

Luke Tremayne (Colonel)	Cromwell's special agent
Harry Lloyd (Captain)	Tremayne's deputy
Andrew Ford	Luke's senior sergeant
John Halliwell (Captain)	Commander, Cromwell's bodyguard

Inhabitants of The Angel

Adam Dale	Wealthy yeoman
Temperance Dale	Adam's wife
Margaret Dale	Adam's sister
Robert Chidlow	Adam's steward
Rose Chidlow	Robert's wife
Rowland Hille (Sir)	Displaced gentleman
Grenville Reeves	Temperance's half-brother
Samuel Wright	Manager of the inn

Others

Miles Baker	Magistrate and politician
Valentine Cole	London entrepreneur
Matthew Craven	Lawyer
Katherine Craven (Old Kate)	A seer
Brian Kendall (Captain)	Showman and soldier
Jasper Nettle (Major)	Officer, London militia
Harcourt Reeves (Sir)	Grenville's father
Cassandra Reeves (Lady)	Harcourt's third wife
Claude, Comte de Sauvel	French naval captain
Emile Tournac	Lawyer

Real Historical Personages

Oliver Cromwell	Lord General of the Commonwealth of England
Thomas Harrison	Senior General and a supporter of religious radicals
Sieur Gentillot	French Envoy to England 1651-2

HISTORICAL PROLOGUE

WITH THE EXECUTION of Charles I in January 1649 England was declared a republic and ruled by a remnant of the House of Commons, popularly known as the Rump. This group annually elected a Council of State which controlled foreign and domestic policy, and was responsible for the security of the young republic. This security was provided by the national army led by Oliver Cromwell— an army increasingly disillusioned by the inactivity of its parliamentary masters. On 3 September 1651 Cromwell defeated Charles II at Worcester. This defeat put an end to effective Royalist activity forcing the King into exile for almost a decade. The victorious army now turned its attention to the perceived incompetence of the Rump. Tension between the army leadership and the parliament rapidly escalated. Both sides, army and parliament, prepared for potential conflict.

 **1**

NORTHERN OUTSKIRTS OF LONDON, AUGUST 1651

SOMETHING WAS AMISS. The government was convinced that goods which passed through the northern parishes of St. Aiden and St. Michael were avoiding payment of the excise. Yet the three excise men sent to investigate the problem, Henry Elks and his assistants John and James Porter, found no evidence of malpractice due in large part to the cunning and lack of co-operation from the local community. The situation improved when, armed with full purses, the government agents resorted to bribery. They set out to buy the information they needed from the drunken sots that inhabited the dissolute alehouses of St. Aiden. At Widow Ketley's notorious establishment a fat man with a ruddy face and enormous paunch was targeted by James, the most outgoing and most obnoxious of the government team. James continually refilled the man's fast emptying tankard from a large jug he had purchased from Widow Ketley's buxom daughter. This saucy barmaid's demeanour had already weakened James's concentration on the task in hand. Her bulging breasts invited later exploration. Bess Ketley was a timbersome wench and given his silver laden purse, James fully expected she would not reject a cuddle-me-cuddle later in the evening.

The fat man was becoming more amenable. James pushed his advantage by placing a small silver coin into the man's free hand as he refilled the tankard yet again. James was anxious to pursue a possible explanation for the agents' failure to apprehend a single excise avoider. 'Is there a way for wagons to move in and out of the city through this area and avoid the highway?'

The fat drunkard signalled for James to sit with him on a low bench at the far end of the room. The lascivious James was already assessing its suitability for a quick cuddle with the brazen Bess, but he was immediately brought back to the task at hand. His cupshot victim was no fool where money was concerned. 'A silver coin buys you very little my boy.' James was not impressed. 'Don't fool with me friend. A silver coin will keep you in ale for weeks, but I will double it if you can tell me about the secret routes wagons use to avoid the highway.' A second coin changed hands and the portly drinker, beaming with the smile of a successful card player answered, 'There are no secret routes or convenient bypasses. In this area all wagons must stay on the highway. The surrounding land is low-lying and much of it under water. The high road runs on top of a narrow water-free ridge.'

James was cross and frustrated. He knew he had been made to look a fool. He tried another possible explanation for their lack of success. 'If all wagons pass along this road do many do so at night?' The informer nodded and whispered, 'Of course! There is much traffic after dark. The inn, The Angel, in the parish of St. Michael to the north, receives and reloads cargoes during the night, and conceals many a suspect wagon during the day.' 'Why the secrecy?' continued James. 'What is being transported that requires the cover of darkness?' The informer smiled, fell back on the bench, snorted and pretended to be asleep.

James now felt free to pursue Bess—but it was not to be.

Everybody's attention was suddenly diverted to the opposite end of the room. A tall dark-haired man, who wore a black patch over his left eye, was pushing James's brother, John, while uttering a combination of obscenities and threats. A crowd gathered, inciting both men to escalate the disagreement. James and Henry moved through the mob to rescue their colleague, but the excited rabble surrounding the two combatants prevented any intervention. Henry was told to hold the monies wagered on John by the gambling drunks. A drinker confided that the tall man did not appreciate the questions that John had asked, and when John confessed he was a government agent the man with the black patch became aggressive. Henry assessed the odds—two dozen men armed with daggers and cudgels, well affected by drink, who hated anyone associated with the government, pitted against three ineffective swordsmen. The only hope was to divide the opposition.

In a moment of inspiration he raised his tankard, and shouting to be heard above the noise proclaimed, 'Before the fight begins, let's drink a health to the King.'

There was immediate silence. Then three men tentatively raised their tankards. 'To the King!' The tall dark haired man stopped his shadow boxing at John and exploded. 'The current Parliamentarians are turds, but the King is worse. The Lord God save us from them both! I will not drink to the King.' The Royalists sympathisers, who appeared in the majority, muttered about religious fanatics, and quickly rallied around John. They were now determined to protect him against this sectarian extremist babbling about the Lord God. Within minutes the room erupted, as everybody joined the free-for-all—except for the fat informant who was now genuinely asleep, and the three government officers who slipped quietly into the night.

The three men who had taken accommodation at The Angel earlier that day returned there to eat, intrigued by James's information regarding the clandestine activities of the transport depot that shared the inn's courtyard. As they ate, as if to validate this information, they heard several wagons clatter over the cobblestones. Their rush to inspect these vehicles was halted. All of the doors leading to the courtyard from within the inn were locked. The excise men climbed the nearest staircase and found a window that fortuitously gave them a view of the courtyard. Intermittent moonlight enabled them to see at its far end a very large building, the external door of which was being closed. The wagons had disappeared, except for one. Several men were tying covers over its load and singing loudly as they worked.

This was an opportunity the agents could not miss. Finally they found a door that gave way to their combined weight and they entered the courtyard just as the sole wagoner whipped his horses into action. Henry challenged the driver to stop. The agents were ill prepared for his response. He turned his team and drove straight at the three officials who momentarily froze. They regained their mobility just in time, diving away onto hard, uneven and dirty ground. Brushing off the combination of mud, manure and soil they ran for the stables. Hurriedly saddling their horses they followed the errant driver.

The wagon headed north. A few miles along the highway it turned off into a thick forest. Passing clouds periodically hid the moon, and the overreaching trees prevented much light entering the woods. The pursuers dismounted, and progressed on foot, inwardly despairing of finding the vehicle in the enveloping gloom. After many minutes tramping through heavy undergrowth the men stumbled into a momentarily moon-drenched clearing. In the middle of a grassy knoll stood the wagon they had been following. The horses and driver were missing.

James raced forward, shouting for the wagoner to reveal himself. Henry ordered him to return to the edge of the clearing. James was not impressed, 'Why? I am not a craven coward like you, Elks.' 'Don't be insolent James. Just think! Isn't it strange that the wagon is left here for us to inspect. The driver knew we were chasing him and his load. Why give us what we want? If we go striding into this clearing, especially when the moon emerges, the driver or his friends, could pick us off one by one.' 'What do we do then?' asked a more compliant John, as James continued to fume and mutter disparaging remarks about his leader.

Henry who was a natural procrastinator finally broke the silence. 'Both of you stay here.' He pointed to a small depression that ran through the open space and passed within a few yards of the wagon. Henry crawled slowly along it. He was only half way to his destination when John shouted, 'I can smell burning cordage.' Any further conversation was lost in the loud explosion that followed. The depression protected Henry from the debris that catapulted in all directions. None of the men were injured. When the smoke cleared they examined what remained of the wagon and its cargo—an amalgam of twisted metal and charred wood. Henry surmised from the evidence that the wagon had been empty except for one or two barrels of gunpowder.

As they cantered back to the inn Henry hardly spoke. James ever ready to provoke his leader exclaimed, 'Has the blast removed your tongue?' Then he noticed that Henry was shaking, and deliberately highlighted his leader's condition. With a sneer on his face he asked, 'What's the problem, sir?' Henry had had enough of his arrogant, disrespectful minion. 'You are a brazen varlet. Anymore stupid talk from you and I'll have the constables place you in the stocks. The locals would have great sport. This is no game. Yes, I am shaking, and I make no excuses. That was an attempt to kill us—a clever ambush. They knew we were staying in the inn. They made considerable noise to attract our attention. Why would anybody be singing loudly at that time of night? Then one wagon deliberately provoked us into following it by driving straight at us. Our enemies are no fools, and they reacted very quickly. Someone from Widow Ketley's told them that we had been alerted to the nocturnal activities of their depot, and they decided to turn it to their advantage.'

Early next morning Henry and his tired men approached the transport barn. Nobody seemed concerned about their arrival. The building was very large, and used for several purposes. Along the far wall were the stalls, stabling a number of horses, including their own. Some were the riding horses of staff and guests; others were larger animals, horses and oxen, for the hauling of the wagons and carts. Six or seven wagons were being loaded or unloaded in the middle of the building by a bustling group of a dozen men. Against the other wall were stacks of goods—barrels and containers of assorted sizes.

Henry approached the overseer, a small man with a slightly hunched back. 'Sirrah, we are government agents who need to inspect the cargo in the wagons, and that stacked against the wall.' The hunchback introduced himself as Ferdy Ferris. He replied pleasantly, but to the point. 'Plain speaking gentlemen! You are excise men. You have been hassling our wagoners for weeks. All the goods in this building have a mark indicating that the excise has been paid, or that they are on route to merchants who will pay the excise when the goods are sold on. Please inspect the loaded wagons first! I want them on the road as soon as possible.' While the men were talking, a wagon suddenly pulled out of the shed, and headed rapidly across the courtyard. James showed an amazing burst of speed, and stopped the wagon by grabbing the reins of its nearest horse.

The driver cursed at the intervention, and turned his whip against James. 'A pox on you scurvy knave! May all parliamentarians burn in Hell.' Henry and John quickly joined James. The driver was pulled from the wagon and shackled to a post, while the excise officers examined his cargo. It consisted of small barrels that were not shaped for beer or wine. Henry suspected they were full of salt, a heavily taxed item, and a good reason for the driver to avoid inspection. Henry opened a barrel and tipping it on its side was disappointed.

A yellow powder spilled onto the ground.

Meanwhile an ever growing and menacing crowd gathered around the inspectors. There were howls of disapproval as the excise men examined each barrel. Eventually a square set, longhaired, ruddy-faced man started to wave a cudgel around their heads. Others began to shout support for their shackled colleague forcing Henry, James and John to form a defensive triangle, and draw their swords. The square set man laughed uproariously, 'Puny swords against a dozen cudgels, and as many staves!' Henry heard Ferdy Ferris vainly trying to get the growing mob back to work—but to no avail. A tall man with strong arms swung his staff at John's feet, which dramatically upended him, to the cheers of the crowd. As he lay on the ground several staves pressed into various parts of his body rendering him completely immobile, while others battered his head with their cudgels. Henry and James could not reach him as the mob used their staves like blunted pikes. The massed staves forced the two officers still on their feet against one of the walls, where they would most likely suffer the same fate as their comrade. They had survived a bomb blast only to be immobilised by massed staves and then cudgelled to death. John was unconscious, Henry prayed, and James thought of brazen Bess.

2

A PISTOL SHOT RANG out. A horseman galloped into the mob. 'Get back to work at once, or you will be out of a job.' They rapidly dispersed leaving the horseman, the overseer Ferdy, the shackled wagoner, and the three officers alone near the far wall of the barn. The horseman dismounted, and introduced himself as Grenville Reeves, owner of the transport enterprise. He apologised for the behaviour of his men and immediately summoned aid for John. James helped carry his unconscious brother into the inn.

Henry thanked Grenville. The delinquent driver turned on Grenville for supporting the prating toads of a perfidious Parliament, and denied that Grenville had any authority over him. He was a servant of Sir Harcourt Reeves. Grenville would have none of this insolence, 'In that case John Hooker take care! Cross me and in the future you will not have access to my depot, nor will you have goods to carry.' John Hooker was seething.

Henry completed his inspection. He was annoyed. He turned on the recalcitrant wagoner. 'All this uproar is for nothing. Why did you try to leave? The sulphur you carry is not subject to the excise. You are free to go.' Henry unshackled the man and returned his whip as James re-emerged from the inn. The driver snarled and spat generally in their direction. Henry gave the nearest horse a heavy slap on the rump, and the animals took off, almost dislodging a very cross wagoner. Henry quickly turned to James.

'Follow that wagon, but at a distance. We don't want another ambush. I want to know where he goes.' James who preferred to be with his injured brother asked, 'Why? The goods on that wagon are not taxable, and therefore no concern of ours.' Henry was fed up with James's general attitude to his job that was dominated by greed, disobedience and laziness. 'Do not query my directives. That yellow powder is sulphur, a vital component of gunpowder. Our masters would be very alarmed if gunpowder is being manufactured in this area without their knowledge. Our experience last night proves that it is readily available. Move!' A reluctant James trotted off after the wagon.

He never returned.

Henry initially thought his rebellious assistant had just walked out. He was horrified when a few days later a shepherd found a body, partly submerged in a water-filled ditch. The victim had been shot in both knees. A local doctor concluded that he did not die from these wounds. By the smell and condition of his clothes, and the odour emanating from his mouth, the corpse, identified as James, had drowned in a container of urine. Henry saw what remained of the body and vomited. An animal had eaten away large sections of it.

Henry was alarmed. He discussed the situation with a recovering John, who was still confined to his bed with several broken ribs. 'Gunpowder is being produced locally. James must have found where they were manufacturing the saltpetre.' 'I don't understand,' confessed a confused John. Henry pontificated, 'Gunpowder is a mixture of charcoal, sulphur and saltpetre. Saltpetre is extracted from animal urine. The liquid is allowed to stand for months over which time crystals develop. James followed a wagonload of sulphur, and then drowns in a tub of urine. It adds up to the manufacture of gunpowder.'

'What do we do now?' asked John. 'I will inform the constable Mr. Dale, who happens to be the innkeeper here, of our discoveries and suspicions; and then return to the alehouses of St. Aiden to find evidence of charcoal, the third ingredient,' replied Henry.

No one was talking until Henry chanced upon a dilapidated hovel, where poultry and pigs wandered around the dirt floor of the drinking chamber. Someone with a sense of humour had painted on a large piece of wood in the manner of a proper alehouse, The Pig's Swill, and a drawing of an overly rampant boar. One local, who was leaving as Henry arrived, warned him not to enter. 'Good sir, flee for your life! The place has been overrun by filthy, base, charcoal burners.'

Henry could not believe his good luck. Details of charcoal burning would complete his knowledge of the third ingredient needed in the manufacture of gunpowder. But he had to be careful. Charcoal burners were considered the dregs of society, and in the eyes of some, scarcely human. They were bad company in normal circumstances, but these could be very dangerous companions, as they made clear to all that their employer had just sacked them unfairly. Henry hid most of his money. He revealed only a few farthings to buy a couple of the more inebriated drinkers further refreshment. It took no prompting for them to rail against this former master who they readily identified.

It was Sir Harcourt Reeves.

The most voluble charcoal burner was the dirtiest, most unkempt creature that Henry had ever encountered. The remnants of several meals were imbedded in his salt and pepper beard, and his face remained blackened by his labours. Much of the ale he attempted to consume was lapped up from the floor by a particularly large pink pig as the liquid dripped slowly through his filtering beard. His friends called him Baa Baa, but he introduced himself as Oliver Lamb.

Lamb's story was simple, and delivered quickly and with enthusiasm. 'Over the last few months we burnt our way through Harcourt's smaller wood, Owl Screech Coppice. Tomorrow we were to move to a larger forest on the other side of the estate, Priory Wood. However the night before last, my brother was caught poaching there by Reeves's bully of a bailiff— churl with a limp, and a mean and spiteful manner, Hammer by name and nature. The next morning this brute rounded us up and forced us from the estate. He wielded his whip against those of us who were slow to respond. We were not paid, and I was not allowed to look for my missing brother, Edmund. He must be dead, probably murdered.'

'That's a pretty harsh punishment for a bit of poaching!' exclaimed Henry. 'It was not the poaching that irritated the bailiff. We poached for months with Sir Harcourt's knowledge, and no action was taken. My brother saw something in Priory Wood that he should not have seen. This led to his murder, and our ejection. From the beginning Priory Wood was out of bounds to everybody.'

Henry was optimistic for the first time in months. A week later under the cover of darkness, he and a still partially incapacitated John, headed for Priory Wood. They skirted the boundaries of Reeves House and entered the wood by a narrow track that led in from the highway. The men cantered slowly through the forest. After twenty minutes of darkness and silence they saw the flickering of tapers. They tethered their horses and moved slowly on foot through the undergrowth. In a small clearing there was an old chapel partly still a ruin, but which had undergone significant renovation. Several men were unloading coffins from a large wagon and carrying them into the renovated section of the building. A man in a white cassock, wearing a large cross that gleamed in the moonlight, appeared to be in charge.

'A nest of Papists!' whispered John. 'I am not sure,' replied Henry. 'It could be the authorities disposing of plague victims, or the reburial of men massacred during the Civil War, or even a gang of ruffians disposing of the bodies of their victims.' John's sectarian view seemed to gain credence when two of the men started to argue in what John thought was Latin, although Henry thought it was more likely Spanish or French. The superstitious and disconcerted John would not be swayed. To him it was Papist gathering. 'Why go to the trouble of putting the bodies in coffins, and presumably placing them in the crypt of an ancient chapel? There are plenty of deep waterholes where criminals could dispose of bodies without fear of their recovery. And there has been no plague in the area for some years. No, this has religious significance. You must inform the government immediately. A Catholic conspiracy is a far greater threat to national security than a few merchants avoiding the excise.'

Henry and John waited. Henry was anxious to inspect the chapel, and ideally, the contents of the coffins. After the wagon was unloaded the coffin carriers wasted little time in the chapel, and within half and hour the wagon, loaded with all the workers, left the scene. Henry and John reached the door of the chapel. Henry was just about to push it open when he heard the sound of heavy footsteps from inside the building. The excise men just had time to hide behind two large tombstones in the adjacent graveyard before the door opened, and a man holding a halberd, and with a dog on a leash, left the chapel. The halberdier carefully locked the door and then moved methodically around the exterior of the building. Luckily for Henry and John he ignored his growling dog as it tried to pull him in the direction of the graveyard.

'Why guard a building full of coffins?' muttered a perplexed Henry. 'Let's retrace our steps and get into the Reeves House estate through its main gate.' This they did, and leaving their horses at the bottom of a long uphill path they climbed towards the manor house. Halfway up the road, they came across a stile over which they entered a large field, at the far end of which were several outbuildings. Two or three mastiffs were tied close to the entrance of each of the buildings. No one could enter them without alarming the dogs that in turn would alert the servants to any intruder.

'Wait here,' Henry whispered to John. A few minutes later he returned carrying his doublet. His sword was dripping with blood. He placed his bloodied doublet on the ground revealing large chunks of a sheep he had just butchered. The task ahead was not easy. Henry had to get close enough to the dogs to feed them the sheep, yet at the same time not cause them to bark a warning to their masters. Henry crawled, as quietly as he could. He was lucky. A gentle breeze took his smell away from the dogs, and he was able to roll a chunk of mutton close to them. There was a brief moment of barking and growling as the dogs battled for the food. This quickly subsided as the rest of the sheep was fed to them. The dogs had not eaten for days. Henry shuddered at the thought.

With John he now entered the nearest building where they were immediately confronted by the overpowering smell of urine. Rows of tubs identified this building as the saltpetre site but the excise men had no time to congratulate themselves. The door of the building, which had been open, was suddenly shut behind them.

In the newly created darkness tapers were being lit near the entrance. A disembodied voice boomed into the high roofed edifice. 'Come out you sheep killing turd!' The number of tapers increased and Henry realised that at least four, maybe more men were closing in on them. Henry tried some bluff. 'We are not trespassers, nor sheep killers. We are excise men checking these premises for illegal goods.'

Before he had finished they were surrounded by a number of armed men. Their leader who was distinguished by a pronounced limp was not impressed. 'So in addition to your criminal activity you are minions of the Parliamentary brazenfaced caterpillars who destroy our nation. This is the second intrusion we have had in recent weeks.' The limp turned to his men, and without warning they opened fire, kneecapping both excise men. Henry and John fell to floor in agony. Their pain increased as they were dragged out of the building, across the rough terrain into the next edifice. The last thing Henry recalled was the sneering face of John Hooker as he untied the dogs guarding the entrance of this second building. Fortunately both men passed out before the dogs ripped into their bodies.

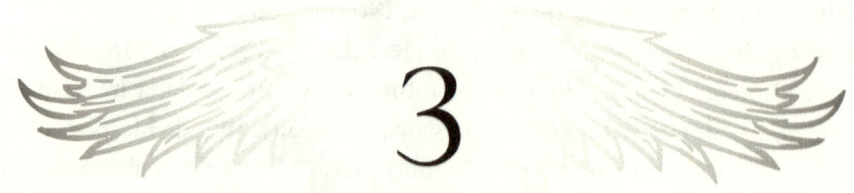

3

CROMWELL'S RESIDENCE, LONDON,
LATE SEPTEMBER 1651

LUKE TREMAYNE, EXPERIENCED enforcer and special agent for the Lord General, Oliver Cromwell, and a Lieutenant Colonel nominally in charge of the cavalry units based at Dublin Castle, was summoned urgently to meet his commander-in-chief. His own regiment currently provided the general's bodyguard, an officer of which ushered him into an inner room to await the general's arrival. Cromwell's appearance shocked Luke. The man was exhausted. Campaigns in Ireland and Scotland, and his pursuit of Charles II from Scotland to Worcester, and the numerous battles he had fought in recent years during serious bouts of illness, had taken their toll. His ruddy appearance had gone, and his agitated mannerisms were more pronounced. He did not take a seat, and Luke remained standing as Cromwell paced erratically about the room.

Eventually he spoke, 'The King is gone but our enemies continue to thrive. You are to delay the return to Dublin of your regiment, and yourself. You will go undercover immediately, and identify the opposition building against us specifically in the outer London parish of St. Aiden in the Field, and more generally in the newer northern extensions of the city. And your regiment, apart from my bodyguard, will be moved from The Tower to an estate on the northern limits of the city, where it can assist you at a moment's notice. I want you to consider what you are about to hear.'

Cromwell motioned to his orderly who admitted a man with dark brown hair streaked with grey and cropped very short. The guest sported a well-trimmed brown beard and wore a bright green doublet with slashed sleeves that revealed a lining of golden silk. He was big man, tall and well proportioned. Cromwell introduced him as Adam Dale, a one-time officer in one of the general's early companies, and asked him to repeat the story he had told him earlier that day.

'I retired from the army six years ago when I inherited my father's estates and a very successful inn, The Angel, on the northern edge of the city. At the time, on the general's recommendation, the Council of State appointed me as an official informer in what was a fast growing, and unruly part of the expanding city. I uncovered a number of developments detrimental to the security of the state. I created a small network of men who reported to me on anything that they thought warranted attention, which I passed on to the chairman of Parliament's security committee. Lately my warnings have been ignored. The committee did not act on my information. The last straw was two months ago. Three excise men were murdered, and the rumour was that they had accidentally uncovered a large cache of arms. The source of this rumour promised to give me the details the next day. He didn't report, and two days later his body was found. His throat was cut, and his body half eaten.'

'Surely that goaded the committee into action!' Luke exclaimed. 'No, quite the reverse. Three days ago I received a letter from the new chairman of parliament's security committee dismissing me from my role, and suggesting I forget everything I had uncovered in recent years. I was furious. I then remembered that the army gathered its own intelligence so I sought an audience with the general which took place earlier this morning.' Cromwell put up his hand to stop Adam's narrative and asked, 'Why do you think you were sacked, and no action was taken on your information about a cache of arms?'

'The reason is obvious. If Royalists, religious fanatics, Papists or social revolutionaries were building up this arsenal the government would have acted. The government did not act because it already knew about the arms. These were government arms being gathered to protect itself from its own army. It is no secret that officers of your army want the government dismissed, and new elections held. Politicians will do anything to prevent this development. The target for whatever is taking place on the northern limits of the city is the army. That is why I came to the general.'

Cromwell thanked Adam and dismissed him. He then signalled for Luke to take a seat with him on a corner bench. 'What do you think of Dale and his story?' Luke was gushing in his praise of Adam, and totally accepted the validity of his report. Cromwell looked pained, indicating his dissatisfaction with Luke's response. 'Colonel this is not the only report I have received concerning disorder and potential unrest in the north of our city. The local parliamentarian, Miles Baker, who has always sided with the army, fears that the local gentry are plotting an anti-army insurrection.' 'Great, with similar reports from two sources the problem is clearly identified, and the evidence should be easier to gather,' commented Luke. Cromwell smiled, 'If only it was that simple. Baker has named his prime suspects.' 'Even better,' added a buoyant Luke. 'I will interrogate those named immediately.' 'You are impatient Tremayne. You have already met Baker's suspected subversive. Baker names Adam Dale as the chief conspirator.'

At last Luke saw the complexities of the situation, 'So, the man who is suspected of preparing a coup against the army rushes forward to warn the army about such a coup. It is a long practiced ploy of troublemakers throughout history to deflect suspicion onto others.' 'It gets even more complicated I'm afraid. Earlier today Adam Dale told me that the leader of the conspirators was Miles Baker. Dale claims that as a member of the Rump, Baker will do anything to prevent the army dismissing Parliament.'

'Do you lean one way or another?' asked a baffled Luke. 'Not really. Miles Baker has a long record of supporting the army on critical votes in the Commons, and Adam Dale has an impressive record as a soldier, and as a government informer and local constable. But we have to start somewhere. You will go to The Angel with Dale.' 'So you suspect Dale as the most likely plotter?' 'Not at all, but his situation creates an obvious opening. You are to go with Dale to The Angel posing as his nephew. Dale has no children, so you will pretend to be the heir who has come to learn the business. You will also be appointed a special constable to assist the local authorities, including Dale, to carry out their responsibilities. Your primary role is to find the cache of arms, and identify the plotters. Secondly you may investigate the murders of the excise men, if you think those atrocities have any security implications. I have a personal connection with the Dale household. My

London lawyer, Robert Chidlow, is Adam's steward and following his recent marriage to a much younger French woman, lives at The Angel. He is a conservative fellow who might make a reliable ally.'

'What about Baker?' asked Luke. 'We don't want to give the impression we are favouring one side or the other in this local feud.' Cromwell thought for a while before he eventually replied. 'I will tell Baker that you are acting for me on a secret mission, and he should assist you in any way he can, without revealing your true identity or activity. He will be delighted, because he will interpret me sending you with Dale, as an indication that I suspect the innkeeper of being the person we seek. In addition I will obtain his permission to encamp your regiment on part of his sprawling estate a few miles north of St. Aiden.' Cromwell waved his hand as a gesture of dismissal and Luke abruptly left the room.

Cromwell's secretary who had been listening outside the closed door was caught by the suddenness of Luke's departure and colliding with him, finished up spreadeagled on the floor. Luke had little time for the general's civilian staff and simply stared menacingly at the embarrassed and immobile clerk.

Luke returned to his regiment which since the Battle of Worcester was camped within the Tower of London. He informed his two senior officers of his latest assignment. Newly promoted Captain, Harry Lloyd, would command the unit in his absence, and his senior sergeant Andrew Ford would accompany him on the mission, pretending to be his servant. Luke would create an identity as close to the truth as possible. He was an active Parliamentary soldier who was taking leave to come to London at the behest of his uncle.

Dale would not be returning to The Angel for some days. Luke had plenty of time to prepare for the assignment. In addition he would fill in time by enjoying himself in long drinking sessions at what had become his regiment's favourite alehouse since their arrival in London, The Green Bottle. When Luke and a considerable number of troopers arrived at The Green Bottle the publican was exuberant. He thanked Luke profusely for the two barrels of Dutch beer that Luke had donated to the establishment to celebrate his regiment's, now delayed, return to Ireland. Luke pleaded innocent of any such donation but suspected that some of his men had made the gift as they were not altogether happy with the local ale, especially a cinnamon flavoured variety, favoured by the Londoners. After a few drinks and without anyone confessing to the gift, and the publican slow to distribute the donated beer, Luke became annoyed. He called out to the alehouse keeper, 'Where is this Hollander beer?'

The alehouse keeper replied, 'The men who brought it insisted on taking it to the cellar. Now that you are here I will send my servants to bring up a barrel.' 'I will go with them,' replied Luke, anxious to taste again a drink he had enjoyed during his service with the Dutch Republic. Its bitterness took getting used to, especially for those brought up on sweet English ale. As the cellar door opened the smell that emerged was immediately identified.

It was the smell of burning cordage. Gunpowder was about to explode. Luke shouted, 'Everybody out!' but there was little time to heed his warning. Luke reached the doorway opposite the alehouse, and sheltered in its cavernous entry from which he witnessed a massive explosion that sent debris flying in all directions. A few made it to the street, others well gone in drink, had not moved. When the dust and smoke cleared there was nothing left of The Green Bottle and the shops on either side. The buildings opposite had all their windows shattered.

Andrew and Harry, who had been late for the drinking session, were walking towards The Green Bottle when it exploded. They ran to the site of the carnage and while delighted to find Luke alive, they were shocked by the dead and wounded that littered the street. They took charge of tending to the wounded and organizing the search for survivors. Luke grieved for the fourteen of his men, who had survived numerous battles, only to die while enjoying a drink with their comrades.

Next day Luke, Harry and Andrew reviewed the situation. Harry, who had not spoken to Luke since the explosion asked, 'What was the owner of The Green Bottle doing with gunpowder, and how did it come to explode?' Luke already had an explanation. 'The publican did not know that he had gunpowder in his cellar. Someone purporting to be from me delivered two barrels of Dutch beer to the alehouse. What were in fact two barrels of gunpowder were taken to the cellar where fuses were prepared. Just after I arrived at The Green Bottle a person who I then assumed to be a servant went down into the cellar. He had awaited my arrival to light the fuse. This was an attempt to murder me' 'But who would want you dead?' asked a troubled Andrew.

'I don't know but it is clear that the general is sending me into a situation that is far more dangerous, and far more serious than he makes out—so serious that someone does not want my investigation even to begin. Details concerning my mission can only have come from one of two sources. Adam Dale may be a two faced traitor, seeking Cromwell's help with one face and trying to murder that help with the other. If he had succeeded Dale would have blamed his opponents and further ingratiated himself into Cromwell's good books. But there is another possibility—Cromwell's private secretary. That dried up jackanape was listening at the door during my discussion with the general. Harry, enquire into his past!'

Luke had been a little tentative about his new assignment. It looked boring and uneventful. The explosion at The Green Bottle had given him a new perspective, and a sense of urgency.

4

LUKE WAS GIVEN a large room at The Angel and Andrew occupied a smaller adjoining chamber. The Angel, in the parish of St. Michael on the Ridge, was an impressive inn. It contained numerous rooms for accommodation spread over three floors. It provided meals for hundreds of people, and it had seven or eight rooms dispensing ale, beer and wine. Adam Dale was at the opposite end of the social scale to the numerous alehouse keepers in neighbouring St. Aiden. Dale was a wealthy yeoman who had reached officer rank during the Civil War, and had married, late in life, the daughter of a neighbouring gentleman—a marriage which brought with it increased landholdings. These added to the vast accumulation of property that Adam and his late father had acquired over the previous thirty years. Although the Dale family had gathered this evening for dinner at the inn to welcome Luke, Adam lived on his favourite estate, rebuilding an already large Elizabethan mansion, which he renamed Dale Court.

Luke's initial meal with Dale's family and guests was a disaster. Most of those around the table oozed resentment at Luke's presence. The sudden appearance of a not previously mentioned nephew, and potential heir, had clearly upset many of the household. A tall soberly dressed elderly man asked Luke provocatively, 'If you are Adam's nephew by the direct male line why do you not have his family name?' Adam intervened, 'My older half brother had some difficulties with the Church Courts, fled the county and took a different name.' The tall man whom Luke soon discovered was Robert Chidlow, Adam's steward, turned towards a mature redheaded woman. 'My dear Margaret were you aware of this missing brother, and his alleged son?' Adam's sister replied, 'No! I knew nothing of this until Adam returned from

London. But it is not surprising. Father married twice and had children by the first marriage. He never spoke about his life before he met our mother.'

'Enough Robert! Where are your manners?' interrupted a petite olive skinned woman wearing a very low cut bodice. This was Rose Chidlow, the prickly steward's wife, whose complexion indicated some southern Mediterranean blood. She was a woman in her late twenties, but decades younger than her husband. She exuded an air of authority, which did not fit her lowly place in the Dale household.

The third woman at the table was the epitome of gentry wealth and elegance. She was tall, with long blonde hair that fell well below her shoulders. She had an alabaster complexion with pale rosy cheeks and large green eyes that were widely separated from each other. She wore an exquisite dark green silk bodice with heavily cuffed sleeves, and a small lace collar. Hanging around her neck was a golden pendant that contained three large emeralds. This was the lady of the house, Temperance Dale, Adam's very young wife.

She glared at Robert, and gave Luke a sensuous and welcoming look. 'Let me introduce my half brother Grenville Reeves, who runs the transport enterprise out of the building at the end of the courtyard, and Sam Wright who assists Margaret in the day-to-day running of the inn. The handsome young gentleman sitting next to me is Sir Rowland Hille, whose late father, Sir Julius, was a long time guest at the inn, following the confiscation of his local estates due to the greed and corruption of the current government.'

Luke was flabbergasted. He stared intently at Sir Rowland as if he had seen a ghost. He finally found his tongue. 'Forgive me sir; you are the spitting image of your father. When as a lad I joined the English regiment fighting in the Dutch army Sir Julius Hille was my colonel. When did your father become a Royalist to incur the sequestration of his property?' The young gentleman replied quietly, 'Father fought for Parliament until the execution of the King. At that point he resigned his commission, and concentrated on his family estates and businesses. He remained loyal to the Parliament and to its army, and did not act against it at any stage.' Luke knew not to pursue the matter.

Luke did not sleep well. He was depressed. He had served the Parliament, and specifically its most able general Oliver Cromwell, for over ten years. They had defeated one King—and executed him. They continually defeated his successor and had forced him into exile. Yet what had been achieved? England was ruled by a corrupt remnant of the House of Commons, which was trying to weaken the very army that had assured its success, and kept it safe from both foreign and domestic enemies.

The army's success had not brought it popularity. Deep down Englishmen could not accept the murder of their King and the abolition of the monarchy. Yet the way events were moving, the supporters of monarchy were in no position to restore the King, and in the short term England would have to accept one of two evils—the continued rule of corrupt self serving politicians, or the rule of a reforming military elite, supported by various groups of religious fanatics, who would use the power of state to benefit a handful of Puritan saints.

In this complex political landscape Luke had not changed his simplistic position. He was a professional soldier loyal to Oliver Cromwell. Although he often disagreed with those around the general, he was driven by the conviction that Cromwell alone, with the support of the army, could bring England the reforms, peace and security it needed.

Next morning as Luke and Adam rode north to Dale Court, Luke revisited the issues that had emerged from the previous night's supper. Sir Julius Hille's fate disturbed him. He confronted Adam who explained, 'Sir Julius remained a fervent parliamentarian. Throughout the forties, he was a parliamentary infantry commander under Sir Thomas Fairfax, and remained so until the King was put on trial.' 'How did a veteran soldier, who had proved his loyalty, time and again, have his properties sequestrated? Sequestration was intended to punish the most extreme of Royalists, such as the Marquis of Winchester, who had used their immense wealth to undermine the parliamentary cause. If we treated every gentleman who disagreed with the execution of King as an enemy, the current government would be in a desperate situation.'

'Sir Julius was the victim of vindictive and corrupt officials determined to line their own pockets. His properties were sequestrated on grounds of alleged Royalist activities. Such activities were a complete fiction. On resigning from the army Julius kept clear of politics. This legalised theft led to his early death, and has bred in young Rowland a bitter hatred against the government for such a criminal act, and against the army for not coming to the aid of one of its most loyal and finest soldiers.'

Luke was genuinely moved by the fate of his old commander and promised to raise the matter with Cromwell. 'It's a pity Sir Julius was treated so shabbily. He was opposing the King's policy in the thirties long before any of the current Rump politicians had the courage to speak out. And as a soldier he gave the early Parliamentary armies the necessary injection of professionalism. If the General had not been busy subduing Scotland he would have assisted his old companion. Why didn't the local Member of Parliament do something to help? The sequestration committees pay a lot of attention to the views of the local politicians.' Adam responded to the question with unusual passion. 'None of us know what Mr. Miles Baker said to the committee, but I suspect he supported the sequestration. After all he received the largest share of Hille's property. Our local member should be the major target of your investigation.'

Luke changed the subject as they trotted through the elaborate gates of Dale Court, 'Your steward is a cold curmudgeon. His behaviour last night was almost unacceptable.' 'Luke, most of the people around that table see their future endangered by your presence. Chidlow is not a warm character. He is a typical puritan lawyer, hard working and principled, who does not abide slackers. He keeps my landed estates and my other businesses running efficiently—and profitably. He is a conservative supporter of the Rump, but he has powerful army connections. He is Oliver Cromwell's London lawyer.'

'He may manage your property, but does he control his wife. She was rather provocatively dressed.' 'Rose is French. Her great uncle Emile Tournac migrated here decades ago. As a foreigner he gained special permission from King James to be admitted to the English Inns of Court, and he built up a large legal practice in London. It was rumoured that he had links with the then King of France, Henry IV. Robert Chidlow worked for him for decades. Three months ago Rose arrived from France shrouded in mystery. Emile claimed she was his nephew's daughter who had been sent to London as a safe haven during the increasing civil disturbances in France. Again there were rumours that she had links with important people.'

Adam continued, 'To everybody's surprise in just over a month she married Robert, a long-standing bachelor, more than twice her age. And Tournac, as a wedding present made Robert his partner. Recently Tournac added a third member to his practice—Matthew Craven the long separated son of Archdeacon Dominic Craven, the former vicar of St. Aiden. Years ago

Dominic was forced to marry beneath his status. His wife was a Mary Ketley, a servant, who has a sister still in service with Sir Harcourt Reeves, and a sister-in-law who runs a very unsavoury alehouse in St. Aiden. Matthew proved an unruly lad, and Dominic, to more readily climb the hierarchical ladder of the Church, simply deserted his wife and child twenty years ago. I did not hear of them again until Matthew Craven appeared recently as the new legal partner of Emile and Robert.'

'This does not really explain Rose's alluring appearance,' commented an interested Luke. Adam pointed an admonitory finger at his companion. 'You misinterpret what you see. Rose is a feisty independent woman, who nevertheless has decorum, dignity and decency. Those half revealed breasts are directed towards her husband, and no other man. It's a French fashion that in no way reflects immorality. Your soldier's instinctive lust will find no response from Rose.'

Luke was not so sure. It could be his first challenge.

He persisted with his questioning. 'Why is your brother-in-law, Grenville, part of your household? Surely his wealthy father, Sir Harcourt, could keep him?' 'He could, but Grenville provides for himself. My father bought the inn from Grenville's grandfather decades ago. However he did not sell the large barn across its courtyard, which remains the base of a once small family transport enterprise which Grenville expanded dramatically during the war. It is his business, and it has no input from his father from whom he has been estranged since childhood. It is convenient for him to live in the inn as some of his work takes place at night. I lease a small part of the building as a stable for my guests.'

Luke changed the focus of his gentle interrogation. 'How is your sister taking the imposition of an unknown nephew?' 'Meg tells me that our mother years ago claimed that father had several children by his first marriage all of whom disappointed him, and whom he disinherited. Your arrival confirms those old rumours. Even if Meg is suspicious of you she will remain silent. She is fascinated by you.'

5

LUKE DIPLOMATICALLY IGNORED the remark, and commented, 'Surely Sam Wright is a senior servant. It's unusual for servants to eat with the household. Social order has not fallen that far?' 'Sam and I went to school together and joined the army on the same day at the outbreak of the Civil War. He comes from yeoman stock, and when he had to retire from the army due to injuries, I invited him as a partner, not as a servant, to help Meg manage the inn.' 'A most interesting household, Adam!' concluded Luke.

'And a most interesting line of questions and omissions, Colonel. You have not asked about Temperance.' 'A gentleman does not pry into the relationship of husband and wife,' replied Luke a little too quickly. 'You should have. There are aspects of my marriage that are very relevant to your investigation. Temperance is half my age, and the daughter of Sir Harcourt Reeves by his second wife, and half sister to Grenville. On my marriage Sir Harcourt transferred many properties to me as part of my wife's dowry. He has fallen on hard times. The marriage relieved him of a considerable debt which he owed me.'

Luke quickly grasped the significance of the statement and could not conceal his dismay. 'You bought Temperance?' 'You could say that. I am anxious to sire an heir to my growing wealth.'

'And create a wealthy scion whose existence will change the fortunes of those around you. If your relatives and friends are upset by my arrival, how will they react to the baby?' Adam was silent for some time and then confessed, 'Bringing you here did have the added value of letting me see how various people reacted to a new player in the inheritance stakes. That knowledge will enable me to better protect Temperance when I announce her pregnancy.'

Luke changed the topic. 'Where does Sir Harcourt Reeves stand in these dangerous times?' 'He is a trimmer. He adjusts his political and religious stance to suit the situation. He has been so adept at this, that the war tripled his family fortunes until recently when a dramatic decline occurred. He has had a finger in many pies especially manufacture, and the accumulation of properties, although he unloaded much of the latter over this last year.' 'Why did he do that?'

'To pay off his debts and ensure that his estranged third wife, Cassandra, receives none of it. The same Cassandra claims his financial decline is due to his ill health. She claims his mind has gone and his renowned business acumen disappeared from the moment he became obsessively religious sometime last year. I do not know the form of this obsession but given reports of certain activities on his estate he may have become a Papist.' Adam suddenly stopped speaking freely, and stared at Luke, 'I trust all these questions are necessary for your investigation. What is your next step?'

'To recreate the activities of the excise men. Did they talk to you about their work? Did they know you were favourable to the government which they served?' 'They knew I was sympathetic, but for most of the period that they were around I was living here at Dale Court. Sam and Meg saw more of them than I did.'

Back at The Angel, Luke decided to question Sam whom he found going down into the cellar. Luke followed and helped him roll a barrel back up the incline that ran parallel to the stairs. When they reached the landing at the top of the slope Luke spoke, 'Sam, I need your help. We don't want the government prying into all our activities. The death of those excise men has already raised problems for all of us. The government is suspicious of activities in this area. For the last few days a detachment of heavily armed cavalry has come up the road from their base in The Tower, and spent all of their time in the parishes of St. Aiden and St. Michael. They claim they are assisting the local constables maintain law and order after the spate of murders that have occurred. Therefore if we can solve those murders ourselves the government might leave us alone.'

'Maybe,' replied Sam, looking Luke directly in the face, and staring at a point behind Luke's eyes. 'I'll be blunt, sir. You are an impostor; but if you are Adam's friend I will help. But if you have forced Adam's hand to accept you as his nephew, I will kill you.' Luke intuitively took Sam into his confidence. 'You are Adam's true friend. He and I are engaged in the same mission to explain the malaise that is enveloping the area; and to solve the murder of the excise men. The only lead we have for their death is that they had uncovered illegal arms. Did any of them speak to you during their stay here?'

'Rarely, they spent most of the day on the road stopping and inspecting wagons, and most of the night in the sordid alehouses of St. Aiden.' 'That doesn't make sense. There are pleasant drinking chambers in this inn, where they were staying, why go down amongst the criminal government-hating classes?' 'It's the one conversation we did have. I warned them that the two things they would get in those alehouses was the pox and a dagger across the throat. They naively believed they could buy information from the permanently befuddled patrons. The money they spent to that end bought them highly dubious intelligence, but it's what led to their deaths. They were not murdered because of the information they sought or obtained. They were stupid. All three had fat purses stuffed full, including silver coins—a fortune for the scum that inhabit those dens of iniquity. Their purses were never found and several local varlets had excessive spending money for weeks after the death of the excise men. The notorious Hooker brothers were demonstrably affluent for a short period. Meg might know more about their movements. She chatted with them most nights. Help me with this barrel into the next chamber, and we can then have a drink!'

Luke and Sam retired to a corner bench with tankards brimful of freshly brewed dark brown ale. Before either had taken their first gulp, calls of 'fire, fire' reverberated through the inn. Both men were initially disoriented, and failed to correctly judge the location of the shouting. By the time they reached the fire Grenville Reeves had it under control. A pile of fodder inexplicably deposited against the wall of the inn, was belching forth a considerable amount of smoke. Workers from the transport depot, and servants from the inn had already formed a line from the nearest well and were passing buckets of water at an impressive speed. Others were hitting the smouldering pile with green branches rapidly wrenched from the hedge that bordered one side of the courtyard. It was largely a false alarm—considerable smoke but no flame.

Luke was nevertheless suspicious. This fire began very close to the wall of the inn, and close to the overhanging thatch of the roof, which if it had not been curtailed, the inn would have been destroyed. The fire was either the result of gross stupidity by whoever placed the pile of fodder in such a location, or a deliberate act of arson. Sam rejected the arson theory and summoned a wagoner from across the courtyard and immediately berated him. 'I am surprised Austin Perry that a man of your experience placed fodder so close to the timber wall of the building.' The wagoner was indignant. 'No, Sam. I placed a tall pile of damp hay well away from the wall. Someone, probably the children who were playing in the area, knocked the top off my pile, spreading it closer to the wall. No need to make a big issue of this. It would have been serious if the hay had been dried but last night's rain created a damp squib.'

Austin moved back to the wagons, and Sam reiterated the explanation that it was an accident. Luke was still not convinced 'So, you don't think it was deliberately lit?' 'No, to what end? If someone wanted to burn the inn down there are several more effective places to start the fire, and straw would have been a much more effective fuel.' Luke was about to concede the argument when he noticed, not far from the smouldering pile a broken piece of curved glass. He picked it up, held it up to the sun with one hand and let the rays filter through to the palm of his other hand. 'What are you doing Luke?' asked a curious Sam.

'Hold out you hand!' Luke focused the filtered rays of the sun on the back of Samuel's hand. He soon withdrew it and complained about the burn. 'Yes, Sam, the glass concentrates the rays. This fire was deliberately lit, especially as the wagoner swears he placed the initial pile well away from the wall. Someone who knows little about agriculture and livestock, and who anticipated a sudden conflagration, lit the pile thinking it would burn like straw. But as you say, to what end?'

Luke and Sam returned to their drinking chamber, and emptied their tankards in a couple of long draughts. Sam rose to refill them. He vomited without warning and fell forward onto the slate floor. Blood poured from his shattered face which had taken the brunt of the fall. Luke rose to assist him, but frothing at the mouth, slid off the bench and slumped unconscious against the wall.

Fortunately Andrew found the two stricken men within minutes. Meg with the assistance of the servants, force-fed both men vile concoctions that ultimately emptied their stomachs. Next morning Andrew waylaid the cavalry patrol. 'Soldier, tell your commander, Captain Lloyd, that the parish may have another two murders. Colonel Tremayne lies close to death, and the innkeeper's assistant is not much better.'

Andrew returned indoors and took his place beside Luke. The doctor concluded that both men had been poisoned, and that apart from exhaustive purgatives there was little that could be done. Time alone would determine who survived and who did not. The reason for the fire was now obvious. It drew Luke and Sam away so that someone could tamper with their drinks.

The two men lay in adjacent beds in a small chamber off the kitchen. Meg Dale did not leave them. Andrew who sat beside Luke was determined that his colonel would not die in vain. He would take over the investigation. 'Meg, is there a connection between the attempt to kill Sam and Luke, and the earlier deaths of the excise men?' Meg who remained pre-occupied with her nursing duties mumbled a disinterested 'no.' Andrew would not be fobbed off. 'Did you talk to the excise men when they lodged at the inn?'

'Yes, I talked to them most nights. They had a monotonous routine. They spent all day on the road stopping and searching the hundreds of wagons that passed through the parish. They then spent the early part of most nights in the alehouses of St. Aiden.' 'So they returned here completely intoxicated?' 'No, they drank little. On their return they had a late meal. By all reports they were never drunk. They went to the alehouses to gain intelligence by listening to the gossip—and by buying information.' 'Were they successful?'

'Not usually, but one night some fool suggested they take a particular interest in Grenville's transport activities. That evening they asked me in detail about his routine. Next morning I saw all three officials at his building, searching wagons and stock. One carter tried to get his wagon away before the officials had inspected it. One of the excise men chased him, pulled him from his wagon and shackled him to one of its wheels. The wagon was searched and partly dismantled. Some time later I noticed this driver heading north up the main road with a re-assembled wagon, loaded with a cargo of small barrels, one of which was spilling a yellow powder. A few minutes later one of excise men followed it from a distance.'

'Did you recognize the driver who tried to avoid the attention of the excise men?' 'Yes, it wasn't one of Grenville's men. It was one of his father's senior servants, one of the Hooker brothers. They look very similar. That was unusual because I know Grenville has paid out a fortune to have the sole right to deliver all goods to all neighbouring estates. He must have made an exception for his father as I have seen the Hooker brothers driving wagons away on a few occasions.'

Andrew was quietly pleased. A lead at last! The Hooker brothers may provide the answers that had eluded Luke.

6

A LOUD HAMMERING ON the inn's door interrupted Meg and Andrew's conversation. A brash young cavalry officer burst into the building, followed by a servant whose attempts to restrain him had been rudely brushed aside. The officer demanded to be taken to Luke's bedside. He was appalled by what he saw. Ignoring Meg and Andrew, the officer fell on his knees beside the bed, took Luke's hand, and prayed silently for more than ten minutes. Finally he arose, pale faced and visibly shaken. As he had orders not to compromise Andrew's undercover role he addressed Meg, 'In the morning I will compile a detailed report of everything you can tell me about these attempted murders. I will be assisting the local constable, and will take up residence in this inn as of now. My men have already made camp on the piece of waste land opposite.' 'And who might you be young man?' asked a bemused Meg. 'I am Captain Harry Lloyd.' 'Not another damn thieving Welshman,' Meg muttered to her self. Andrew smiled.

Harry was shocked by this second attempt on the life of his colonel, who over the years had appeared invincible to the young officer. Luke's overall appearance did not suggest a speedy recovery. The earlier explosion at The Green Bottle and now the poisoning had put an end to months of good cheer and self-confidence for Harry. He had been promoted to Captain after the Battle of Worcester, and was delighted to be assigned as a captain in Luke's own company within the regiment which had become his home. He had little confidence in the assertion of those at the inn that Luke was out of danger. Harry slept badly, but did not hear anything unusual during the night.

He only became aware of trouble when a badly bleeding and beaten trooper fell into the inn as Sam unlocked its main door the next morning. A gang of ruffians armed with cudgels had attacked the three tents containing the troopers, beaten them senseless, and stolen their weapons and horses. Harry was furious. He summoned the inn's household and exploded, 'To murder three government officials is bad enough. To attack six soldiers so close to thousands of reinforcements within the city of London is plain stupid. I will return, not with a few troopers to camp innocently on the waste land opposite, but with a company of cavalry which you, mistress innkeeper, will feed and shelter. The army will not tolerate this insult to its honour.'

During the next week the inn had several of its rooms converted into hospital wards containing Luke, Sam and the troopers who suffered broken bones, bruised limbs and concussion. Most of the other chambers housed the troopers that Harry had imposed on the establishment. The courtyard and stables were overcrowded with the horses of two companies of cavalry. Adam, who knew Andrew's real identity took him aside. 'Get rid of that arrogant young Captain and his men. To flood the parish with soldiers will not help Luke's investigation. They are getting in the way, and antagonising the parish. It is the last thing that Luke needs.'

Andrew, still outraged by the attempt to poison Luke, was not a sympathetic listener. 'Maybe that is what the parish needs—a fine taste of army steel,' replied Andrew, barely able to conceal his cold fury at the turn of events. He irrationally turned on Adam. 'This is the second attempt on Luke's life since he began this assignment. Who did you tell about his mission?'

'I told my friend and business partner, Valentine Cole. You don't think that my indiscretion is responsible for these outrages?' 'Somebody, somehow has heard of what Luke is involved in—and is determined to stop it. If it wasn't you, who was it? And who is responsible for this latest assault on the troopers?'

'Who knows? It might be a spontaneous attack by locals, or an assault organized elsewhere. Frankly, stealing the horses and weapons is sufficient explanation without looking for deeper motivation,' Adam concluded blandly.

Harry and Andrew reported to Luke as soon as they thought he was well enough to comprehend their concerns. Both were convinced that Adam Dale had leaked the information that had provoked two attempts on Luke's life. Andrew passed on Adam's admission that he had told a Valentine Cole of what he had proposed to Oliver Cromwell. Harry, who on Luke's instructions, had investigated the background of Cromwell's secretary, Zephaniah Scroggs, agreed. He explained that Scroggs had worked for leading Puritans within the city but had been recommended to Cromwell by the general's own lawyer, and current steward to Adam Dale, Robert Chidlow. If Scroggs was the blather mouth he was nevertheless clearly linked to Dale.

Luke was not convinced. An associate of Adam Dale may have recommended Zephaniah Scroggs but it did not prove that the secretary reported to Adam. There could be an entirely different puppet master pulling the strings. When he had time he would dig deeper into Scroggs's background.

The situation at The Angel changed dramatically over the following weeks. Luke and Sam fully recovered, and Luke quietly ordered Harry to take his company out of the inn. He was to immediately implement Cromwell's order to move the whole regiment from The Tower and relocate it on the estate of the local magistrate, Mr. Miles Baker.

Luke and Sam, vitally concerned in any investigation into their poisoning, met with Andrew in one of the drinking chambers of The Angel. As Sam carefully drew from a fresh barrel of ale, Andrew asked of Luke, 'Who wants you dead?' Luke responded, 'I don't think that that is the first question. Who was the poisoner trying to kill? Was it Sam or myself? He was not after both of us. We had just met and to any outsider had nothing in common.'

Sam disagreed. 'No Luke, we do have something in common. Until you arrived the same group who resent you resented me. Adam's family wanted me treated as a servant, and not as Adam's partner. But with your arrival my threat to their inheritance fell into insignificance. But if you died my threat to their future prospects would be re-activated. It seems straightforward to me. This is an attempted double murder— to remove in a single blow the two prime beneficiaries to Adam's legacy.'

Luke did not agree. 'The fear that either of us will usurp the legacies of Adam's relatives and friends is not urgent enough for action to have been taken so quickly. My credentials would be challenged in the courts as an imposter, and you Sam would be accused that as a servant you used your position to unduly influence your master. Forget the greed, envy and ambitions of the household and the tensions within the family. After all, we are not the greatest threat to the existing beneficiaries. It is Temperance. When she produces a son for Adam that son would inherit the Dale estates without challenge. No, the attempt on our lives is political. Sam, are you a member of any group whose activities some might fear?'

'In these chaotic times any views other than those pronounced by the current establishment can arouse alarm. Look at the government's reaction to a few murders. Two companies of troopers are imposed on the inn. Come with me to an alehouse in St. Aiden this evening and your question will be answered. I shall introduce you to many with similar views to myself which might explain some possible antagonism.' That evening Sam and Luke entered the rear door of a small house in St. Aiden. Luke realised that this back chamber of Goodwife Blunt's residence was a small alehouse. There were rows of benches lined up in imitation of the pews in the local church. In one corner of the room three barrels rested side by side on a large table. Men were filling their tankards, and then taking a seat on the benches. At the far end of the room were three stools. Sam sat on one of them, and motioned to Luke to sit on the bench opposite. The patrons were all male, and their dress indicated that they were moderately well off. There were no women present. Sam stood up—an action that brought immediate silence. The congregation stared at his companion making Luke distinctly uneasy.

Sam acted quickly, 'My friend, Luke Tremayne, has spent thirteen years as a soldier, and recently retired to assist his uncle at The Angel, but he sympathises with our aims.' Luke's anxiety intensified. He had no idea what these aims were, let alone his alleged approval of them. Sam addressed the meeting. 'Brothers, the time is right for us to confront this corrupt government. It has ignored all the reforms that the nation craves. Now that the army has returned from Scotland, its officers are holding the politicians to account, and the recently demobilised soldiers are demanding the pay that is owed to them. All want a say in the government of the country. Yet we are playing no part in this agitation. The religious fanatics have usurped our position. Four years ago our Leveller petitions and demonstrations influenced the government of the day, and we had so infiltrated the lower ranks of the army that they achieved a role in army affairs. All these gains have now vanished. We must resurrect our political aims for an annual parliament, an equality of electorates, law reform and fair payment of our troops.'

A snowy haired man responded, 'Demonstrations are useless. A couple of murders and military force is immediately dispatched to the area. Our leaders are in gaol, and the army is not exerting any influence to free them, or to put our manifesto, *The Agreement of the People*, to the Rump. We must find a new approach.' 'So what do you suggest brother Walter?' asked Sam. 'We must flood London with pamphlets setting out our aims, we must speak covertly to as many apprentices and soldiers as we can, and we must somehow counter the influence of the religious sectarians on the people of London, and on the officers and ranks of the army. The people, not the saints should rule. We must act before the army imposes a rule of the godly upon us.'

'Is that a possibility Luke? Has the army been taken over by the religious extremists? Will it replace the Rump with a parliament of saints?' asked Sam. Luke responded, 'Brothers, fear not, the army will not blindly follow the whims of the fanatics. The majority of officers are aware of the unpopularity of the saints. But one has to recognise that at the moment, Major General Harrison, who does have the support of the Lord General, Oliver Cromwell, leads a number of officers who would respond positively to the demands of these extremists. Cromwell is sympathetic to their cause, and they return the compliment by suggesting that Cromwell is God's agent on earth, about to destroy the evil Parliament, and to introduce godly rule.'

Luke continued, 'But have no fear. Cromwell is an English gentleman with a high regard for property. When he becomes aware how far some of these sects will go to destroy established society, he will withdraw his support. As you know each of these conflicting groups limit the saints to their own narrow membership. What I am suggesting is that any open confrontation with the sects might win the support of the Rump administration, but it may not be supported at the moment by the real power in the land—the senior officers of the army. You must convince Cromwell and his officers that a government of puritan saints is not the solution to England's growing anarchy, but a guarantee for escalating chaos.'

7

THERE WAS A long silence as the gathering inwardly digested the import of Luke's advice. Finally Sam asked, 'And how do we do this?' Luke was warming to his role as adviser to the reforming, if not revolutionary Levellers. 'A simple approach with two prongs—turn the saints against each other. There are dozens of competing sects with very different beliefs, and there is no greater hatred than that exercised in the name of God. Secondly turn the army against them. If they can be blamed for the recent murders and for the growth of violence and immorality, it will force senior army officers to act decisively—at least at the local level. Can the mob that attacked the trooper tents be depicted as a group of religious fanatics?'

The snowy haired man, whom Luke later learned was a printer, Walter Sheffield, responded, 'Unfortunately, no. Those men were the scum of society primed by many hours of drinking, and a small fortune in bribes. They were a mob bought by powerful interests from outside the area to do a specific job. Someone wanted the army out of the way.'

'Why would that be?' asked Luke. Walter was surprised at the question, 'That is a naïve question coming from a soldier. There are countless illegal activities taking place across London. Local government has collapsed and the committees of the counties that surround the city ignore the parishes that have in reality become part of greater London. The county gentry are only interested in the rural areas of their jurisdiction, and the London authorities on the whole refuse to cross the county borders into the new suburbs of the city. Within this vacuum of law enforcement, crime, treason and religious deviousness are flourishing. Only the army could restore order to these areas which is not in the interests of several powerful people.'

'And that might be the very motive behind whoever ordered the attack on the soldiers,' interjected Sam. 'We are looking in the wrong direction. Attacking an army patrol invites retribution—a massive military intervention. Those who attacked the army may want a bigger army presence in the area.' Sam's interpretation provoked a heated debate. Walter still believed the army should be hunting its enemies—criminals who feared for their livelihood. Others warmed to Sam's view that perhaps the assault was not by criminals protecting their empire, but by lovers of law and order who wanted a massive army intervention in the local situation. The debate continued for another hour. Sam closed the meeting and Goodwife Blunt entered the room with plates full of food. As the group ate and drank Luke singled out Walter and asked him to expand his views on the current political situation.

'Everyone is two faced. Their expressed beliefs are far removed from their basic loyalties. As a bard suggested, these times are out of joint, but two basic facts are clear—everybody hates the army, but every political interest needs the army to achieve its goal. The Rump will only bring about reform if the army pressures it, the King will return only if the army supports him, the religious fanatics can only take over the nation if the army supports the saints, and we can only achieve social reform and democracy if the soldiers use their arms to impose our democratic revolution.'

'Where does the murder of the excise men fit into this broader political landscape?' asked Luke. 'The two possible answers are easy to form. Either they were murdered because of political considerations, or they were the victims of local criminals after their fat purses.'

Luke assessed the Leveller. Walter would do what he could to alter the balance of power in favour of the middle and lower orders, but sensible enough to know that those with power would not give it away voluntarily. The only immediate vehicle for change was the army. Perhaps it was the Levellers who had attacked Harry Lloyd's patrol to bring more troops into the area where the locals might indoctrinate them. Luke downed the remnants of his drink and asked Walter, 'Who would be my best informant on local feuds and family secrets?' 'You don't have to go far. Your landlady at The Angel, Meg Dale, has lived here all her life and her role in the inn has put her at the centre of gossip for decades. Also get her to take you to Old Kate, our local seer.'

The next evening Meg and Luke found themselves hovering around the blazing fire in the hall of the inn. Meg shocked Luke out of his relaxed reverie. 'Who are you Luke? Adam must have a very good reason for foisting you on this household as his potential heir—and his reasons must have been very serious, and very urgent. After all we daily expect Temperance to announce she is with child, which will put an end to any disputed inheritance. Reasons serious enough for Adam not to consult his only sister, issues serious enough that someone tries to kill you twice.'

Luke replied openly, 'After my current assignment is complete I will be gone. The family need not fear my intrusion. I am here to assist Adam solve a number of problems which worry him, and the government.' 'Why would Adam need outside help to deal with local problems?' 'There lies the problem Meg. It is not clear whether the troubles arise out of local antagonisms and interests, or whether they are being stoked by outside interests who have wider political and religious agendas. I really need your help to understand this local situation. What do the locals think motivated the murder of the excise men, and who do they deem responsible?'

'The parish is convinced that their killing had nothing to do with high politics. The excise men were foolish enough to display purses full of silver coins, and one of them showed a lewd interest in a popular barmaid. This infuriated the regulars. The agents' investigation into the transports that moved in and out of the parish upset some smaller and probably shady entrepreneurs. And their humiliation of one of the wagoners was strongly resented by his fellow carriers. The Hooker brothers openly declared they would get their revenge.'

Luke trusted Meg. He continued his confession. 'There is another aspect to my investigation and far more important than the fate of the excise men. The army fears that armed insurrection is being prepared on the outskirts of London, and that groups in this area are gathering an arsenal to strike against us. It was Adam who alerted the army to the problem. That is why I am here. But I am no fool. Adam's co-operation and cordiality could be a cover to hide his own part in this conspiracy. Where do the local landowners stand in the looming confrontation between army and Parliament, and towards the young lad who wants to be King?'

'Luke, you are a realist. Nobody likes the army—apart from its own leadership, and some of the religious fanatics. Even less support the present government, but with the Royalists in disarray there is no alternative. The populace has never forgiven the execution of the King, and whatever the government or the army does, they will never win over the hearts of the people. Despite this if the army and the current republican government came into conflict, a large number of the political nation, including Royalists, will accept a military dictatorship as a better option than the chaos and anarchy that is offered by the continuation of the corrupt Rump. Most gentry in this area have not committed themselves to any one position. That is why they have survived the constant changes of government since 1642.'

'Your views on the attempt to poison Sam and myself?' 'Personal not political. Sam unfortunately drank poison that was meant for you. You were a victim because you are an outsider who has intruded himself, quite dramatically, into our family.' 'Are you admitting that the attempt to murder me was a family affair?' 'Your presence has seriously disconcerted many of the family and above all their servants, some of whom may have tried to take matters into their own hands.'

'What about the attack on the soldiers encamped on the village green?' 'Hardly serious. A few local lads took advantage of the situation to express their dislike of the army, and to show how effective they could be. The powers-that-be should not underestimate the so-called mob.'

'So you don't believe that this was a well organised assault with the assailants brought in from outside to attain the objectives of their puppet master?' 'No, and if the victims had been a group of squatters or a band of tinkers no one would have reacted. Just because it's the army that is attacked, people exaggerate its importance, and read into a simple outburst of communal violence, some world shattering conspiracy.'

'You said earlier that the local landowners have kept their options open and have survived the changes in government without much loss. Who exactly exerts power in this region?' 'That is fairly easy. Most of the land in St. Aiden was part of one of Miles Baker's many estates. He has made a fortune out of its break up and the creation of hundreds of small tenements. St. Michael was nearly all part of Sir Harcourt Reeves's lands, but the largest landowner in the wider region covering parishes to the north was the late Sir Julius Hille. As you know Hille's silence over the execution of the King found him designated as a Royalist, and his lands were confiscated by the government.' Meg anticipated Luke's next question. 'His lands were distributed between Miles Baker, Sir Harcourt Reeves and my brother Adam Dale.'

'Your brother is devious. He told me that Baker received much of Hille's property but did not mention his own share of the spoils. I did not realize your brother was such a wealthy and powerful local figure, despite not being a member of the gentry. How did he come to participate in the spoils of the Hille sequestration?' 'Being a gentleman is not a major factor in this area. There are three yeoman families—the Dales, the Coles and the Cravens— that have as much land, wealth and influence as their gentry neighbours, the Reeves, the Bakers and the Hilles.'

'So if there is any high politics at work in this area it would involve one or more of the families you mention.' 'Yes. Baker is a member of the Rump and regularly attends its meetings, but keeps himself independent of the many factions that have emerged, but in a crisis he has always backed the army. Reeves has been non-political for over five years. During the first Civil War he was an avid Parliamentarian but since then has been a political recluse. Baker and Reeves used the civil conflict to enrich themselves, and are not going to allow principle or loyalties to endanger their position. A younger son, Augustine, runs the Coles estates. The eldest, Valentine, moved to London decades ago, and is now a very successful entrepreneur. The Cravens are the only locals who initially supported the King and some of the family were Papists. And the matriarch of the family is a centenarian—the local seer Old Kate. One of her grandsons, Archdeacon Dominic Craven was deprived of his benefice at St. Aiden by the Parliament for insisting on retaining the traditional Book of Common Prayer. Had the King and Archbishop not been beheaded, Dominic would be a bishop of the Church of England, although a scandal involving his wife and child may have hindered his promotion.'

8

'NOW I AM getting somewhere. Take me to Dominic and Old Kate!' 'No point with the old crone. Fifty years ago the whole of London followed her visions and prophecies as if they were fact. Her prediction of Queen Bess's death caused her to spend a year or so in The Tower. A similar prediction that Charles I would be executed was ignored. She is too old, and dominated by the one obsession that all events since the King's death are punishments from God for that abomination.' 'I will talk to both,' re-iterated a determined Luke.

Three days later Luke and Meg made their way into the countryside, joining up with many people heading in the same direction. Passing through an extensive wood they were confronted by a large low hill. A line of persons wound up its gentle contours to a semi-derelict chapel just below the peak. Meg's view that Old Kate had lost her appeal was patently wrong. Luke was impatient and cross. It would take days waiting in line, and he did not have the time.

Meg ignored the queue and rode up a much steeper incline directly to the ruined building. There she accosted a tall shorthaired man dressed in black and wearing a large silver cross. He was delighted to see Meg. After a lengthy chat they motioned for Luke to join them. The man in black led them further into the building, and inserted them at the head of the line of supplicants.

In the candle lit chamber Luke could just make out a very old, wizened hunchbacked woman. She was in a trance-like state as she placed her hands in a blessing on a kneeling recipient. Behind her was an altar-like table on which candles and incense were burning, and holy pictures exhibited. When

he heard the old woman mumbling in Latin, Luke was convinced he had
stumbled across an illegal Catholic ceremony. He expressed his outrage to
Meg who quietly berated him. 'There is much tradition in this ritual, but
old Kate is no Papist, and her assistant who led us here is her grandson,
Archdeacon Dominic Craven, a priest of the Church of England.'

Half an hour passed. Dominic signalled for them to kneel before Old
Kate. She caressed Meg's face. Luke realised that the seer was blind, and
was therefore quite surprised when she announced, 'Ah, the young Margaret
Dale! You have ignored my advice for decades. Why waste my time now
when the die is cast, and the secrets of your past are about to be revealed?'
She then ran her hands over Luke's visage, and with a mischievous grin
announced to Meg, 'The man beside you would make a more suitable lover,
than the one you currently cherish. Repent your ways, and the Lord might
yet save you.'

'Enough, you old hag! I am not here to listen to your ravings. My
companion seeks guidance on the malaise he considers envelops this area.'
Old Kate held Luke's head tightly in her hands. She then turned towards the
altar, raised her arms and invoked the Archangel Gabriel. She engaged in
incomprehensible mumbo jumbo for some minutes. She replaced her hands
on Luke's head. He almost passed out. The hands were red-hot, and Luke's
whole body went into spasm. As he struggled to bring his trembles under
control she announced, 'The malaise that covers London is a punishment
from God for those who murdered our lord the King. The murderer-in-
chief, with Satan's help will escape justice, because those that seek his death
are an even greater abomination to the Lord God. One day you will see the
light, and return the King to his rightful place. Then God's bounty will once
again flow through the land. Meanwhile the nation must choose between
two evil beasts.' Old Kate fell back exhausted, and Dominic carried her to
a trundle bed behind the altar.

On their way down the hill Meg and Luke did not speak. Luke was still
recovering both physically and emotionally from the traumatic effect caused
by Kate's laying of hands. He gradually began to consider the import of her
utterings. Meg anticipated his thoughts. 'Well Luke did you learn anything?'
Luke still could not speak. After ten minutes of silence he finally found his
voice. 'In addition to the physical reaction which has taken me completely
by surprise, there are things she said that are difficult to explain away. How

did she know that the malaise I mentioned might involve an attempt on the life of General Cromwell—in her parlance the murderer-in-chief? I never mentioned any details. However her prediction that I will one day become a Royalist is laughable. Although I did find during my adventures in Scotland that the young Charles is quite a likable lad.'

Luke, now feeling much better, tried to lighten the conversation and chided Meg, 'And who is this unsuitable lover?' 'Long out of date. Kate thinks I am still a young wench with an array of lovers. She disapproves of them all.' This discussion, and the seer's suggestion that Luke would be a suitable lover for Meg, led him to discreetly peruse his female companion. Meg was a decade older than Luke, but her long dark red hair revealed no wisps of grey. Her pale peachy complexion remained unwrinkled, and her large dark brown eyes were alert and sparkling. She was short and her low cut, tight fitting bodice revealed large firm breasts that excited Luke's interest. She had a narrow waist and expansive hips. This was a woman with a curvaceous body that appeared twenty years younger than her chronological age.

His sensual fantasy was suddenly quenched by the realisation that, given his cover story, this was his aunt with whom he could not embark on a relationship. Meg, who was responding to his initial emanations, did not make it easy as she took his hand as they walked their horses back towards The Angel. Luke returned to his experience with the seer in an attempt to modify his unfortunate physical response to Meg. He asked more about Dominic. She responded prosaically, 'We have known each other since childhood. He is Kate's youngest grandson. We went to school together and in my youth he was one of my sweethearts. Harcourt's father appointed him as the vicar of St. Aiden in the early thirties. He strongly supported the reforms of Archbishop Laud to bring the beauty of holiness back into worship. He was dismissed by Parliament after they executed the Archbishop.' 'I thought as much,' railed Luke. 'The man is a covert Papist, and Old Kate the focus for the Catholic opposition to the government. Dominic is probably a secret convert to Catholicism—a priest who manipulates the old woman in the interests of Rome. The whole charade is a cover for a Papist plot against the army and its generals.'

Luke's anti-Catholic tirade annoyed Meg, and quashed her sensual desires. She berated him. 'Luke, your anti-Papist obsessions blind you to reality. The Archbishop's liturgical reforms were popular with the common people. A good dose of catholic ceremony has always been part of the Church of England. On the other hand your Puritan changes to the way we worship are not popular. Dominic was, and is now, responding to popular demand. Good Catholic ritual in worship is in no way related to our ingrained hatred of Papists as enemies of England. Dominic is as anti-Papist as you are, and as a schoolboy wanted to fight against Catholic Spain.'

Luke lapsed into total silence. Meg's blast redirected his thinking from the religious to the personal. Luke had detected several nuances between Meg and Dominic, which she had only partially explained. And why did old Kate raise the question of Meg's past lovers in his, and Dominic's presence? Dominic still interested him and he questioned Meg further. 'You mentioned yesterday a scandal involving Dominic, his wife and son. Adam said he simply walked out on his family, is that true?'

'When Dominic became vicar at St. Aiden in the early thirties he had a ten year old son who was a little wild. Dominic had married one of his parent's servants, a woman well below his status, who was soft in the head, and fell under the influence of religious fanatics. She simply disappeared and took her son with her. Dominic was glad to see both go, and took no steps to find them. He made up the story that he had left them because, although it gave him the reputation of being callous, it was more acceptable than admitting that his wife and child dominated him, and had cast him aside. Some benefactor took pity on the boy, and provided an education that enabled him to become a lawyer.'

Luke relapsed into silence as he struggled to decipher the meaning of Old Kate's prophecy. Her prediction that the plotters against Cromwell would not succeed because they too were an abomination to God intrigued him. In the old woman's parlance this could only refer to religious fanatics and libertines. Or was it all a clever ploy to divert attention away from a plot that if not Catholic, was anti-Puritan and Royalist.

Before they reached the main road the pilgrims on either side of the track leading from the chapel stood aside for two wagons drawn by large black horses with black ribbons around their necks. The wagons carried many coffins. 'What's this all about?' Luke asked Meg, largely to confirm his own assessment of what he sensed was further proof of Catholic superstition. 'They are probably being taken to be blessed by Old Kate. Following the wagon you can see a multitude of mourners.' Luke was convinced that a traditionalist religious conspiracy was afoot. It may not be Papist, but it could be equally threatening to the security of the nation. Luke had had enough.

He sent Meg back to The Angel alone. He turned around and still leading his horse, joined the rear of the funeral procession. Two things were immediately evident. The people around him were genuine mourners, and by their clothing or lack of it, were extremely poor. Luke moved beside a young man who seemed to displaying less grief that most. 'A sad day good fellow.' 'Not really, it's my great grandfather. No one knows his exact age but he was well over four score.' 'Why bring his body to Old Kate?' 'We are not here to see that ancient crone.' 'Then why?'

The young man looked furtively around as if those near him would eavesdrop on his conversation, 'These are strange days. Our parish church lost its vicar when Parliament replaced him with a man who does not conform to our traditional Book of Common Prayer, and some of the other mourners come from parishes in which the laity now perform the service. Great grandfather lived scores of years according to the rites of the Church of England, and it is only fitting that he be buried according to them.' 'But it is now against the law,' thundered Luke.

'It's against the illegal claims of a group of Parliamentary and Puritan turds,' responded the young man with a passion that Luke had not expected. The mourner continued, 'Archdeacon Craven is brave enough to conduct a traditional burial service according to the Book of Common Prayer.' 'So Craven and his grandmother are not Papists?' asked a somewhat deflated Luke. 'No way, when he was vicar at St. Aiden he was as strongly opposed to the Catholics as he was to the Puritans. He always preached that our English church is the true church between the heresies of the Papists on the one hand, and that of the Puritans on the other.' 'I am very relieved that what happens on that hill is not part of a Papist conspiracy.' Another problem confronted Luke. He turned to the young man and asked, 'How you can afford such expensive coffins ?'

'We can't. The coffins do not belong to us. After the archdeacon has read the burial service from the Book of Common Prayer the coffins will be used to return the bodies to the parishes from which they have come. We poor folk will then bury our kin in a shroud.' 'Then where do these coffins come from?' 'They belong to a gentleman who has similar views to us. He lends them to those who want their deceased to have a decent and proper burial service.' 'And who is this kind gentleman?'

'The man who used to have the rights to appoint the vicar of St. Aiden, and is still a powerful local gentleman, Sir Harcourt Reeves.'

9

LUKE'S MIND WAS racing. He speculated that Sir Harcourt's new found religious obsession was to preserve traditional Anglican worship and that he had not, as Adam had suspected, converted to Roman Catholicism. The young man seemed pleased to chat and surprised Luke with his next comment. 'I notice you are well-armed. We could have done with your assistance a few miles back in the middle of the woods. There were originally three wagons but the last one was set upon by a gang of ruffians who forced the wagoner to turn around and leave the procession.' 'Why would anybody want to steal a wagonload of coffins? Did the robbers say anything?' 'They said little. The only words I heard were directed at the wagoner and they were clear—" you stupid fool Hooker".'

Luke noted yet another reference to the Hookers.

He was still not totally convinced that all the mourners were innocent Anglicans, pining for the traditional form of burial. He followed the procession to Craven's service. If the coffin lids stayed down during the service it was Anglican, if they remained open at least some of the mourners were Papists. The service indeed was conducted from the outlawed Book of Common Prayer just as Luke remembered it from his childhood. In the semi-gloom of the smoking candles and failing light he noticed only one of the coffins was open. He would be forced to shelve his theory of a Catholic conspiracy, but the precise role of Sir Harcourt, the fate of the third wagon and the role of the notorious Hooker brothers warranted further investigation.

As Luke trotted home he heard the pounding of many horses, fast catching up to him. Wild thoughts went through his mind. Could these horsemen be after him? No, he had done nothing at Old Kate's to warrant such attention. But it would be wise to be cautious. He pulled off the road, and sheltered in a small coppice from which he had an excellent view of the highway. Luke was relieved. The mysterious horsemen were two troops of cavalry from his own regiment led by Harry Lloyd.

Luke saw his senior sergeant, currently masquerading as his servant, Andrew Ford, riding beside the young Captain. Luke followed the cavalry into St. Aiden. On reaching The Angel Luke was greeted by Meg who explained that there had been a large-scale riot earlier in the evening. She had sent Andrew to get the soldiers. A hundred or more men had fallen on selected houses in St. Aiden, and few in St. Martin. The houses were smashed to the ground, and the thatch and beams of the partially demolished structures set alight. Neighbours had stopped the blaze spreading to surrounding buildings. Seven men were missing, believed kidnapped by the demonstrators.

By the time Luke reached the scene Harry's men were busy helping the parishioners stamp out the remaining embers. The cavalry had no conflict on their hands as the rampaging mob had melted away. Only one of the rioters, who had been knocked out by a falling beam, was apprehended. Later in the night the trooper watching over the shackled rioter was cudgelled unconscious and the prisoner disappeared.

At dawn Harry informed the magistrate, Miles Baker. Baker according to established practice sent authorization to Adam, who had been constable for both St. Aiden and St. Michael for years, to carry out the investigation. Harry returned to The Angel later that day where the inhabitants were having their midday meal. He informed Adam of the magistrate's request and handed him a sealed letter. Adam withdrew from the gathered company to read it, and when he returned ten minutes later he was in a foul humour. Adam was totally perplexed by a postscript that Baker had added to the letter. He had appointed Luke as a special constable to assist in the enquiry.

Adam was not aware that Baker knew of Luke's competence in such an area. Adam was distraught. Was Luke an agent of the man that Adam suspected of being behind the corruption and disorder in the area? Had General Cromwell and Luke deceived him? Normally if the constable wanted assistance he appointed his own additional men. It was unusual for the magistrate to interfere. Without Baker's interference Adam would have naturally included Luke, but now he was suspicious of everyone's motivation. Had it been a mistake to seek Cromwell's assistance?

After Adam withdrew Harry handed another letter to Luke, who although excusing himself remained at the table. He was delighted with what he read and when Adam returned to the room was about to inform him of its contents. Adam could not prevent his anxiety overflowing into a tense and rapid series of questions directed at Luke. 'I have been ordered to include you in my investigation. Do you know Miles Baker? Why would he single you out, unless he too is aware of your real identity?' There was a sudden hush around the table as the dinner guests picked up on Adam's unguarded comment.

Luke sensed that this interference by the magistrate had hit a raw nerve and Adam needed to be pacified. He replied cheerfully. 'No Adam, I do not know Baker nor does he know me. My letter from him simply states that on the advice of Captain Harry Lloyd, who emphasised my experience in these matters for the army, he wanted me to continue to assist you. As for my former identity as a senior officer working for General Cromwell, Baker would know no more than whatever Captain Lloyd told him.'

Although he managed to conceal it from the gathering, Adam was greatly relieved on two accounts. There was a simple and logical explanation for Miles to include Luke, which did not involve any conspiracy of the others against him. And Luke had cleverly covered his slip of the tongue. Before the meal had finished an agitated trooper reported at length to Harry. Harry immediately asked that Adam and Luke accompany him into an antechamber so that he could update them.

Harry was upset. 'This is far more serious than we thought. My men have uncovered six male bodies in the rubble. Even more worrying is that they did not die as accidental victims of the fracas, or from the fire. Their necks have been broken and their skulls crushed.' The three men hurried to the scene of the killings, which was guarded by several troopers who ensured that none of the bodies were moved, despite the pleading of their families. After a brief inspection Luke concluded, 'This is not an irrational mob hitting out at property and authority. Seven houses were specifically targeted and destroyed, and in all but one, the male head of household is dead. We have six premeditated murders.'

Luke was feeling uneasy. He knew virtually nobody in St. Aiden yet each of these men seemed familiar despite their disfiguration. The last body he definitely recognised. It was Walter Sheffield, the printer. Then it became clear. All of the victims had been at the Leveller meeting.

Luke and Adam attempted to question the victims' families. Luke was staggered at their reaction. Mary Sheffield, Walter's widow, made it clear that she and the other widows and orphaned children had nothing to say. The community refused, as one, to co-operate with Adam's official enquiry. Luke was appalled that popular distrust of authority had reached such a level that these families were happy to allow the murderers of their husbands to escape. Without the help of the families the enquiry would get nowhere. Perhaps he as an outsider, and Sam's friend, might get further than Adam.

The next day Luke visited the murder scene on his own. He was making his way through the debris when a tiny little girl, no more than three or four, grabbed his hand. She led him down a narrow street that ran at right angles to the highway and was bounded by a terrace of small two-storied houses. He was alert. Was this to be the third attempt on his life? Luke had one hand in the little girl's, the other rested on the hilt of his sword. Halfway down this narrow side street, which Luke realized led to the water lands, the child ran through a darkened doorway. Luke followed her into an even darker room. Sitting on a bench were four women, one of whom was Mary Sheffield. Standing along the far wall smoking pipes were several elderly men. Luke relaxed. Mary spoke, 'Thank you for coming Mr. Tremayne. Walter said you were a good man, and could be trusted, despite your relationship with Mr. Dale. For God's sake punish those who murdered our husbands!'

'Why did you refuse to speak to Mr. Dale?' asked Luke. 'He ordered Walter's death.' 'What makes you think that?' demanded a now disconcerted investigator. 'Walter was a Leveller who had much experience in bringing people onto the street in large demonstrations. Until recently the apprentices of the City of London were usually willing participants. Many apprentices have now become religious radicals, more concerned about the next world, or effecting changes here only for the benefit of the self-defined saints. They turned their back on the political reforms advocated by the Levellers. Even more seriously, hundreds of the apprentices became involved in a conflict between two powerful employers. One of the apprentices told Walter that the battle between The Fox and The Wolf, heads of vast commercial and criminal networks, was more important to their future than any theoretical plans the Levellers might be advocating. If you supported The Wolf or The Fox you would obtain and keep a job. If you wasted time on political reform you would be taught a lesson.'

'Was Walter expecting an attack of this nature?' 'No, Walter was taken by surprise. He believed the Levellers had become so ineffective that nobody was concerned about them anymore,' replied a deflated Mary. 'But my lad knew this attack was coming,' said the woman sitting next to Mary. 'He was drinking in a London alehouse. He was told that easy money could be had if he presented to a certain tavern between the hours of ten and noon where he would be paid and armed. Certain people in St. Aiden had alienated an important person and were to be taught a lesson. The plan was to smash up a few houses and deliver a beating to specified individuals. The next day, after the beatings had escalated into arson and murder my son asked his informant what had gone wrong. He was told that three men joined the group, encouraged the mob to rampage and burn, and appeared to be particularly brutal towards some individuals. They were led by a man who was exceptionally tall and strong.' Mary Sheffield interjected, 'You can see why I suspect Mr. Dale. Most of people in St. Aiden work for Mr. Dale or his relatives. The motive is clear. Our husbands upset a ruthless employer.'

'You don't think it was of a more general political nature? Did Walter target any one in particular in his various campaigns? Did his recent pamphlets name individuals who might seek revenge?' asked Luke. Mary motioned to one of the men who opened a chest and brought to Luke a number of pamphlets. Mary continued, 'I cannot read Mr. Tremayne. There may be something in the detail that infuriated someone in authority.'

Luke was pensive. 'Even if there is, to kill six men seems a bit heavy handed. Even to beat six men severely would be an over-reaction. To give Walter a severe beating would have been sufficient. No, it is the extreme reaction that worries me. The killings sound almost manic. Why did Walter and friends have to die?' Luke immediately realised the insensitivity of his remark as Mary and the other women began to weep. He apologised, and left carrying a large pile of pamphlets.

He read the pamphlets, but they did nothing to clarify the situation. Walter had attacked everybody—the government, the army, the religious extremists, the London merchants and the great landowners of the realm. Both the attacks Walter made, and the remedies he suggested for improvement, were all of a general nature. Walter was politically astute and did not name individuals, although someone within one of the groups targeted may have taken offence. Luke was frustrated on two counts. There was no way of telling from the pamphlets who that individual might be, and secondly the murders, beatings and arson seemed too extreme to be explained away by any of the motives so far canvassed. He needed more information. He would start with Grenville Reeves as a major employer in the local parishes.

10

GRENVILLE HAD A moon face dominated by two very large blue eyes, one of which was slightly turned. He wore his chestnut blonde hair long, and as one of those rare creatures, a working gentleman, his doublet and breeches were a tan colour, and his lace cuffs and collar reduced to a minimum. He was initially wary of Luke's request to talk over a quiet drink. Luke knew that Grenville would reveal little unless he was completely relaxed. Through an hour of solid drinking Luke kept Grenville entertained with tales of his soldiery and womanising. Grenville slowly responded by several unguarded comments about his lust for Rose Chidlow, and how his sister, Temperance, was wasted on Adam Dale. Luke saw an opportunity. 'If you have such an opinion of Adam, why dwell under his roof? Are you here on behalf of your father to keep an eye on your sister?'

Grenville laughed, 'Sir, you know nothing of our family—if you can call it a family. I never knew my mother. She died in giving birth to me. When I was four, father wanted no further part in my upbringing. Meg, who had lost two children of her own years earlier, took me in. She brought me up. Temperance is my half sister, born to father's second wife, who also died as a consequence of childbirth, although some months after the delivery. Temperance was also sent away—to a distant relative in the West Country. Father only recently reclaimed her so that he could marry her off to Adam, a man old enough to be her grandfather. Temperance and I were never welcome at Reeves House. Father blamed us for the death of his wives. Since his third marriage to the notorious Cassandra, father has become a recluse. Surprisingly his only regular visitor of late is Mistress Chidlow. She assisted Robert in keeping father's accounts. Rumour has it among my wagoners that Robert ignored his husbandly duties, and wasted his nights with Rose teaching her bookkeeping. No wonder she was ripe for the plucking. Poor father ignored her charms having turned to religion, some say to escape his current wife. I live at the inn, not only because it is the only real home I have known, but it is very convenient for my work.'

Luke after refilling Grenville's mug confidentially asked, 'Are your transport activities relevant to my enquiry?' 'You're not suggesting that my workers were amongst the rioters?' 'Well were they?' retorted Luke. 'No, my men work long hours, and have no time to loot and burn. The rioters according to my men were the unemployed, recruited from the alehouses of the inner city, directed by a few men with military expertise.'

'The origin of the rioters is important, as is their target—seven Leveller families within St. Aiden. The printer, Sheffield, has attacked employers who took advantage of the times to cut wages. You are a large employer. Did these attacks cause your workers to agitate against you?' 'Yes, the Levellers, especially Sheffield have consistently advocated ridiculous nonsense about the rights of the workers. What rubbish! If I did not employ these men in various aspects of my transportation business at rates which I determine, they would be unemployed. Most know that they work for less, or not at all. Why would I want to kill a few Levellers? They are a spent force, and irrelevant to my commercial interests.'

Grenville rose, put his hand on Luke's shoulder and confided, 'My workers know that if they cause trouble they will be dismissed, and would not find any other employment. Be warned! There are greater powers than you or I that control the market, and manipulate the masses of the city. I am sure Sheffield died because his activity upset one of these key people who decided to make an example of his small Leveller cell. Cross these men and you will suffer the same fate.'

Luke's initial instinct was to take umbrage at this threat, but he remained focussed. 'Grenville, who are these greater powers?' 'Luke don't probe too deeply. At the moment there is an escalating conflict between the network of commercial and some say criminal interests controlled or protected by The Fox, and that of a relative newcomer whose opponents mockingly label The Wolf.'

'Which of these crime chieftains sent the mob against the Levellers?' 'People in this area, including myself, are protected by The Fox so it is most likely to have been The Wolf.' 'Is this attack on the Levellers a warning to you and other local employers that you should change allegiances?' 'Maybe, but on second thoughts it could just as well be a warning from The Fox.'

'What makes you think that your own protector might do such a thing?' 'The Levellers appealed to the apprentices, journeymen, and masters of the skilled trades, the same groups that provide support for The Fox. The Levellers were competing for support from the same elements of the London work force as The Fox.' 'And The Wolf does not?' 'No, at least not until lately. His initial support came from the unskilled workers, recent migrants from the country, and the unemployed—and more recently from the thousands of demobilised soldiers who are desperate for work. As the rival leaders battle for support The Fox does not want his traditional pool of support, essentially the apprentices of London weakened by the ridiculous demands of the Levellers.'

Grenville suddenly felt he had said too much and staggered from the room without further comment. Luke, also legless, fell onto his bed without disrobing. He was soon asleep, spread sideways across the bed. Some time later he heard a gentle knocking, that seemed to echo around his head. The knocking became louder, and a voice called his name. He stumbled to the door and opened it slightly. Standing before him, holding a large flickering candle, and wearing little more than a flimsy chemise over which she had hastily draped a blanket, was Rose Chidlow.

For a moment Luke thought Adam's assessment of this woman as a faithful wife with puritan sexual mores, was wrong, and he was about to live out Grenville's sexual fantasies. He was brought back to reality when he noticed blood on her hands. Rose pleaded, 'I need your help. Meg said I could trust you, even if you are not her nephew. Come quickly something horrible has happened to Robert.' Luke followed Rose to her chamber. She showed Luke a considerable amount of blood on the outside of the door, splattered over the handle, and pooled on the floor. 'Mistress Chidlow, what happened?' asked a now thoroughly awakened Luke.

'Mr. Tremayne, my husband and I sleep in separate chambers. Every Sunday and Wednesday he comes to my room to perform his husbandly duties. He told me earlier this evening that he had to go out until late, and would visit me around midnight. When he did not arrive I decided to go to his room—which I occasionally do to surprise him. As soon as I opened my door I saw the pool of blood. I turned to re-enter my room to get a blanket to visit you, and found my hand covered in blood from the handle of the door.' 'Mistress, stay here. I will get Meg to be with you.' 'Meg is in London tonight.' 'Then, as we do not know what has happened, lock your door, and do not let anybody in until I return. I will try to find Robert.'

Luke woke Andrew. They agreed after inspecting Rose's door and the floor in front of it, that someone who was about to visit her, had been savagely beaten. Andrew suggested that the person had been smashed in the face, and was probably bleeding from nose and mouth. Luke was more pessimistic. The amount of blood suggested far more serious and probably fatal wounds. They then went to Robert's room. His bed had not been slept in, but his outdoor clothing had been removed, as had his doublet. It fitted the picture of a husband about to visit his wife.

After they left the room Andrew pointed out spots of blood leading away from Rose's door. Somebody, who was still bleeding, had been dragged away from the door. The two men followed the intermittent spots along one of the hallways of the inn that ended at a side door that led into the courtyard. As Luke opened the door a gentle breeze extinguished his candle and Andrew suggested they wait until daylight. Luke would have none of it. He removed a lighted taper from the entrance to the barn, and both men followed the trail of blood.

This led them down a sidetrack, which fell away from the ridge along which the highway and most of the houses of St. Aiden and St. Michael were built. Soon they had left the houses behind and were on a damp path that meandered through the waterland. Given the moisture there was now no hope of finding any spots of blood, but these had been replaced by several fresh footprints and marks of someone being dragged along. Suddenly there was a piercing scream. Luke extinguished the taper. Both men realised that they were almost unarmed. Andrew had dressed quickly, and had no weapons at all. Luke, although he had fallen asleep fully clothed had had time to unbuckle his sword. Consequently he carried only a small dagger concealed in his leggings.

It was drizzling, but the moon emerged at intervals enabling Luke to see that tall rushes now edged the ever narrowing path. Then they heard further screaming which was very close, followed by absolute silence. A few minutes later they heard the sloshing of several feet coming closer and closer.

Both men froze. The probable murderers of Robert were returning up the path. Luke and Andrew dived into the reeds and waited. Two or three men passed them.

A very wet Luke and Andrew regained the path. Luke insisted on continuing the search for Robert. After an hour of walking along damp and waterlogged paths Luke called a halt. 'Either Robert was one of men who rushed past us, or his body has been deposited somewhere off the path. In the morning we will get Harry and our men to thoroughly search this path and the surrounding wetlands. A body could be hidden anywhere. It may even have sunk, as some parts of this wetland are a foot or two under water.'

Next morning the news of Robert's disappearance, and assumed murder, spread through the two parishes. When Harry's troop of fifteen men arrived to search, there were as many local parishioners ready to help, including some of Grenville's wagoners. If Robert's body was to be found it would not be far away from where the abductors had brushed past Luke and Andrew. Unfortunately they could not remember where this was. Eventually Harry found a site where the reeds on both sides of the path had recently been trampled. Luke limited the search to three to four yards on either side of the path, and five minutes walking distance beyond the point where he and Andrew had broken the reeds. There was nothing. Just as Harry was about to end the search, Sam Wright who had wandered down to assist, approached Luke. 'Haven't they told you of the other paths. If you wade through a few yards of this tall common reed that the locals harvest for their thatch, you reach paths that move in other directions across the wetland. These paths are often little more than stepping-stones of tussock sedge. Follow me!'

They followed. Sam was soon on a path that ran at right angles to the one they had originally taken. They had travelled only a few yards when they were stopped in their tracks. Their movement had upset hundreds of ducks that then tried to take wing. These flapping wings forced the men to bend down and protect their heads. As the men knelt a pair of sanguine white swans, also disturbed by the ducks, crushed the grass-like bull rushes and revealed, just off the path, the foot of a man. On closer inspection it was attached to a body, the upper portion of which lay under several inches of water. It was lying face down. Sam turned the body over.

It was not Robert Chidlow.

11

'GOD'S TEETH!' EXCLAIMED Sam, 'It's John Oakes. You met him at the Leveller meeting. He is the missing seventh head of household.' 'The ruthless varlets,' muttered Andrew. 'He must have escaped the murderers during the riot but they relentlessly tracked him down. They knew who they were after.' 'We do not know that for certain,' responded Luke. 'He has been strangled, but there is no sign of the beating and the crushing of the skull suffered by his friends. He could have been killed anywhere, at anytime.' Sam organised for Oakes's body to be removed. He would be buried with his six fellow victims the following morning.

Luke, Sam and Andrew continued their search in the area where the body had been found. Andrew suddenly shouted, 'What's that glistening in the sunlight?' Caught on one of the reeds several feet in from the path Luke saw what appeared to be glass or a precious stone reflecting the sun's rays. Luke reached the glistening object—two large diamonds that were part of a large golden ring. It was attached to a severed hand.

Sam gasped. 'I have seen that ring many times. Its owner bought it to celebrate his wedding. He only wears it on festive occasions. Visiting his wife was clearly such an occasion. This is Robert's ring.' Luke shook his head in disbelief. 'Why sever a hand and still not take a ring worth hundreds of pounds? This Chidlow affair does not make sense as an abduction, a robbery nor a murder.' Luke redirected the searchers to the area where the hand had been found. Suddenly two men who had ventured into a pool of deeper water began shouting. Luke and Andrew waded towards them. 'What have you found?'

The man who had beads of water dripping off his face, and whom Luke recognized as Grenville's wagoner, Austin Perry, replied, 'If you feel with your feet there is a large wooden box resting in the mud. It's fairly new and has not been here long. I kicked at it, and it did not splinter or cave in, and when I put my head under the water I saw its surface has not gathered any accretions. I am sure it is a coffin.' 'Why hasn't it floated to the surface?' asked Andrew. 'There are two large stones resting on the lid, and by now it is probably full of water,' replied Perry.

'Let's get it up and ashore before the light fails,' commanded Luke. The men kicked the rocks off the lid and on Luke's signal they put their heads under the water to see the handles of the coffin that they quickly raised to the surface. When they reached dry land they placed it on a hand drawn cart that had been requisitioned for the purpose. A couple of men pulled the cart to the courtyard of The Angel where Luke insisted that it be opened carefully and in good light. He expected to find the body of Robert Chidlow.

Luke was sure of one thing. This coffin was identical with those he had seen earlier in the week—one of the community coffins Sir Harcourt Reeves provided to assist Anglicans transport the bodies of their loved ones to places where they could receive a burial service according to the Book of Common Prayer.

The coffin was unloaded in the courtyard of The Angel. It was now dark and several troopers held tapers around the coffin, as Luke carefully prised open the lid. There was a frenzied silence of expectation, followed by sighs of disappointment. There was no sudden stench of a decaying corpse. There was no abandoned shroud. There were no precious effects of the deceased. There was nothing. The coffin was completely empty.

Luke reviewed the situation with Adam, Sam and Andrew. 'Gentlemen, our enquiry has taken an unexpected turn in the recovery of another body. It complicates the abduction, and probable murder of Robert Chidlow. Finding the Leveller's body so close to where we discovered Chidlow's hand suggests that the same persons are responsible for both atrocities. Did Robert have any links with the Levellers?'

'Quite the opposite.' replied Sam. 'Robert detested the Levellers. He looked down on them as artisans acting above their social and economic status. He might have been behind the attack on the Levellers. Profit was Robert's god and paying workers more, as the Levellers consistently demanded, was anathema to him.' 'Be fair Sam,' interrupted Adam, 'Robert was not a likeable character, but he was a godly man. His puritan morality with its accompanying social discipline took the fun out of life for those around him, and he would have self-righteously paid the Levellers as little as he could—but he would never be a party to their murder.'

Luke remained focussed on two questions. Why was Robert taken in the first place, and why was his hand severed? Sam was adamant. 'Rule out robbery as a motive. That ring is worth a King's ransom, yet it was left behind.' Andrew had a simple explanation for Robert's abduction, 'He discovered too much about the riot, and the Leveller murders.' But Luke immediately dismissed that explanation.

'No Andrew, if the exercise was to silence Robert why not kill him here in the inn? Why remove a hand?' Sam quietly answered, 'The severing of the hand was a warning, disappear and keep quiet—or you die.' Adam nodded, 'I agree. Robert was a man of principle. Severing his hand was an act of torture. Tell us what we want to know, or we will progressively dismember you. After his hand went, Robert told them what they wanted to know. I suspect the perpetrators were unknown to Robert, or they would have killed him outright.'

Andrew retained his pessimistic and simplistic explanation. 'No Adam, Robert was known to his kidnappers— and he is dead. His body is somewhere deep in the wetlands, and the hand was severed for the ring, but the killers lost it while disposing of the body. Maybe an animal ran off with it. These killers are no petty criminals. They are agents of someone important. Robert's disappearance and the mass murder of the Levellers are related. Both events have more to do with economic gain and survival than with who rules England.'

'And where does the coffin recovered from the wetlands fit in?' asked Sam. 'I can help you there,' said Adam. 'A week ago Grenville mentioned that he had complained to his father that one of Sir Harcourt's wagoners was suspected of pilfering. A day or two later one my servants said the Hooker brothers were moving through the alehouses of St. Aiden selling pistols and swords very cheaply. I assume that John and William Hooker, in addition to the thefts that Grenville was aware of, had helped themselves to a coffin full of arms. They dumped the empty coffin in the wetlands.'

Luke was stunned. Was this a slip of the tongue? Why did Adam associate coffins with arms and ammunition? He obviously knew more about the transport of weapons than he admitted. Luke immediately poured cold water on his own speculation. 'It makes a nice story, Adam, but every time I checked a coffin it contained a body, not weapons or any other illicit goods. The offer of cheap weapons is a mere co-incidence. No, this coffin was stolen to carry Robert's body to the wetlands. Further searching will find it'

'If that was the case how did the body escape the coffin, and where was it now?' riposted the ever-practical Andrew. Following this comment a frustrated Luke threw up his hands and refocused the group's attention on the mulled wine that was a specialty of The Angel.

Next day Luke questioned Rose, 'Was Robert troubled by anything in the last few weeks?' 'Yes, when he returned from London two days ago he was very agitated, but when I asked him why, he told me it would be safer if I knew nothing. Then the night before last he told me he had to meet someone to resolve the troublesome matter.' 'So you do not know what the matter was, or whom he went to meet?' 'No, but he was dressed in his most expensive shirt and doublet. He was meeting someone of wealth and power.'

'Rose, you assist Robert in his work. In addition to running Mr. Dale's enterprises what else was Robert working on?' 'In recent months Robert expanded his activities and spent much time in the city but his new clients were all Puritan merchants and none of their problems could have led to his abduction.' Luke was not convinced. It was an avenue that he should follow up. For the moment he changed the direction of his questioning.

'Did Robert have enemies?' 'All lawyers have enemies. Robert was not popular with the inferior sort because he acted on behalf of the masters in reducing wages and keeping conditions limited. But he had little dealings with the either the apprentices of the City, or the unemployed who are blamed for the recent disturbances. I see no link between Robert and the local rioters.' 'Except,' interrupted Luke, 'that Robert's hand was found close to where the body of the seventh Leveller was recovered. That would suggest the same people were responsible.'

Rose did not answer and took from a small bag that hung from her waist a folded paper and handed it to Luke. 'I found this in Robert's doublet—the one he removed just before he was taken.' Luke unfolded the paper and was disappointed. It was a bill advertising a forthcoming bear-baiting event at the Northbank Bear Gardens. *Old Joachim, a ferocious bear will battle six dogs at once. In smaller enclaves around the Garden, cock fighting and other entertainment will take place.*

Rose picked up Luke's disappointment. 'But there is more. Yesterday I visited Goodwife Sheffield and the other widows to offer my sympathy. She mentioned that around their charred houses a number of bills advertising the bear baiting had been found. The rioters discarded them during their demonstration. If the rioters had the same bill as Robert had in his pocket, it may suggest a connection.' 'Indeed it might,' agreed Luke. 'The government has banned plays; bear and bull baiting and cockfighting will be next. I can see why the apprentices might be interested in directly defying the government, but why did Robert have such a bill? Did your chat with Mary Sheffield reveal any other useful information.'

'Yes, red ribbons.' 'What do you mean?' 'It has became a custom in recent years for demonstrators to wear a coloured doublet, sash, band or ribbon to identify their cause. The Levellers wore sea green, and the Royalists white. Apprentices usually displayed some aspect of their trade. The group that ran riot here, according to Mary, wore red ribbons.'

Luke reported this to Andrew who quickly concluded that, 'These rioters wanted to be recognised. Or rather they wanted to make clear to everybody who they were, and what their act represented. This was neither a simple apprentices riot nor a random outrage by unemployed vagrants. It was organized, specifically directed against the Levellers, and by someone who was making sure his victims, and innocent spectators, knew who he was, or at least what he stood for. Discover the origins and nature of this red ribbon group and we will know a lot more.'

'Too obvious,' mused Luke. 'Someone wants us to think that these Red Ribbons are responsible.' 'Let's ask around. If the Red Ribbons had a message to deliver it would be meaningless if nobody knew what it meant. You and I will spend tonight in the alehouses of St. Aiden looking for answers.' Luke, remembering the fate of the excise men, decided to rely on the effects of intoxication to loosen tongues without any obvious display of bribery.

Their reception was worse than anticipated. Luke's association with Adam, and his formal role in the investigation of the riot and murders, isolated him from the inhabitants of every alehouse they visited. The atmosphere ranged from cold to hostile, although the hostility was manifest in withdrawal rather than aggression. This organized boycott continued until they entered an unnamed two-room hovel in which a bouncy voluptuous woman with large breasts, and unnatural reddish hair dispensed warm ale from a large jug. The ale had a strange aniseed flavour and was very sweet, but sold for half the cost of other ales. The barmaid was immediately attracted to Luke, and when he presented his tankard for a refill she made clear her intentions, 'I'm Jolly Joan. It's on the house, love. As long as you earn it after I close down.' With that she swirled her breasts in a rhythmic motion that quite disoriented Luke.

12

ANDREW WAS NERVOUSLY aware that several men were reacting angrily to Joan's interest in Luke. They nodded knowingly to each other in preparation for action. Luke was completely oblivious to the growing tension. Andrew had to act. He sprang, with his dagger drawn, at the throat of their apparent leader. 'Let's all drink quietly together,' he advised as he motioned for the would-be troublemakers to return to their drinking. The man with the dagger to his throat was not fazed. 'Whatever you do to me, my three friends here will be onto you before your comrade can draw his eyes away from Joan's breasts.' Andrew did not like his bluff being called, and was confused as how he should respond.

Fortunately Joan stepped in and restored harmony. 'Calm down Jack! If you cause any trouble you will answer to Big Bill. He's asleep in the back room, and you know what he's like if he is rudely awakened.' She then turned to Luke and asked, 'What brings a fine gentleman to our humble abode? Perhaps you have heard of my well known generosity?'

'You are perceptive as well as generous. My friend and I have been to most of the alehouses in the parish seeking…' 'Information without offering anything in return,' interjected Jack. 'You are the special constable and army officer working for the high and mighty Mr. Dale,' slurred one of his intoxicated companions. 'Yes, you are right on both counts. I am trying to solve the murder of the Levellers, and discover as much as I can about the red-ribbon-wearing rioters.' Luke was astonished at the reaction.

All of the drinkers walked out of the ale house without uttering a word. Joan feigned anger. 'See what you have done. All of my customers have fled. You will now have to pay tenfold for that,' as she grabbed his hands and placed them on her breasts. 'Tell your man to go home, and I will bar the front door.'

Luke, turned on by the thought of gaining more information, rather than the opportunity to share in Joan's generosity, nodded for Andrew to leave. She barred the door, and ran her hands over Luke's body. She was very effective in arousing Luke's baser instincts, but he was determined to use their mutual arousal to obtain the information he needed. 'Joan, why did your customers run out of here when I mentioned the Red Ribbons?' 'How would I know,' said Joan cheerfully, as she plunged her hand down the front of Luke's breeches.

Luke removed it, and moved to unbar the door, saying, 'That's not good enough Joan. You know very well why those men left.' 'Not really, my sweetie, but given the murders, everybody is on edge. If the Red Ribbons were responsible, you do not want gossip getting back to them that you have been mouthing off about them to the authorities. The lads are only protecting themselves. No one trusts a stranger, let alone an officer in our ever-victorious army.'

Before Luke could reply there were sounds from the back room. Big Bill was stirring. Joan responded immediately, 'All right, I don't have much time. Take me quickly, before he fully awakes, or we will both be in trouble.' 'The Red Ribbons—who are they?' insisted Luke. As he slipped between Joan's legs, she combined utterances of delight, with an answer to his question, 'There is a major war going on in what your ilk would call the criminal world. A new man is trying to take over the interests of the existing crime chieftain. The henchmen of this new man wear red ribbons to remind everybody that it would be wise to join him.'

Big Bill's snoring began again, indicating that he had fallen back to sleep. Luke and Joan had a mutually satisfying hour. Joan was overjoyed with the experience. Luke was pleasantly surprised. What could have been a sordid one minute explosion turned into a series of climaxes. Joan's final reaction was to talk incessantly. Luke used it to follow up on the Red Ribbons. 'Tell me more about these crime masters?'

'When authority collapsed early in the civil war London crime became organised. One man controlled the harlots of Southwark, another robberies in Westminster, a third the highwaymen along the northern road. However over the last five years one man, The Fox, has exercised control over most criminal activity, and many of the commercial enterprises in London. He protects us. Recently a rival has entered the field, and is trying to take over from him.'

'This rival I understand is called, at least by his opponents, The Wolf. Do you know the real names of The Fox or The Wolf?' 'No, both work through their minions. It is dangerous to ask too many questions.' 'Did the Levellers, and Mr. Chidlow ask too many questions?' probed Luke. 'Maybe. The Levellers were disappointed that their support was drifting away not only to the religious radicals, but to one or other of the crime bosses who could more readily provide and protect jobs. Work and wealth are more important than the vote, or law reform.'

'Have many apprentices joined the Red Ribbons?' 'Until very recently, no. Most apprentices stayed with The Fox in their own self-interest, as he and their masters, and the City of London authorities are close allies. The poor Levellers! They are crushed between the religious fanatics on the one hand, and the network of criminals, entrepreneurs and their workers on the other.' 'If they were such a spent force why murder them?' Luke asked.

'The Wolf wants to scare us all, and make us rethink our links with The Fox,' whispered Joan. 'The Wolf gets his support from the unemployed and the recently arrived country labourer?' asked Luke. 'Yes, and most importantly during these violent times, from recently demobilised soldiers, and some who are still serving and who have not been paid. Old Bill said the riot that preceded the murder of the Levellers was organised with military-like precision. He was really impressed.'

'And Chidlow, why was he abducted and probably murdered?' 'All of the landowners, shopkeepers and tradesmen in this area, including their lawyers, stewards and bailiffs are protected by The Fox. The Wolf probably kidnapped Chidlow, who had access to the commercial secrets of the Dales, Sir Harcourt Reeves and many other allies of The Fox. When he failed to extract information from Chidlow concerning his clients, The Wolf killed him to show us that The Fox could no longer protect even those very close to him. Cutting off his hand was warning to others.' 'Was it a warning to you?' 'Not directly. I am too far down the chain to be of interest or influence, but I depend on a regular supply of grain to make my ale which I must obtain from Grenville Reeves.'

'So if you told Reeves you would no longer buy grain from him and would obtain it from another source you might find all hell would break out.' 'Yes, but why would I do something so stupid?' Luke ignored Joan's negative response and continued, 'Joan, I have a proposition for you.' 'Just keep repeating what we have just gone through, and I will agree to anything,' purred the still sexually aroused wench.

'My proposition is dangerous. I want you to tell Reeves that you have a new source of your grain. I will approach the Red Ribbons to see if they can supply and protect you. It might bring the crime masters and their local representatives into the open.'

'And get me killed. You must be mad.' As she untangled herself from Luke there was a loud hammering on the door. Joan ran to the back room and woke Old Bill, who instinctively reached for a short heavy cudgel that lay in the corner of the room and strode straight towards Luke, and swung aggressively in his direction. Joan redirected him to the door. Luke drew his sword and stood diplomatically behind Bill as the giant demanded to know who was without. Luke was relieved to hear Andrew's voice, but was surprised to find that he was accompanied by six armed troopers.

Luke left immediately with his heavily armed escort. Andrew explained that he had only just escaped Jack and his friends, and realised that they would be lying in wait for Luke. Harry and his patrol had stopped at The Angel for a few drinks, and Andrew asked for assistance to rescue Luke from a difficult situation—albeit one of his own making.

Back at the inn Luke updated Andrew and Harry on the Red Ribbons and his plan to approach them with the offer of new business. Andrew was wary, 'Jolly Joan has not agreed, and why deliberately undermine Grenville Reeves who is an important local figure—and could prove a good ally? You do not have to use Jolly Joan or Grenville Reeves to gain access to the Red Ribbons. Create a fictional business that seeks protection from them. Upsetting Grenville, and endangering Joan will not be helpful.'

As Harry and his men were about to leave The Angel they had to delay their departure as the relatively narrow way was occupied by a large wagon drawn by two black horses and a number of heavily armed outriders. Given the consistent drizzle the load, was covered, but Luke was sure he knew the contents—more coffins. He turned to Harry. 'Arrest the driver, confiscate the wagon, uncover the load and open one of the coffins!'

Andrew once again advocated caution. 'No Luke, this is lunacy. Your anti-Catholic obsession has got the better of you. There is nothing illegal in transporting bodies across the country, if endorsed by the local bishop. Now that the bishops have no authority, anything goes. Whether the bodies are Catholic, Anglican or one of the many varieties of reforming Puritanism is irrelevant. Do you want to raise the ire of dozens of grieving relatives?' Luke took a while to calm down. 'Maybe you are right Andrew. Nevertheless, Harry follow that wagon as far as you can!'

Next morning Harry reported back. Before Harry had opened his mouth Luke anticipated his findings, 'I can tell you where that wagonload of coffins was heading. The corpses were being taken to what passes for a mountain in these parts to receive from Dominic Craven the banned burial rites according to the abolished Book of Common Prayer.' Harry, initially put out by the interjection, now had a broad smile on his face, and winked at Andrew. 'Is that so Colonel?' 'Yes, Meg and I saw wagons loaded with coffins heading that way the other day.' Harry was enjoying the moment. He shook his head slowly. 'Well you are wrong, sir.' Again Harry procrastinated, leading Luke to declaim, 'Spit it out man, where did it go?' 'The wagoner circumnavigated Sir Harcourt Reeves's estate and then entered it through the woods on the far side of the property.' 'And?' asked an impatient Luke. 'The coffins were unloaded and placed inside a former derelict, but now partly renovated chapel.' Luke was silent.

Harry persisted. 'Come Colonel we need action. Talk has got us nowhere. Two issues require urgent attention—the coffins and what they contain, and the Red Ribbons.' 'You are right Harry,' said Andrew, 'but as the coffin issue is largely based on Luke's obsessive assumptions about a Catholic conspiracy we should concentrate on the Red Ribbons.'

Luke, somewhat put out by the telling banter of his subordinates, finally rejoined the discussion. 'Many of the red- ribboned murderers carried bills advertising a series of entertainments at a new Bear Garden which they may attend in great numbers. But these bills are interesting for a number of reasons. I have never heard of this Bear Garden. It is on the north bank of the river—all established bear gardens are on the south. The entertainment is in late winter in unfavourable weather. This is traditionally a warm weather event. No wonder it is being scheduled to start at noon, when normally bear baiting began in late afternoon.'

'Even more surprising it is to take place on the Sabbath and within the City of London. Parliament and the City authorities have opposed bear baiting and cock fighting for almost a decade. Such activities are barely tolerated during the week, but they are already totally forbidden on the Sabbath. This event is a deliberate affront to the authorities. Someone wants to show them where power really lies within metropolitan London. And that someone could be the arch conspirator that we seek.'

13

I T WAS OVERCAST and cold. Luke and Andrew left their horses within The Tower at the barracks that their regiment had recently vacated. They walked along the river to what had been for centuries rows of dilapidated hovels. These had been demolished over the past few weeks and the area had become a hive of building activity—except for its total suspension on this and every Sabbath day. Today activity on the site surprisingly far exceeded its weekday levels. The event they witnessed, stretching across the site to the banks of the river, was not a clandestine bear baiting. It was a full-scale traditional fair with a range of events and exhibits that would be anathema to the Puritan city authorities.

The noise of enthusiastic participants and spectators, and the shrill blast of a variety of woodwind and brass instruments including fifes, shawms and crumhorns; the rhythmic beat of the tabor, a snare drum that reminded Luke of many a forced march; and the exciting melodies from a host of fiddles, created a cacophony of sounds. The site had an outer line of hurdles along its street frontage, and then an inner more tightly fenced area for the paid entertainment associated with the bear baiting. The outer area was filled with tents in which customers could see and listen to a mix of free and paid exhibits and performances.

There were several puppet shows, including the ubiquitous Punch and Judy. Luke gave a farthing to a young girl who was collecting the money, and he remained long enough to realise that the puppets were being used to promote quite revolutionary propaganda. This was not simple entertainment. Luke and Andrew avoided the tents containing the deformities of the age—conjoined children, the bearded woman, six legged sheep and four legged geese. In a very large tent a group of minstrels and actors were performing a range of ballads that ranged from the bawdy to the obscene, focussing exclusively on fornication and defecation. As soldiers they had heard most of them before, but were a little surprised that in many, the words had been changed to insult the late and present kings but also to denounce the current republican government.

What intrigued Luke was not that attacks on the current government received resounding cheers of support from the audience, but that every negative reference to the monarchy was booed. Luke was surprised that the singers continued to attack the monarchy when the audience was overwhelmingly sympathetic to the Royalist cause. Their persistence suggested that these actors and singers were on a mission to denigrate both Royalist and republican solutions to England's problems. But whom did they represent?

Another tent contained life size wax models of important people, real and fictional. St. George and Robin Hood represented the former, while former monarchs dominated the latter. There were several figures, who had made a name for themselves in the Civil War including the former commander of Parliament's forces, Sir Thomas Fairfax, and the successful sailor, General-at-Sea Robert Blake. Luke was miffed. There was no Lord General Cromwell. He questioned the proprietor over this omission. Amazingly the man broke down, and almost wept, 'Please sir, do not tell the organizer of this fair that the model of the general is missing. Part of the condition of having a tent here was that we should if possible attack the King and the current government, and advance the role of the reforming army.' Luke was pleased that these entertainers were supporters of the army he served.

'Then why have you broken the agreement?' he asked of the proprietor. 'Why is there no Cromwell?' 'These models take a considerable time to make. I have already made at least six of Noll Cromwell. Every time my back is turned someone decapitates him with a sword, or chops into his body with a dagger. I also have trouble keeping the model of the late King Charles. People steal the whole figure, or parts of his clothing. Many kneel before the model, and the area around it has become a shrine. I receive countless requests to make models of the King from visitors willing to pay considerable sums.'

Luke left the tent of the wax modeller depressed by the failure of the fair's organiser to modify public opinion, and by the overwhelming support that remained for the monarchy. He rejoined Andrew who had strayed into an adjacent ale tent. After a few drinks the two walked quickly along the side of the enclosure which contained cages of wild animals. The lions, the wolves and some young bears were all clawing at the bars to escape their captivity. Above the roaring of the big cats a series of trumpet calls were heard. Luke ascertained from a man on stilts that this was a preliminary blast informing the public that they should pay their entry fees to the inner enclosure. Proceedings would commence in half an hour.

The inner enclosure contained a large pit dug by the building workers. At one end there was a hastily erected grandstand to give the wealthier customers an unimpeded view of the fight. On the far side a natural terrace gave similar advantages to other paying customers. On the left of the pit was a collection of tents and wagons containing the competing beasts and their owners. Along the river frontage there were six or seven smaller pits around which a number of men were beginning to assemble with their fighting cocks. While the main entertainment took place those obsessed with cockfighting could place their bets continuously throughout the afternoon. Makeshift hurdles fenced the whole inner area. To prevent the nonpayer from entering this inner enclosure the perimeter was patrolled. Today, given the size of the crowd, it was clear to all there were insufficient men for the task.

Luke fully expected that at any moment the Puritan London authorities, who held extreme views on such useless and blasphemous pastimes, would stop these well-advertised activities. Yet there was no sign of any formal agents of repression. Luke and Andrew approached the designated entrance to the inner enclosure. Luke sensed trouble. There was a considerable delay as the customers attempted to pay, and enter through the only gap provided in the makeshift fence. The men collecting the money were an unhappy lot. Luke, trying to be amiable despite his long wait in the queue, asked the collector why there were not more people allocated to assist him, and why only one gate had been provided. 'Sirrah, my fine gentleman. You tell me. We normally have four entrances and several dozen men controlling the perimeter. They have not turned up today. Maybe it is too cold for the white livered churls, or more likely they have been delayed by those out to destroy my master's livelihood.'

Luke wanted to probe the nature of this opposition, but the irate crowd pressing to gain entry made it impossible to continue the discussion with the gatekeeper. It was well past noon when a Master of Ceremonies finally entered the ring to a combination of pipes and drums and a series of trumpet blasts. He was greeted by boos, catcalls and a barrage of miscellaneous objects. Those who had not yet entered the enclosure added to the outburst. Luke and Andrew, both big men intimidated a group that had occupied the front row of the tiered stand. They quickly made room for the two men. Obtaining some degree of attention, the Master of Ceremonies announced that as a prelude to the fight between Old Joachim and the best of English mastiffs there would be a series of entertainments beginning with Tommy Pitt and his team of tumblers and vaulters. The catcalls and booing continued until Tommy and his team began to achieve great heights in their acrobatics, and began to engage the audience. Their ability to vault over two or more horses, and vault on and off these beasts amazed Luke. Then one of them, blindfolded, climbed a pole, and walked across a tightened rope, to a post erected on the other side of the pit. The same man then appeared to slip and fall, hurtling headfirst towards the ground only to be stopped by a rope attached to his ankles that left him inches from disaster. The crowd erupted in clamorous approval. Then Tommy Pitt took a basket of eggs and two lighted candles and performed a series of somersaults without breaking the eggs nor extinguishing the candles.

The Living Giant, Gerald the Great, replaced Tommy Pitt and his troupe. Gerald was a strongman who began by showing off his flexed muscles to the audience that led many women to swoon. Luke was surprised that this seven foot giant with such a remarkably strong body, had hair almost to the ground. He soon understood why. Six men wheeled a cannon into the pit. Gerald tied his hair around the cannon and unaided dragged it around the small arena. Again the crowd erupted into spontaneous applause. Gerard was followed by *Flight The Wonder Horse* who answered questions from its master by tapping with its front hoof, and changing into a series of different gaits and paces according to a variety of whistles. As a finale its trainer left the enclosure, both inner and outer, and apparently walked away down the adjacent street. Those on the tiered stand heard a high-pitched whistle and

Flight disappeared, and according to the ringmaster found its trainer well away from the enclosure. A few minutes later man and horse galloped back into the pit.

Luke was interested in the next item as a number of wooden targets in the shape of humans were placed at one end of the enclosure. The crowd's attention was directed to three marksmen at the far end of this immense vacant block standing on a slight embankment. Luke estimated the distance as several hundred yards. The Master of Ceremonies announced that the first shot would be to the left kneecap, the second to the heart and the third to the head. Luke turned to Andrew, 'A crown that they miss two or more of the nine shots.' 'You're on,' replied the sergeant. The first musketeer fired his three shots—all of them on target, as did the remaining two. Luke handed over his crown and wished he had had musketeers like that supporting his cavalry at Worcester.

As there was a lull in proceedings Luke, ever the optimist, looked around in vain for anyone wearing red ribbons. After another fanfare of trumpets, and then to the eerie beat of the tabor, a large brown bear was led into the ring, and tied by a rope of limited length to a stake placed against one side of the pit. Immediately uproar emerged from the section of the crowd standing at one end of the enclosure. Luke could make out a litany of complaints—*It would not be a fair fight. The bear was blind. The bear had no teeth. The bear had no claws. The result had already been rigged in favour of the dog owners who did not want their animals hurt. Management had been paid a fortune to protect the dogs, and the heavy betting that had already taken place, had been done so under false pretences.*

In listening intently to these complaints Luke had not noticed that a large group from outside the enclosure had crashed through the undermanned hurdles, broken up the crowd on the terrace, and combining with the discontents already within, started a major brawl. Luke and Andrew drew their swords and made their way to the edge of the pit. They would cross it and leave the enclosure on the far side, well away from the affray. The bear was safely tied to its stake, and despite the noise had settled down and was watching the events with a bemused expression. The complaint of the discontents that the bear was blind was clearly false. As were the other complaints—this bear had sharp claws and gleaming teeth.

The mob began to rip up the tents and set fire to the tiered stand. Luke and Andrew turned back and joined several armed gentlemen in putting out the blaze and restoring order so effectively that within five minutes the main mob had dispersed.

14

B UT SMALL AFFRAYS continued. On the far side of the enclosure four men set upon one of the bear garden's attendants. Instead of beating their victim the quartet picked him up, and threw him into the pit—at the feet of the bear. The fall incapacitated the victim. He could not move. The bear stirred, slowly rose onto all fours, and began to sniff at the still body that had disturbed his repose. Apparently Old Joachim was not attracted by the man's smell, and seemed unlikely to immediately slash the body with his razor sharp claws, or rip into parts of the body with his gleaming teeth. But the man was not out of trouble. The bear placed a heavy paw on his chest, and lay across the human body providing itself a soft mattress for his afternoon sleep. The man regained consciousness, and sensing his inability to move, screamed for help. The bear pressed even more heavily upon him.

Andrew ran to the bear and pricked it several times with his sword. After a minute or two of these gentle jabs the bear finally responded, and uttering deep guttural growls moved towards Andrew, who quickly retreated to safety beyond the limits of the bear's chain. Meanwhile Luke scooped up the man who screamed with pain as he was moved. He was shaking uncontrollably, and Andrew who often carried with him a flask, poured pain-numbing whisky down the throat of the injured man. After several minutes the victim regained his composure, and asked for the Master of Ceremonies. While Andrew looked for the ringmaster, Luke asked the victim to identify himself. 'Joseph Muggs. I work for Black Brian, the Master of Ceremonies. During the week I am an apprentice gunsmith. The disruption of the performance and the attack on me were part of The Fox's plan to destroy our Bear Garden, and ruin its promoter.' A very interested Luke drew a deep breath and asked with feigned innocence, 'Who is this Fox? And why is he out to destroy the Bear Garden?'

'The man who operates this Bear Garden, and other enterprises, has challenged The Fox for control of many of London's activities, including public entertainment. Usually men wearing red ribbons protect the Garden. Today I assume the London militia, as is its want, detained most of them. How convenient! We did not have enough people to control the crowd. Consequently The Fox was able to disrupt the performance with false accusations, and finally his viperous toads smashed their way into the enclosure. I was taking the admission money to Black Brian when I was attacked. I threw the bag of money into the bear pit. The would-be robbers were so furious that they tossed me after the money. I must find it.'

At that point Black Brian arrived and quickly assessed the situation. Andrew went to retrieve the bag which had fallen close to the bear, but still looked intact. Black Brian found a wide plank in one of tents that had been used for a makeshift bench. Two of his men lifted Muggs onto the board, and carried him in the direction of one of the larger tents. Luke commented to Black Brian, 'A nasty business. Muggs claimed it was the work of The Fox.' 'Muggs has a good imagination. This was the work of some dog owners, who resent the way my master gives the bear a fighting chance. In our bear fights more dogs die than in other encounters. The dogs are very valuable property and in most situations a company of dog owners can exert considerable pressure on the entrepreneur to mutilate and weaken the bear. Not so with my master.' 'And who is your master?' probed Luke.

'Sorry sir, that gentleman does not want his interest in bear baiting to be known, particularly not in this town and especially with the present government. Given the determination of the traditional bear pits to protect their interests, and those of the dog owners to exert theirs, he is wise to remain unidentified. Even if I knew his identity I would not tell you.' Luke understood the reluctance of Black Brian in the circumstances to reveal the name of his employer. Andrew returned and handed Brian the bag of takings that the bear had conveniently thrown beyond the extent of his chain.

Luke tried another approach, 'Who is The Fox? Muggs seemed quite convinced that he was responsible for the disruption.' Black Brian appeared irritated, 'Sir, it does no one any favours to be asking about The Fox. I bid you good day.' With that Black Brian entered the pit and untied the bear that had fallen asleep in the fading winter light, and gentle flurry of light snow.

Luke was not a happy man. 'The ingratitude of the man! I rescue one of his senior workers, and he refuses to answer a couple of civil questions. I will find out more about The Fox, and I know just the man who can help me. He has lodgings near here. When I first joined Cromwell's Ironsides, at the beginning of the war, Jasper Nettle joined on the same day. As young newcomers we spent a lot of time together. He is now a senior officer in the London Militia, and is responsible for policing the more unruly sections of the city. His men should have been here today, preventing the entertainment in the first place, or restoring law and order once the fracas had broken out.'

After several fruitless enquiries Luke was finally successful in locating Major Jasper Nettle. He was directed to a tavern, The Black Horse, by a passer-by who scurried away as if anticipating some frightful calamity. Pushing their way through the crowded public house Luke and Andrew realised that most of the drinkers were militiamen. There was not a male civilian in sight, and the noise created by the raucous throng was incredible. Everybody was singing, or rather shouting the words of a popular ballad about a lusty young smith who made his tool available to various damsels. The chorus of 'With a jingle dang jingle dang, jingle hi ho' took the level of raucousness to unbearable levels.

The gathering started up on another ballad, this one dedicated, not to fornication but to defecation—The Jolly Brown Turd. Luke recognised that the man leading the singing swinging his tankard with exaggerated movements, and stamping his heavy boots to keep the rhythm, was Jasper Nettle. Nettle who had an impressive baritone voice suddenly broke into a new rendition of this scatological ditty in which he made numerous salacious references to the high command of the army. Luke lost his composure. He became icily furious.

These London militiamen had no time for members of Cromwell's national army. An out-of-control Luke, headed for Nettle, but found the tail of his coat being tugged on with such force that he was pulled back. It was Andrew. 'Don't be a fool! Given the location, and the company, and their high level of intoxication and camaraderie, this is no place for an officer of the hated national army to confront Nettle. You do not know how he and his friends might react, and in your current mood you are not likely to be diplomatic. There are only two of us. Let's sit quietly in the far corner and await a better opportunity.'

Andrew's caution was well placed. A group of militiamen, having seen the two strangers began to provoke them, indicating that unless they left immediately, they would be forcibly removed. Luke and Andrew feigned obsequiousness, and quickly departed. A little down the road on the opposite side of the street was another alehouse, from where the exit of The Black Horse could be watched. It was well into the night before The Black Horse began to empty. Eventually Nettle with three of his comrades stumbled into the street. His friends were legless, but the Major was less affected by drink than Luke had hoped. He approached the Major, 'God's Blood! my old partner Jasper Nettle.' Luke extended his right arm in salutation. Nettle stared for a few seconds into Luke's face that was in the shadow of the tavern's external taper. Nettle moved to where he had a clearer look at the stranger. 'Zooks! it's Master Blue Eyes. How are you Luke?' They hugged and Jasper farewelled his friends, and motioned for Luke to re-enter The Black Horse with him, where he directed Luke to one of the vacated benches.

'What are you doing in the city? As a senior officer in our glorious army I expected you would be on duty in Ireland or Scotland. The government has been trying to detach a few of our London companies to reinforce you, but the city fathers have so far refused to co-operate.' 'You are right. Until recently I was on service in Scotland, but I took leave after Worcester.' Luke thought it politic not to reveal his real situation, as he had not seen Nettle for years, and knew nothing of his current political or religious allegiance. He repeated his cover story. 'I am heir to an inn to the north of the city, but am currently assisting the Middlesex authorities investigate several murders.'

'I heard that old Noll Cromwell used you as some sort of investigator. Have you seen the General of late?' Luke again lied and turned the conversation away from the past. 'Jasper, I need your help. During the course of my enquiries I keep coming across references to a mysterious master entrepreneur, some say criminal, The Fox. Who is he and where can I find him?' Luke was not prepared for the response. Nettle raised his arms, and made to club Luke with his clenched fists. At the last minute he smiled and pretended he had been play-acting. After a long silence Nettle whispered, 'A piece of advice. Never ask about The Fox.'

Luke responded provocatively, 'Why not? You are responsible for keeping law and order in the City. Why are you not hunting him down? Even worse you now protect his identity.' This time Nettle reacted diplomatically and softened his response. 'You were always on a mission Luke. You have spent too much time dealing with the priggish Scots, and the barbarian Irish. This is London. Imposing discipline through the sword is not the answer to the city's problems. Englishmen cannot be coerced and bullied over the long term. General Cromwell should remember that if he considers forcing reforms on an unwilling city and country. I am responsible for order—and The Fox is a person that I need to have on my side. As for the law, it is increasingly an ass. Enough of these questions! It is good to see you again after so many years, but it is late, and I must retire. Fare thee well.'

Jasper walked out of the tavern without any further comment. Luke followed at a discreet distance. He would discover the location of Jasper's lodgings for a future confrontation. Andrew, who had sheltered in The Black Horse's entry while Luke talked to Jasper, rejoined his colonel. It was very dark, and the gusts of snow further limited visibility. It was futile. They could not see Jasper, nor his footprints. They struggled along the slippery cobbles and constantly lost their footing. It was a miserable night, and as Luke struggled to his feet after yet another fall he heard something behind him. He felt a tremendous blow on the back of the head. He crumpled to the ground and passed out.

Luke had no idea how long he had lain unconscious on the street. He eventually became aware of six or seven men hovering around him—and they were doing nothing to assist. They were his attackers. He lay still, feigning unconsciousness, despite the cold numbing every member of his body. One voice asked, 'Do we finish him off?' He was answered by a voice that Luke recognized. It was Jasper Nettle. 'No, the death of a senior officer, and one of Cromwell's close associates would provoke army intervention in London, which is the last thing I want. Luke will recognize this as a warning. Just to remind him, place that small wooden carving of a fox in his pocket. What about his companion?' 'I hit him too hard,' said another of the group, 'He is dead.'

 **15**

BEFORE LUKE COULD take in the death of Andrew, Jasper reversed his man's assessment. 'No, he still breathes. Go back to The Black Horse and get a flask of strong water. Leave it beside Tremayne. Let's go!' Luke waited several minutes until he was sure a flask had been placed beside him, and all the assailants had left. He struggled to his feet and discovered that the extreme cold had temporarily removed the shocking headache he had experienced on first coming to. His eyes gradually adjusted to the dark. He could just make out a crumpled body some yards away. It was Andrew. Luke cradled him in his arms hoping that the body warmth would somehow encourage him to wake up. Just then he heard voices, and saw lights heading his way. It was the watch. Luke called for help.

The commander of the watch was suspicious. At first he suspected that Luke was an assailant who was in the process of robbing his victim. But the lump on Luke's head supported his story that he and his friend were set upon by several club wielding thugs. As Luke placed all his possessions on a cape that one of the watch had laid on the ground, including his weapons, the commander of the watch uttered a cry of alarm. 'Bejesus man, you have upset the most powerful man in London—The Fox. Leaving behind a small wooden fox is his way of warning the recipient of his immense displeasure. You are lucky to survive this attack.'

Luke went on to explain that their horses were stabled with the cavalry mounts in The Tower. During the discussion Andrew regained consciousness, and was given considerable swigs of strong water. Two of the watch assisted Luke with Andrew until they reached the army barracks. It was too late to return to St. Aiden, and the two men spent the night in the onetime barracks of their regiment. Luke would take advantage of his location to visit the Lord General in the morning. There was something seriously amiss in the leadership of the City militia.

Next morning Cromwell did not waste time with civilities. 'I did not expect to see you until your mission was complete. I trust this visit does not indicate that you are experiencing difficulties?'

'To be honest I am in trouble, and have come up against resistance to my enquiries by leading figures in the London establishment. I have come across frequent mention of The Fox. Nobody will elaborate, and my sergeant and I were set upon last night and beaten as a warning. None of this in itself is sufficient reason to bother you, except that man the city authorities have placed in charge of maintaining law and order is working for The Fox.'

'And who is this treacherous officer?' 'One of my fellow troopers in your original company formed in 1642—Jasper Nettle.' Cromwell grinned and then laughed aloud, 'That takes me back, as does your complaint. The two of you were constantly complaining about each other in your mutual determination to become my senior cornet. You continued in the cavalry, but young Jasper, having convinced me of the importance of artillery, moved into that area. He was a great asset in the siege of many a Royalist town and castle. He did not join the New Model Army but took a position within the London Militia. Are you sure that your old rivalry has not warped your view of the situation?' Luke thought it politic not to comment, and redirected the discussion, 'Sir, do you know anything about The Fox that might be useful to me?'

'Tremayne. I don't have time to concern myself with London criminals. The civilian authorities, aided by the militia are totally responsible for law and order in the city. The army is concerned with the defence of the republic from external and internal enemies.' 'That is my point sir. I suspect that the internal security of the republic may be threatened by as yet unknown activities of leading London criminals, aided by senior militia officers. Yesterday the opponents of The Fox were detained by Nettle, rendering one of their enterprises unprotected. A mob recruited by The Fox then destroyed the event.'

'Proof Tremayne, and I will act! At the moment all you have is that many people are frightened of The Fox, and your allegation, based on very little, that your old opponent—responsible for law and order in the city—is part of his network. Now what's the situation in St. Aiden and St. Michael?' Luke provided a lengthy summary of the situation as he saw it. There was a major problem brewing in the area, but he had not been able to penetrate the local conspiracy of silence, or effectively assess the deliberately misleading information provided by those he had questioned.

Cromwell began to pace the floor with increasing speed, and reddening face. He finally spoke. 'Luke you must uncover as a matter of urgency the real loyalties and intentions of Adam Dale and of his rival Miles Baker. It is time you paid Baker a visit. He may be the subversive element in the area. As you know I ordered Lloyd to move your whole regiment, other than my personal guard, to Baker's estate on the pretext that the northern approaches to the city need more intense surveillance. The officers are billeted at Baker Grange, and the men have erected tents on a designated part of the estate. I also asked Lloyd to raise your name favourably with Baker with regard to assisting him as a special constable.'

Luke returned to The Tower to collect Andrew and their horses. He pondered the irony that the militia of London might be more loyal to the Parliament than its own national army. Since the victory at Worcester until Cromwell's recent order, Luke's cavalry regiment had been stationed in the Tower of London, although the defence of The Tower was in the hands of the recently raised militia units of the Tower Hamlets—a separate body from the militia of the City of London, or those of Westminster, or the borough of Southwark. These units were urgently raised when the army was in Ireland and Scotland and the parliament feared internal insurrection. With the return of a large portion of the army that had been in Scotland, and the scaling down of activities in Ireland, the metropolis now faced potentially conflicting armed forces. The national army was officially controlled by the Parliament, but in reality obeyed its high command led by Oliver Cromwell. The militia of the City of London was dominated by the merchants and guilds of the City, and the same mercantile clique that provided a large minority in the Rump. The militias of Southwark, Westminster and the Tower Hamlets represented local vested interests, and obeyed powerful local identities.

As he was in The Tower Luke questioned the senior officers of its militia regarding The Fox, the Red Ribbons and their colleague in the London Militia, Major Nettle. Most of the Tower officers were drawn from the merchant and artisan inhabitants of the Hamlets, usually selected because of their previous experience in the national army. They all knew of The Fox. He controlled many of the commercial and criminal activities of the city. He essentially provided protection for those who paid him, and terrorised those who did not. Until recently most businesses paid protection and enjoyed the benefits it gave. In recent months there had been growing unrest—more affrays and riots as The Fox and his mysterious rival, The Wolf, battled for control. The Tower officers blamed the spate of murders within their jurisdiction on this conflict. The victims had upset either one or the other of the powerful leaders.

The Red Ribbons were an essential part of this contest. They were labourers, building workers, recently demobilised soldiers and the unemployed who provided the manpower to help The Wolf undermine the activities and interests of his adversary. None of them knew anything about The Wolf other than his orders were delivered by a lawyer, and executed by a showman who was also an experienced soldier.

As for Major Nettle the officers of the Tower Hamlets were divided. Because he took strong action against the Red Ribbons, often for no clear reason, a Dutch born captain with a very deep voice, suggested that Nettle was a partner of The Fox, and engaged in several corrupt activities with him. Another, with a homegrown London accent, strongly resented such aspersions. Nettle was an honourable officer who had managed to keep a lid on potential disorder by his diplomacy towards The Fox, and his resolute action against the Red Ribbons. A young officer with a short Spanish beard agreed. It was common sense to support The Fox, 'The Fox can maintain order better than the authorities. Why undermine him? We could never control the eastern and northern outskirts of the City if we were in conflict with The Fox. The Fox not only controls crime in the city, he regulates many aspects of legitimate commerce, especially transport.'

Luke was unhappy. Before heading back to The Angel he and Andrew revisited the site of the previous day's entertainment. They entered a lane heading for the river but immediately stopped. The alley was full of men, armed with staves and cudgels, heading towards the river. To avoid involvement Luke and Andrew moved on to the next lane that ran parallel with the one they had just left. It too was full of armed men chanting in unison as they headed towards the river, and the building site which had been the location of the aborted bear fight.

Andrew suggested they return to The Tower and alert its militia to potential disorder. 'No point,' replied Luke. 'We are now in the City. The Tower militia have no jurisdiction here.' Just as Luke spoke, a large body of horse galloped past them, and turned into the narrow lane. Luke recognised the sash of its commander. These were units of Nettle's London militia— the legitimate military authority within the area. Andrew expected the horsemen would disperse the mob, which was chanting itself into a frenzy. He teased Luke on his negative assessment of Major Nettle in maintaining law and order. Within seconds he was eating his words. The militia unit took no preventative action. It fell into line behind the mob—to a suspicious Luke, a position from which it could prevent the mob retreating, but in no way prevent its attack. They were not there to prevent an affray. They were part of it. Luke turned his horse, and galloped several alleys passed those occupied by a mob. He turned into the first that was relatively empty, and galloped to the riverbank.

He and Andrew reached it just as the mob poured from the lanes onto the land that the previous day had been the Bear Garden. It had reverted to a building site but with only a dozen or so men erecting some wooden scaffolding, and a few others digging drains and footings. It looked as if the builders had been warned of impending trouble, and withdrawn their labour force. As soon as they saw the mob the few workers remaining retreated to the riverbank, as the intruders began smashing up the site. Luke could now see the militia located behind the rampaging mob quietly observing the scene, and ensuring that no one left the site. Luke's instincts were to ride into this melee of destruction and put an end to it, but two horsemen were no match for a hundred or more cudgel and stave wielding men. Suddenly there was uproar.

16

EMERGING FROM BELOW the riverbank, where they had been obscured from Luke by the low tide, and disembarking from several barges were wave after wave of red-ribboned men. Standing on a slight ridge directing the river-borne defenders, now turned attackers, was Black Brian, sword raised aloft. Behind him a row of musketeers appeared, and quickly fired their first volley over the heads of the advancing mob. Then a man somersaulted himself directly at the mob and hurled a well-primed grenade at the advancing party of louts. It was the tumbler from the Bear Garden, clearly an experienced, as well as an agile grenadier. The Red Ribbons, in addition to grenades, and a dozen musketeers, were armed with swords, pikes and daggers. As more barges pulled up to the bank disgorging more red ribboned, well-armed men, the cudgel-bearing mob retreated, and in their haste enveloped the watching cavalry, unhorsing several of the militia. Completely surrounded by the retreating mob they were in no position to seek immediate aid for their poorly armed friends.

A few of the more stupid assailants did not retreat, and staggered forward to engage the advancing Red Ribbons who showed no mercy to their inadequately armed opponents. Cleverly sidestepping the cudgel swing of a leading assailant, a red-ribboned swordsman plunged his weapon into the chest of his startled opponent. Without withdrawing the blade, with his other hand he drove his dagger into the stomach of his now expiring victim. This was quickly becoming a massacre. On a crisp command the pursuing Red Ribbons threw themselves on the ground to allow their musketeers an unobstructed field of vision to fire several volleys into the retreating masses. After the fleeing mob had disappeared up the alleyways Luke was horrified to see the large number of dead and wounded. Their companions did not stop to render assistance, nor did the Red Ribbons whose marksmen had taken an unnecessary toll. The Red Ribbons were unrelentingly ruthless—to Luke another example of overkill.

Andrew muttered in admiration, 'An ambush if ever I saw one. An uneven skirmish between a well disciplined military force and a poorly armed, intoxicated rabble.' Luke nodded in agreement, 'Yes, and where did they obtain those accurate musketeers? We saw them yesterday. Then they put on a good display for entertainment. Today they were shooting to kill.' Luke and Andrew were so stunned by the turn of events that they did not notice a platoon of Red Ribbons encircling them. Any potential nastiness was cut short by the arrival of Black Brian, resplendent in a short bright red cape, who jocularly proclaimed, 'You have come on the wrong day Mr. Tremayne. This was not a bear fight.'

'I noticed that', said Luke with no sign of humour. 'The rout of your opponents was very professional.' Black Brian responded. 'It had to be. The Fox is determined to prevent my master developing this site, and sent his loathsome scabs to destroy it. And did you notice that the London Militia was there encouraging them?' 'You seemed to be forewarned of the attack,' observed Luke. 'My master has friends close to The Fox,' answered an unthinking Brian.

Luke's mind was churning. If only he could uncover a person who had interests in both camps his investigation would be getting somewhere. But for the moment he was overcome by the unnecessary loss of life, which mirrored the similar overkill of the Levellers. 'Why did you massacre the Levellers in St. Aiden and St. Michael last week?' 'We didn't. The Fox suspected, quite rightly, that information was flowing from his camp to that of my master. To embarrass us, and remove his perceived enemies he had his men wear red ribbons when they went on their killing spree. The real Red Ribbons were detained by The Fox's notorious ally, Major Jasper Nettle—the same ploy he used yesterday to remove our protection from the bear fight.'

Luke was not convinced. It was a common defence to claim that your enemies disguised as your own men committed the heinous crime. 'What about the disappearance and dismemberment of the lawyer Robert Chidlow?' 'I know nothing of that, although I know of Mr. Chidlow. He is partner of Mr. Craven who acts as the spokesman for our master, The Wolf.' Luke was increasingly perplexed by this arrangement. How could a man who was central to the activities of the Fox, Robert Chidlow, be a partner of a man, Matthew Craven who was clearly acting for The Wolf? Chidlow's disappearance must be related to this dilemma.

Luke turned on Brian. 'What about yourself? This operation was well planned and executed. You are no common showman.' 'I was—before the war. I was conscripted by Sir Thomas Fairfax and eventually commanded his personal company of infantry. I was Captain Brian Kendall of the Parliamentary Foot. When the New Model Army was created in 1645 I did not join it and became a garrison commander in Yorkshire, but last year I resigned and moved to London to make my fortune amongst the gamblers involved in cock fighting, and bull and bear baiting.'

'And where did you get your musketeers?' 'Suffice to say they are on loan to my master in return for services rendered, by military men that have no time for Nettle and his Fox loving militia.' 'I assume that your master has the barge men of the river in his camp.' 'Yes, The Wolf now controls all goods on the river that are not unloaded from sea going vessels, and is, through their apprentices obtaining influence in many river and warehousing crafts and professions.' 'And how did you become involved in leading the military wing of the Red Ribbons?' 'Very simply as I refused to pay protection money to The Fox my entertainments were constantly disrupted, and my actors and acrobats intimidated. Mr. Craven approached me with an offer from The Wolf to train a few retrenched soldiers to assist his men combat the minions of The Fox. When the London Militia came out clearly on the side of The Fox, I was asked to recruit and train a rival force.'

As they spoke a man wearing a red ribbon galloped out of one of the lanes and immediately confronted Captain Kendall, 'Sir, Major Nettle is headed this way with a company of cavalry and what appears to be a regiment of foot.' 'How much time have we?' asked Brian. 'The cavalry will be here within minutes. The infantry are probably half an hour away.' Luke was astonished, 'Where did Nettle get so many horsemen? By law, the militia is not allowed to recruit cavalry.'

'Our friend Nettle is no fool. Those horsemen are technically not cavalry. They are dragoons—mounted infantry. Forgive me Luke, I have a few things to do before Nettle arrives.' Kendall barked a series of orders and as quickly as they had emerged the Red Ribbons disappeared. Dozens left by the many barges that were ready for just such an eventuality. Those that remained transformed into building workers, intent on resurrecting the edifices that the mob had demolished.

As predicted within minutes some thirty horsemen galloped out of three parallel lanes that ran to the river. At their head was Jasper Nettle who was surprised on two accounts—the virtual desertion of the building site, and the presence of Luke Tremayne. Luke took the initiative with a deliberately misleading comment, 'Thank God you have arrived Jasper. We came across a mob trying to destroy this site. I noticed a detachment of your men here. Thank goodness they went back for reinforcements. Unfortunately everybody has disappeared—except for the dead and wounded. Maybe your men can help organize their removal?'

Nettle was livid.

Luke rode back to The Angel with a smile on his face. On his arrival it immediately disappeared. Sam could not hold back his surprising news. 'Luke, you are in charge of the inn for some time to come.' 'What do you mean Sam? Where are Adam and Meg?' 'Adam is at Dale Court. He said if you had any problems you would find him there. He told the staff that it would give you a chance to gain experience in running the establishment, and I was here to assist.' 'What is that devious Adam up to? He knows anything to do with running the inn, is simply a cover. Gaining experience at running the inn at this time in my investigation will simply take away valuable time and energy from the enquiry.' 'Maybe that was his intention,' muttered a suspicious Andrew.

'What about Meg?' continued Luke, ignoring Andrew's comment. 'There is a lot you don't know about Meg. She has been very kind to me so am not going to reveal her life story. Suffice it to say she was thwarted in love, but has maintained a close relationship for decades with an innkeeper in the City. She spends much of the year with him.' Luke thought for a while and commented, 'Isn't it strange that Adam and Meg have both left the inn? Has it anything to do with the attempt on our lives, the murder of your Leveller friends, and the disappearance of Robert Chidlow?'

'Probably, although I cannot see a connection. Everybody is concerned with the growing tension throughout the city. Adam and Meg are anxious to protect their business interests, and turn a handsome profit before the growing incompetence of the Rump, and revolutionary ambitions of the army destroy the commerce of London.' 'Do they belong to a network of likeminded persons?' 'Yes, My Leveller friends always claimed the Dale family was associated with the most powerful man in the City—The Fox. That is why they do not trust Adam, and why their families refused to assist with his enquiry.'

'Is The Fox a criminal or simply a sharp entrepreneur?' 'In these times if you oppose the Rump you are considered a criminal. Since the wars began where do you draw the line between criminal and legal activity? Of all the extended family Grenville certainly has direct links with numerous shady elements, as transport is a dangerous, and yet very profitable enterprise.'

When they were alone Andrew gave Luke the benefit of his assessment. 'You have been snubbed by the Dales for pursuing the Leveller enquiry, and upsetting Nettle. Perhaps he and Adam or Meg are allies.' 'It is too soon for that level of reaction. I only confronted Nettle two days ago. Adam and Meg organised their departures before that. Now that our relationship with the Dales appears to have chilled, it is a good time, as the general suggested, to meet their local rival. Tomorrow we will visit Mr. Miles Baker.'

Next morning Luke and Andrew headed north. Baker Grange had been a collection of out-houses of a Benedictine monastery. The current owner's great grandfather who had been one of HenryVIII's supporters, joined them together, and created the very large manor house. The Bakers remained Protestant during the reign of Catholic Mary, and were found in the parliamentary Puritan opposition to Elizabeth, James and Charles. During the Civil War Miles Baker remained a member of the increasingly radical House of Commons surviving its many purges. He supported the actions of the army leaders, although he was not present during the trial and execution of the King. More recently during the absence of many of its army members on service abroad he had defended their interests against the majority of the Rump. Now that the security threat was gone his political rivals planned to disband all but a few regiments. On the surface Miles Baker was a very staunch ally—but was he?

17

THE MANOR HOUSE at Baker Grange was built into the side of a lengthy tree lined ridge and was reached by a winding, relatively steep way. As Luke and Andrew approached the entrance to the house a man emerged, collected his horse from a waiting servant and galloped away from the house in their direction. On seeing them he slowed, doffed his hat, and then accelerated down the slope.

'Someone is in a great hurry. Was that Baker?' asked Andrew. 'Don't know. I have never met him.' With that reply Luke dismounted, tied his horse to a hitching post, went through a small entry portico and hammered on the large double door. A diminutive servant opened it. Luke introduced himself as an envoy from the Lord General Cromwell who had urgent business with Mr. Baker. The little man ushered the two soldiers into a small chamber off the entrance hall. They were immediately aware of raised voices in the next room.

Suddenly the door to their chamber burst open, and a tall aristocratic woman with a myriad of brightly coloured skirts each slightly shorter than the one it covered, and a neckline that left nothing to the imagination, strode into the room. She let forth a stream of oaths that were better suited to an army camp than a genteel drawing room, and began to throw a number of loose cushions back at the door through which she had come. 'Men are loathsome turds, especially relatives. I agree with that French woman who said the more she saw of men the more she admired dogs.' Then she saw Luke and Andrew and intensified her tirade. 'So my sycophantic churls, are you the bum boys of my husband, or the cuckolding and cuckolded friends of my brother? Or the brainless hulks who assist my obsessed lawyer?'

Luke attempted a safe response. 'So which of these vile men just rode off in a desperate hurry?' The woman paused to look Luke up and down as if examining a prize beast. 'What's it to you my pretty blue-eyed boy?' With that she took Luke's head in two hands and drew it down upon her breasts which had largely escaped any covering. Her rampant nipples were clearly displayed. Luke, somewhat taken aback by this turn of affairs, was struggling with a verbal and physical response when the woman pushed him aside, drew herself up to full height, and pulled her bodice up over her bosom. 'Let me introduce myself. I am Lady Cassandra. The turd you saw running out of here was my hard working lawyer whom I enjoy teasing. He has no sense of humour. And you gentlemen—where do you fit into this convoluted and topsy turvy world?'

Luke explained he was an envoy from Cromwell on urgent business with Miles Baker. Lady Cassandra moaned a little and mumbled something about always needing a soldier to satisfy her unfulfilled needs. Once more Luke could hardly believe his ears as much of Lady Cassandra's conversation suited the bawdy house, and definitely not the drawing room of a Puritan politician. Miles Baker must have a full time job keeping his wayward wife under some sort of restraint. She was a total embarrassment.

Luke had it all wrong. A well-dressed gentleman in a golden jerkin over a white shirt with a small collar and small cuffs, and breeches of tawny brown, tied at the knee with golden ribbons, entered the room. 'I am Miles Baker. I regret you had to witness the behaviour of my sister. Her mission in life is to embarrass and harass every man she comes upon. Her husband has thrown her out. That is why she is here. Instead of going quietly she has taken her husband to court on the most outrageous of charges, and has employed an expensive lawyer to plead her case. Even when they lived together she terrified Harcourt with her knowledge of the black arts and her ability with potions and poisons. I think he expected at any moment to be poisoned. My sister is an interesting but destructive woman.' Before he had finished Lady Cassandra left the chamber but not before she gave Luke a squeeze on the buttock. Miles ushered the two soldiers into the adjacent room, which housed a magnificent library.

Luke went straight to the point, 'Mr. Baker, the army, having returned from service in Scotland, is concerned with the level of disorder and violence in this region, and the suggestion that certain groups are arming for a coming showdown with it, should it fall out with the Parliament. The General has heard that it is members of the Rump such as you, who are behind this conspiracy. Conversely, there is evidence pointing to a group of yeomen and gentry in the vicinity of St. Aiden and St. Michael led by Adam Dale who might be responsible.'

'I can assure you Colonel that I put my faith in the army a decade ago and have no intention of changing my position. You are well advised to investigate Adam Dale, his notorious sister Margaret, and the trimming and twisting Sir Harcourt Reeves, my erstwhile brother-in-law.' 'Lady Cassandra is Sir Harcourt's wife?' asked Luke, already seeing the potential for information from the litigious virago. 'The third. It is one reason why I took my sister in. She has considerable information on her husband's political activities. It was her evidence that I passed on to General Cromwell. There is no doubt that Sir Harcourt and the Dales belong to a large commercial and, I believe, criminal network that is plotting against the army. Have a word with Cassandra's lawyer. He took her case largely to get himself as much information as he could on Reeves and his friends.' 'And what is this lawyer's name?'

'Matthew Craven. He is in partnership with a Frenchman Tournac and Adam Dale's missing steward, Robert Chidlow.' 'Chidlow could have been murdered,' announced Luke. 'That fits with what Craven told me recently. Chidlow discovered more and more irregularities in the Dale accounts. He probably confronted Adam Dale, and was killed to keep him quiet.'

'Sir, have you heard of The Fox?' 'Of course, a shady business man who took advantage of the wars, and in recent years, declining local authority, to built up a vast network of protection. He controls many legitimate and criminal activities in London.' 'Do you know who he is?' 'Yes, he is a local lad, Valentine Cole. His family farms the lands between the Dales, and that of the Reeves. He grew up with Adam and Margaret Dale, Dominic Craven and Harcourt Reeves. They were a wild lot in their youth. Rumour has it that Valentine was thwarted in love, and ran off to London where he made his fortune by fair means and foul.'

'Have the Dales and the Reeves kept up their friendship with this Valentine Cole over the years?' 'To be honest I would love to be able to say that they are all part of The Fox's criminal conspiracy but I have no evidence. I am not very close to any of those families. Matthew Craven raised the same question with me a week ago. I hear you are related to Adam Dale yourself, and are heir to The Angel.' 'Mr. Baker, my role with the Dales is not what it appears to be. The general has sent me there to uncover precisely what is going on—from the murder of three excise men, to the massacre of the Levellers, several other murders and now the disappearance of Chidlow. Adam knows my true mission and identity but none of the others have been informed.' 'I would not be too sure of that. Adam is a follower. He tells his sister everything.'

Luke left Baker Grange with as many questions as he had answers. As expected Miles had tried at every point to blacken the name of his enemies, yet when it came to the critical issue he had no tangible evidence to link Adam Dale and Harcourt Reeves to The Fox. Lady Cassandra was a handful, but she would be useful in pursuing Sir Harcourt. Above all, Luke was intrigued by Matthew Craven. His link with Robert Chidlow on the one hand, and with The Wolf on the other; and his current relationship, if any, with Archdeacon Dominic Craven and Old Kate needed unravelling.

News travelled fast. Adam who had retired to Dale Court for the duration was waiting for them at The Angel. He was disconcerted. He poured Luke and Andrew a drink, and immediately, nervously yet aggressively, questioned Luke. 'What are you up to? Why were you at Baker Grange? I hope you have not fallen for the forked tongue of that unscrupulous dissembling knight.' 'Calm yourself Adam. I have just been doing what you and General Cromwell suggested. I have been interrogating Baker about his possible anti-army activities. He denied any such behaviour, and as you predicted, suggested that you and your friends were the more likely source of unrest and disorder. But he did raise two interesting points. He told me that The Fox, about whom everybody else I spoke to refused to comment, was indeed Valentine Cole, a childhood friend of yours. And secondly that your ally Sir Harcourt Reeves's current wife is Baker's sister. She is determined to bring him down. Do you still have links with you schoolboy friend?'

'Of course, for decades we have worked along with Valentine, through a commercial cartel of certain goods and services related to transport, property development and public entertainment. Grenville plays a major role in our co-operation with The Fox.' 'What about Cole's alleged criminal activities?' 'I am not certain that that aspect of The Fox's reputation is deserved. Much of his so-called criminal activity is simply the result of the collapse of law and order in the newer outer suburbs of London. The Fox has stepped in to protect legitimate businesses and prevent unnecessary competition. The London authorities appreciate his efforts.'

Luke had strong evidence of this last assertion, but changed the direction of his probing, 'Did the partnership of lawyers that included Rose's great uncle and husband reveal any political or religious bias during the last decade?' 'Emile Tournac and Robert Chidlow were the epitome of professional neutralism, although they had quite contrasting political and religious views. Robert was not only my steward, but also carried similar roles for a number of other persons, including Harcourt Reeves and Oliver Cromwell not all of whom I knew, and many with very different views than mine. He was a Puritan and a strong supporter of the Parliament during our civil strife. Emile Tournac, given his French Calvinist origins may have secretly deplored the execution of the King, and felt deep sympathy for his fellow Calvinists in Scotland during the recent conflict, but this did not stop him from acting for both traditional Anglican and religious radical clergy removed from their ministries by the Rump. During the monarchy he had an intimate association with the royal court, which was rumoured to have been personal rather than ideological—although some believe like a lot of French Calvinists he converted to Catholicism. He was certainly a confidante of the Queen, Henriette Marie.'

'I gather Tournac took in another partner recently who has taken up the cause of Lady Cassandra Reeves.' 'Crazy Cassie! Did you meet her? She fell under the influence of one of her servant's when she was at Reeves House. Harcourt had to sack a bunch of them who were convinced that God was about to destroy existing society and create a world of equality. The girl filled her ladyship's head with ridiculous concepts that women were the equal to men, that the laws must be changed to allow eldest daughters to inherit their father's property, and that married women should be able to divorce their husbands for the mildest indiscretion—and then claim the bulk of his estate. Cassie has taken poor Harcourt to court hoping to achieve some of these ludicrous claims.'

'What intrigues me, and should concern you, is that a lawyer who is a partner of your missing steward, is now representing a woman who is determined to bring down your friend, and partner in several enterprises, Sir Harcourt Reeves. Did you have any cause to suspect Robert of disloyalty?'

18

'NEVER. ROBERT, IF anything, was too loyal and too conscientious. Many a time I told him not to bother about minor discrepancies, and a few unpaid debts.' 'Is his dismemberment, and possible murder related to his work with you, or with other activities?'

'I would be stupid, given the other murders and general disorder in the area, to believe that his death is unrelated to his activities here. Robert was no dissembler. He was too honest for the role that a steward is forced to play. If Robert has been killed, it would be to stop him revealing a truth. Maybe he was worried about his new partner's relationship with Lady Cassandra, especially given his and Rose's business association with Sir Harcourt.' 'Accepting your point Adam, my task is now to uncover whether the truth that Robert was about to reveal was detrimental to Sir Harcourt, Valentine Cole, Miles Baker, The Wolf or yourself?'

A highly agitated Sam burst into the chamber and announced, 'Mistress Chidlow has disappeared.' Adam was relaxed, 'What do you mean disappeared? She is visiting friends. Since her husband vanished she has a need for company, and has spent a lot of time at Reeves House.' 'Come with me!' requested Sam. The men followed him into Rose's chamber and he took them to two large chests that rested against the wall. He opened both and explained, 'All her possessions have gone, as has Tamsin, her maid servant.'

Luke was now concerned, 'Did she leave of her own freewill, or has she been kidnapped? In either case is it related to the disappearance of her husband?' 'Let's not speculate, this may explain everything,' announced Adam, as he produced an unsealed letter from her small table. He carefully perused its contents. 'Relax! Rose is with her great uncle. She apologizes for her sudden departure, but as his partner, Mr. Craven, was in the area she left with him.'

Sam was not convinced. After Adam left he confided in Luke. 'I don't think Rose left willingly. This morning she told me that she was going to ask Adam whether she could take over Robert's role as steward.' 'No woman can take that role,' pontificated Luke. 'Correct, but Rose suggested that I become the nominal steward, and she would look after all the legal and financial aspects of the position. An hour or so before she departed she had no intention of leaving.' 'Don't stress yourself Sam. I will visit her great uncle tomorrow and discover the truth.'

Luke's composure was ruffled on entering his own bedchamber. He took his goblet from a sideboard and was about to half fill it with canary wine when he saw that it contained a small object. It was a ring. He recognized it immediately. It had been on the severed hand of Robert Chidlow. Rose would never have left without it. Or did she leave it behind to alert Luke that she was in trouble? Luke could never resist a damsel in distress. In the morning he checked with Sam that the note left by Rose was written in her own hand. It was.

Luke and Andrew found the chambers of Tournac, Chidlow and Craven not far from the Inner Temple. Luke climbed a narrow staircase which opened into a large room. Several young men sat at desks laden with piles of papers. The man facing the top of the stairs appeared to be the senior clerk, and asked Luke whether any of the legal gentlemen expected him. Luke replied that he was on urgent business regarding a family matter, and needed to see Mr. Tournac. The clerk looked annoyed, but wandered to the far end of the chamber where several doors led from the large room.

Luke followed him into a library chamber. A small silver haired man, dressed in black was slowly dismounting from a small set of steps, carrying a number of large tomes. Before he had alighted, the top volume slid off the pile, and crashed to the ground. Luke retrieved it, and placed it on a table that was incredibly small for the rest of the room. Emile Tournac introduced himself. Luke informed the lawyer that he was Colonel Tremayne, and an acquaintance of his great niece, and that he wished to speak to her. 'I am sorry Colonel that you have had a wasted trip. Rose arrived here yesterday, but left first thing this morning for France.'

'Why? I thought given her recent trauma she needed to be with family.' 'Exactly so Mr. Tremayne. This is not a suitable establishment for a young woman who needs the comfort of female companions. As my partner Mr. Craven had business in France, he kindly offered to take her to my sister in Bordeaux.' 'Surely Mr. Tournac this is not the time to visit regional France. Remnants of the Civil War continue to plague much of the rural countryside, and Bordeaux faces invasion from Spain at any moment,' advised Luke somewhat pompously. 'Mr. Craven has all the right political connections. Rose will be safe.' Luke was getting nowhere and changed his focus, 'I am having a bad day. I had also hoped to see Mr. Craven. He has a case which interests the army and which may bear on a number of crimes committed in a couple of the parishes north of the city. Some people seemed surprised that you made Mr. Craven a partner? Have you known him long?'

'My reasons for inviting him to join me are my own. To your second question, I have known of him since he was a baby. I encouraged him to become a lawyer. Matthew has built up a lot of commercial interests and has considerable influence in parts of the city. He works in many fields, and when he asked to work with me, to pay me back for the assistance I had been to him in his early days, I was delighted. Robert Chidlow is a conscientious lawyer but his overdeveloped morality does not permit him to take cases that would make our fortune. Matthew is much more pragmatic.' 'And has the association proved fruitful?' 'Profitable, but risky.' 'Which annoyed Robert Chidlow?' 'Initially yes. Until recently there was tension between the two, but in the last few weeks they appeared to have reconciled, and were allies on a number of cases.' 'Can you tell me which cases these were?' 'Colonel what transpires between the client and his counsel remains confidential. Unless I obtain permission from them to reveal information, I can tell you nothing.'

Andrew who had accompanied Luke did not enter the building. He tied the horses to a rail, and went to relieve himself behind a few shrubs at the side of the premises. This site overlooked a side entrance to Tournac's property that was well below street level. The side door opened and two men emerged carrying a number of bags which they placed on a small cart which rested against the wall. They made an unusual pair. Andrew recognised both. One was the strongman from the Bear Gardens who had his long hair contained under a rather large hat. The second was the athletic vaulter and tumbler, Tommy Pitt. Two women followed them to the cart. They were not struggling, and willingly clambered aboard. One was Rose Chidlow and the other her maid Tamsin. They dangled their legs over the back edge of the vehicle as the strongman pulled it out of the small yard up into the street. Rose was deliberately avoiding Luke. Why?

Andrew followed them on foot. Soon he could smell the river, and given the slope of the alley knew they were heading directly to the Thames. Eventually the cart reached open ground, which Andrew immediately recognized as the location of the bear baiting, and the battle between the Red Ribbons and allies of The Fox. The cart did not progress far into the field. It sank into the mud of the churned up building site. The strongman could have undoubtedly freed it, but instead he picked Rose up, and carried her across the muddy terrain. The tide was almost at its ebb and the strongman held her above his head and he sank up to his knees as he crossed a large expanse of ooze to reach a large barge. He repeated this activity several times until both women and their luggage, and Tommy Pitt were safely aboard the barge. Finally he gave the craft a powerful push which sent it rapidly into the middle of the Thames where the bargemen relaxed, as the last efforts of a receding tide pulled them down stream. Andrew ran back to Tournac's, mounted his horse and galloped to London Bridge hoping to identify the barge that contained Mistress Chidlow and ascertain the direction she was being taken—was it across the river to Southwark, or downstream to an ocean going vessel?

It was useless. The river was full of barges and Andrew could not identify the relevant one. An unhappy Andrew arrived back at Tournac's chambers just as Luke emerged. Andrew explained what had happened in detail and emphasised that he recognised Rose's companions as members of Brian Kendall's troupe. Luke decided to observe Tournac's chambers from an adjacent alehouse to see who visited the Frenchman. After two hours located in The Book and Quill which conveniently provided a view of Tournac's front entrance Andrew gave a horrendous sigh. 'I'm a fool. Visitors could have come and gone through the side door.' He rose to take up a new position overlooking the side door, but Luke restrained him.

'Too late. Let us apprehend the first man who attempts to enter or leave the lawyers' premises through the front door.' The wait was finally rewarded. A medium sized clerk dressed in dark grey with a distinguishing brown doublet left the building. The two soldiers bounded out of the alehouse, but before they could engage with the clerk, a band of youths draped in red sashes swept him up. Trotting behind the noisy band of artisans was Captain Brian Kendall, again wearing his bright red cape.

Momentarily he was taken aback to see Luke and Andrew. 'Gentlemen you are a long way from home'. 'And what bit of showmanship are you engaged in at the moment?' asked Luke. 'The Red Ribbons are about to right a few wrongs created by The Fox. Ride along with me and see what good we are doing.' 'Another time Captain. We must return to St. Michael on the northern road.' 'That is exactly our destination—as soon as I gather my full quota of men, and a number of large wagons.' Luke was puzzled. 'Then we shall accompany you, but at a distance, as we are not part of whatever you have in mind.'

Luke and Andrew trotted behind the ever-increasing number of men, most of whom were displaying a red ribbon or sash. The group halted at a small open field, which had recently been created by the dismantling of a number of decayed houses. After half an hour a big cheer went up from the waiting group. Coming down the slight hill was another large body of men and six large wagons. Their leader was Joseph Muggs, who seemed fully recovered from his encounter with the bear. 'Joe is my deputy for this engagement. These are our people from south of the river,' explained Brian.

What happened next surprised Luke.

19

ACH OF THE large wagons contained only a half load of tanned leather hides. The empty space was quickly filled by most of the gathered throng. The dozen men, who did not board the wagons, covered their companions loosely with large sheets of fabric. The caravan that moved slowly north consisted overtly of one horseman Brian Kendal, six wagoners, and a dozen men armed with cudgels and daggers, and what appeared to be six wagons laden, given the information painted on the side of one of them, with leather products.

Luke quizzed Brian, 'What are you up to? It looks like another ambush.' 'Quite the reverse. My men are here to prevent an ambush. The six wagoners brought numerous raw hides down the northern road to the tanneries in Bermondsey. They were accosted in the parish of St. Aiden by a gang who demanded protection money on the pain of the destruction of their goods and wagons. These ruffians were agents of The Fox, who is determined to keep his control of land transport in and out of London. As these wagoners are returning with a much more valuable cargo of finished leather goods, further demands are anticipated. My master has just given his protection to these wagoners for much less a consideration than that demanded by The Fox.'

On entering St. Aiden Luke saw hurdles placed across the road. He motioned to Andrew, and the two of them disappeared down a side street towards the water lands, and sloshing along its sodden paths and riding parallel to the main road they were soon able to rejoin the highway well beyond the obstructive hurdles. They quickly dismounted, and strolled back down the highway in the direction of what appeared to be a major traffic jam. Brian Kendall was arguing with a man whom Luke recognised as one of Grenville Reeves's leading hands. The man waved his hands in the air and from concealed positions along the edge of the road some twenty heavily armed men appeared—more than enough to deal with Kendall's visible gang. The intention of Reeves's men was clear. They would give the wagoners, and their pathetic guard a beating, and confiscate sufficient goods to pay for the protection that the wagoners had refused to accept.

Suddenly one of Kendall's men produced a cornet and a couple of discordant blasts were sufficient for the covers to be thrown off, and dozens of men disgorged from the wagons. Reeves's men were surrounded, and brutally beaten as the Red Ribbons once again showed great discipline, little humanity, and no mercy. No one escaped. Luke and Andrew watched from the doorway of an adjacent tavern. This was no time to show their hand, or get embroiled where one party had overwhelming superiority. After some twenty minutes a blood soaked man half stumbled, half walked towards them and then collapsed. He was obviously recognised by the wench who had joined Luke and Andrew in the alehouse entrance. She summoned help from within the house.

The Red Ribbons moved on. Luke and Andrew assessed the carnage. Twenty bodies were strewn across the highway—most motionless and quiet. A few were stirring—moaning and groaning in pain. Four or five were dead, and an equal number might soon join them. Just as the two men completed their rounds, offering assistance where possible, a contingent of horsemen arrived from The Angel and its adjoining transport depot. Grenville Reeves immediately approached Luke. 'What are you doing here? I thought you were in the City.' 'I was but on our return we noticed a disturbance on the highway, and wandered down to see what was happening.' 'And what was happening?'

'Your men attacked the red ribboned escort of a group of wagons. But they were led into a trap. The wagons were full of additional men, and you were outnumbered. I am sorry to say several of your men are dead.' Grenville did not speak further. He was distraught. He arranged for the disposal of the dead, and succour for the injured. The survivors were taken to The Angel.

Later that day Luke was in his room at the inn when a musket shot was heard, followed by another. He ran into the hallway and looked out of a street-facing window. On the ground spreadeagled in the mud was Brian

Kendall. Luke ran down the stairs, and was soon comforting the dying showman. Two shots had entered his back. He was coughing up blood and was paralysed. But it wasn't Brian. It was Joe Muggs who was wearing Brian's distinctive red cape. The assassin had killed the wrong man.

Andrew arrived angry and disgusted. 'Margaret Dale shot him in the back. She just left her room with a smoking musket. From her window she had a perfect shot into the street below.' Luke stared at Andrew, and without replying re-entered the inn and bounded up the stairs where he confronted Meg, sitting on a bed with a tankard of ale in her hand. A musket rested against a chair. Before Luke could speak Meg bluntly denied her role, 'No Luke, I did not shoot that murderous churl. But I salute whoever did. That murderer had at least four of Grenville's men slaughtered in cold blood. These were innocent men simply ensuring that those who used our roads pay for their protection, against the dangers confronting any traveller. Without our protection operating through Grenville's vast transport network, trade in this area would become haphazard and random. The man that died was a danger to law, order and the peaceful operation of business. What are you going to do, Luke? Arrest me?'

Luke was seething. Shooting someone in the back, unless they were deserting their post or position during battle, was alien to his sense of professional conduct. He would however distance himself from this investigation. He liked Meg, and hoped she had a simple explanation for her possession of the offending musket. He replied, 'I will do nothing. The constable, your brother must report the matter to the local magistrate, Miles Baker. This is not a matter for the military.'

Luke ran downstairs, and found Andrew who had stayed with the body. Luke whispered in his ear, 'Meg denies her role in the murder. She thinks the victim is Kendall. Conceal the real identity of the body. Take it to the regiment's camp at Baker Grange! And find Captain Kendall and take him into custody before he is seen by the people here!' Andrew too was still seething. 'Luke, don't be taken in by the smooth talking witch. This is cold-blooded murder. I do not believe a word of Mistress Dale's explanation. I saw her with the musket in her hand. The local constable, her brother, cannot be relied on. I will report the matter directly to Mr. Baker. I will not stay here at The Angel any longer. It compromises our position.' Andrew rarely showed his emotions, and for a veteran soldier who had experienced horrendous events, and witnessed the most inhumane treatment of man by man, he was deeply moved at the shooting of Joe Muggs.

Andrew gathered his few possessions, and escorted the covered wagon carrying the body of Joseph Muggs to the encampment of his regiment on the estate of Miles Baker. He reported to Captain Lloyd who within the hour arrested Brian Kendall. Brian was several miles north along the highway leading a caravan of happy leather merchants. Harry explained to the surprised prisoner, 'I am sorry Brian to inform you that your sergeant Joseph Muggs has been murdered, shot in the back outside The Angel. The murderer thinks that he has killed you. Muggs was wearing your cape, and he was shot in the back. Colonel Tremayne wishes you to remain hidden on this estate.'

Kendall was visibly upset by the news of the murder of his faithful servant and sergeant of many years. After a long delay he replied, 'If Tremayne believes that by going into hiding I will assist in uncovering the murderer then I will oblige. Could I get a message to a friend of mine who can make arrangements to cover the death of Muggs and my absence ?'

Harry replied in the affirmative, and instructed a trooper to be ready to take a message from Kendall as soon as he had written it. Kendall withdrew, and Harry and Andrew proceeded immediately to the manor house to inform Miles Baker of the murder. Baker listened intently to Andrew's account of the episode from meeting Kendall and the wagoners, to his apparent murder. Harry and Andrew did not to tell Baker the real identity of the victim. Baker probed Andrew on whether he had seen Meg Dale fire the fatal shots. Andrew confessed that he had not seen the shot fired, but had seen Meg leave a highway-facing room with a smoking musket.

'Thank you sergeant. I will conduct the formal investigation myself, but I cannot see any good coming from it. Margaret Dale will deny the charge and present a dozen witnesses to support her position. It will be your assumptions against the sworn evidence of her supporters. She has only to claim that she entered the room and saw a man shoot the horseman who then dropped his musket, and escaped from the chamber. She picked up the musket and ran into you as she was leaving the room. Knowing how ruthless the Dales can be, they might even find a man who will confess to the killing.'

Miles Baker knew his enemies well. Four nights later Luke was awakened by a disturbance beneath his window. In the moonlight he saw two men half carrying half dragging another along the road. Luke followed them into the water lands. Soon a variety of rushes and the discordant croaking of innumerable frogs surrounded him. Luke heard one voice exclaim, 'This is Witches Deep, the only hollow in all these wetlands. Drag our friend this way.' 'Let's make sure first. Slit his throat!' commented another. 'Don't be an idiot. How many suicides cut their own throat?' 'Many, in this situation it is plausible. Our friend fearing justice walked to Witches Deep, waded out into its depths and slit his own throat. That will fit their story perfectly.'

'Is this varlet still wearing his own dagger?' Before an answer could be given the noise of revellers was heard coming along the path. The first man acted quickly. He gave the victim a mighty blow to the head, and with his companion waded into the deeper water, and threw the unconscious man as far as they could. They quickly left the water and ran back up the path, avoiding any contact with the revellers, who were staggering and drinking their way slowly from one tavern to another. Their diversion into the wetlands was to capture wild ducks, which would be roasted and eaten at the next tavern.

Luke splashed into Witches Deep just as the revellers hove in sight. They mistook Luke for one of their own who had got ahead of the main group. Luke called out for help. Two men jumped in to oblige and were disappointed—the catch was not a duck. Luke cradled a body in his arms. The man was still breathing. His clothing had trapped sufficient air to keep him afloat. Luke lied, informing the revellers that the man was dead, probably murdered. He convinced them that they had not seen a body, otherwise they might all be considered implicit in the murder. There was a shout of joy further back along the path and eventually a man emerged waving a quacking duck in his hand, soon followed by a second. The throng moved rapidly to the next alehouse for more ale and roast duck.

The victim stirred.

20

LUKE PUSHED HIS flask of whisky to the man's lips. He drank heavily, and then lapsed into unconsciousness. Luke could not take the man to The Angel. It probably housed the very men who had tried to kill him. Luke laid the body on some dry tussocks and partially covered it with the drier reeds he pulled from the wetland, and returned to the inn. He saddled his horse, returned down the track, slung the inert body across the horse, and rode to his regiment's encampment at Baker Grange. Andrew was pleased to see his commander, and half apologised for his dramatic departure. He was heartened by Luke's story which confirmed his own conviction that evil resided at The Angel. Andrew was certain that the threat to General Cromwell emanated from that establishment, and that Adam Dale had constructed a vast cover up by persuading the general to send Luke and himself to the inn. It prevented any real investigation into his sordid activities, and put him in the perfect position to monitor any adverse developments and take immediate action. He was not amused when Luke using the name of the inn poked fun at this view by suggesting that they were now probing an Angelic Conspiracy and seeking an Angelic Assassin.

The victim was nursed back to health in the army camp, and on Luke's express orders, his presence was kept secret from everybody. Miles Baker was not told. A few days later Harry Lloyd arrived at The Angel. The victim wanted to talk to Luke who hoped for some earth shattering revelations. He was disappointed. The victim who had a pronounced limp said no more than he was the senior servant of Sir Harcourt Reeves, and that he had been kidnapped, beaten, and left to drown in Witches Deep. He did not know who his enemies were, and wanted Luke's help to disappear to relatives in

Southwark without being seen by the locals. He convinced Luke that it was safer that his enemies assumed he was dead.

Later that day Miles Baker informed Luke of the results of his formal inquiry into the murder of the man many believed was Brian Kendall. Grenville Reeves swore that at the time of the killing he was just passing the main door of the inn when he heard a shot. He saw a man collapse into the middle of the highway, and another scramble down from a first floor window of the inn and limp away. He recognised the fleeing man as Tom Hammer, his father's senior servant. Meg Dale said she was in the hallway of the inn when she heard a shot. She entered one of the front rooms of the inn and saw a man escaping out of the window. A musket lay on the floor. Grenville further deposed that on the orders of the local constable Adam Dale he with several members of the watch went to his father's estate and arrested Tom Hammer. Under interrogation he admitted not only to the murder of Captain Kendall, but also to that of three excise men. Grenville was bringing the murderer to Mr. Baker when he broke free, ran towards the water lands, and threw himself into Witches Deep. Adam claimed that his men searched Witches Deep and the surrounding wetlands, but did not find a body. Sam Wright gave evidence that parts of Witches Deep were extremely deep and that the body may never be found, adding that eels would quickly strip the body clean of flesh, making any identification impossible.

Luke sat through the Quarter Sessions meeting as the other magistrates listened to Mr. Baker's report, and received the depositions of the witnesses. They concluded that Tom Hammer had murdered Captain Kendall and the excise men. As he was deceased the matter was now closed. The court, many of whom seemed to be dozing, were awakened out of their slumber by a sudden intervention from the audience. A man dressed in black except for a bright blue coloured jerkin was on his feet, 'Your worships, I rise on behalf of the widow of Captain Kendall. As Hammer's body has not been recovered it is possible that he survived. I would like you gentlemen to issue a warrant for the arrest of Tom Hammer on the charge of murder. This may only amount to an empty gesture, but it would be a more fitting end to this sorry tale.'

Luke recognised the man immediately. It was Matthew Craven. The magistrates discussed the request for a few minutes, and acceded to his petition. As they left the court Craven approached Luke. 'Mr. Tremayne, May I have a few words with you. There is a pleasant inn just around the corner.' Luke recognised The Book and Quill immediately. Seated in a small nook Matthew ordered ale, and to Luke's delight two mutton pies. As both men crammed the pies into their mouths conversation was at a standstill. Eventually clearing his throat with a long draught of ale, Matthew came to the point of the meeting. 'Brian's men tell me you were present during his last fateful trip and were sympathetic to his cause. With his death our organization is without a military leader. I am authorised by my master to offer you that position.'

'But you know nothing about me. I am not whom I appear to be,' responded Luke, almost caught off his guard. 'Don't fool yourself Colonel Luke Tremayne, currently a special agent of Lieutenant General Cromwell, and commander of an elite cavalry regiment, currently stationed on the estates of Mr. Miles Baker, although officially part of the establishment at Dublin Castle. You are at present residing at The Angel in St. Michael at the behest of Adam Dale, purporting to be his nephew, although the reason for this charade eludes me.'

'Given your statement, if correct, that I am currently a serving officer under General Cromwell you can see that I am in no position to accept the offer of your master, who I presume is the mysterious Wolf.' 'Correct Colonel, but your command of the military arm of our organization would greatly assist the General. The armed militias around the capital are not necessarily supporters of the national army. Your own experiences with the militia of the City under that two-timing rogue Jasper Nettle bears this out. You could be the man that cements a large part of the City in support of the army, and its commanding general.'

'Thank you Mr. Craven. At the moment I cannot accept, but on the principle that mutual enemies might make us allies I would like to maintain contact with you. On another matter of mutual interest. Where is Rose Chidlow? I know your men whisked her away on a barge.' 'Colonel, Rose has been removed for her own safety. If she had stayed at The Angel she would have met the same fate as Tom Hammer. The Dales suspect that one of their inner circle is betraying their secrets and activities to their enemies.' 'Was it Robert Chidlow?' 'I am not sure that anyone was betraying the Dales and through them The Fox, but they certainly were looking for an explanation for the problems they have recently confronted. Initially they blamed the local Levellers who were getting in the way of their nefarious activities. I have no doubt that the Dales ordered the deaths of those men.'

'Maybe, but you are avoiding the question. Where is Rose?' 'She is safe, that is all I can say.'

Luke returned to The Angel and was surprised to see that Adam and Temperance had joined Meg, Grenville and Sam for the evening meal. Andrew remained with the regiment. This suited Luke who could play up his support for the Dales, and indicate that any negative feelings had stemmed from Andrew, who had formally returned to military life. He clearly was not suited to the role of a personal servant. The company celebrated their exoneration by the court, and the acceptance of their version of events. Luke decided to set the cat among the pigeons.

'Friends I hope this celebration is not premature. I hear gossip in the alehouses of St. Aiden that their patrons rescued a body from Witches Deep on the night that Tom Hammer disappeared.' 'If they did find a body what happened to it?' asked a pale-faced Grenville.' 'There are two possibilities. Either Hammer after being rescued subsequently died, or he recovered and lives with information that may be detrimental to this household.' Grenville felt sick, and Meg nearly choked on a mouthful of wine. Sam intervened, 'No need for anyone to worry. I spoke to one of the nocturnal duck hunters, who in catching a bird saw a body sinking into the deep. Hammer is definitely dead.' The jovial atmosphere returned, but Luke was furious with Sam and anxious for him to explain his surprising intervention.

Later that evening the two men withdrew to a distant nook for their usual nightcap. Luke could not contain himself, 'Why did you take the heat out of the discussion which I had deliberately provoked to test reactions.' 'To save your life, Luke. You did not think through the implications of your comment. If Grenville had followed up your insinuation that the duck hunters had seen a live body, he may have also discovered that they had also seen you with the body.' 'God's Blood, if anyone here knew that, my credibility with the Dales would be shattered.'

'Precisely, but don't worry! I mentioned the problem to Andrew and seven duck hunters have been conscripted for service at sea. They will not return until long after your period here has passed. But you must find Tom

Hammer. Send him abroad for his own and your safety.' Luke knew, if necessary there was a more direct way to silence Hammer.

Luke retired and lay across his bed with only his outer garments removed. He fell asleep and was awakened by a shadowy figure gently tugging at his shirt. It was Meg, dressed only in flimsy chemise, which was transparent at all the sensual parts of the body. Large breasts, rigid nipples and the reddish lustre of pubic hairs had an almost instant effect on the sexually starved colonel.

But the awakened Luke was not an easy target. He jumped up from the bed, and as Meg snuggled in between the sheets, Luke paced up and down the room. 'No, Meg. Do you take me for a fool? You know I am not convinced by your story, nor by the amazing supportive tale your friends and servants told the magistrates. How convenient it was for you to find a killer, attribute three other murders to him and then for him to commit suicide before his guilt could be legally established. This visit is to convince me that your version of events is true.'

21

'OF COURSE, LUKE. What else can I do? I value your friendship but you continue to avoid me. I did not shoot Kendall, although given the opportunity, I would have. The man in the chamber who escaped out of the window was Tom Hammer. Whether he killed the excise men I do not know. Grenville claims to have extracted that confession from him after some serious interrogation. Tom Hammer was Harcourt's personal bodyguard, and responsible for discipline amongst the servants. He was in charge of the gunpowder complex, and keeper of Harcourt's mastiffs. He had a very unsavoury reputation. It is not an unreasonable assumption that he was responsible for the murders of the excise men, and one or two missing charcoal burners, and several of Harcourt's servants who have mysteriously disappeared.'

Luke noted the reference to a gunpowder complex, but kept focussed on Hammer. 'If what you say is true was Hammer a disturbed multiple killer, or was he a loyal servant who simply exterminated people on the orders of his master? Did Hammer act with or without Sir Harcourt's connivance?' 'Unfortunately we will never know,' responded Meg, trying to conceal a faint smile. As he led a frustrated Meg from his chamber, Luke had an even bigger smile on his face. He would know, very soon. He would re-question Tom Hammer.

Next morning Luke returned to his regiment's encampment, and sought out the trooper who had escorted the disguised Hammer through London to a small tenement in Southwark. Luke, accompanied by the trooper and Andrew, had no difficulty in relocating the site. A large sign above the entrance to a small courtyard read *Hammer and Sons, Suppliers of Sea Coal.*

Although Luke was dressed in civilian clothes Andrew and the trooper were in military dress, and carried an array of weapons.

Their arrival disconcerted the workers. One group peered out of a large barn-like complex, while others quickly disappeared from sight. Luke dismounted, and headed towards the barn opening when a tall man with a shiny leather apron emerged to meet him. 'What can we do for you sir? Is the army short of coal?' 'No, my good man. I am not here to purchase coal, but to enquire about a relative of yours.' 'Not another group after Tom?' 'What do you mean?' 'Tom is my half brother. I had not seen him for years until last week when a soldier dressed like your friend brought him here one evening. Tom was wearing a wig like some Royalist gentleman, and had his face covered. I sensed he was in trouble. He told me he had been falsely accused of murder, and needed a place to hide.'

'You implied that others been after him?' 'Yes, you are the third group. The first man I have seen around on many occasions. He is an agent of The Fox who controls most business in this area. Tom saw him coming, and pleaded with me to deny I had seen him, and to say that I had just recently received news that he had committed suicide somewhere along the north road. I did as Tom asked, and The Fox's man went away contented.' 'And the second visitor?' 'That had quite the opposite ending. Two days ago a lawyer with a detachment of Southwark militia appeared with a warrant for Tom's arrest. He tried to escape through the back of the premises, but there were more soldiers waiting for him. They took him away.' 'Where is he being held?' asked Luke.

'That's the strange part of all this. I went to the two nearest gaols. He was not there. I then saw the commander of the Southwark militia who claimed none of his men were engaged on any such policing activity. I finally went to the local magistrate who knew nothing of the proceedings. Tom has disappeared off the face of the earth.' 'Don't worry Goodman Hammer. I don't know where Tom is, but I know who has him.'

As they returned to The Angel, Luke and Andrew considered the situation. Obviously the Dales were aware that Tom had relatives in Southwark, and had The Fox send a man to check on the situation—just in case he had escaped Witches Deep. And then the wily Matthew Craven had executed the warrant for Tom's arrest. The so-called Southwark militia were probably well armed Red Ribbons. But why did Craven take Hammer, and where was he now?

Luke had an answer more quickly than he anticipated. At The Angel there was a message that Miles Baker wished to see him as soon as possible. Luke proceeded immediately to Baker Grange. Miles led him into the library where Harry Lloyd, Matthew Craven, and the Lady Cassandra were seated. Craven opened proceedings, 'Colonel, I wonder whose side you are on?'

Luke was taken aback as Craven continued his accusations, 'You have misled Mr. Baker and myself on two vital points. I discover that two men you said were dead are both alive. Captain Kendall, whom you concealed in your camp on this very estate, wrote a letter to me explaining the situation and seeking my advice. I am the go-between for him and his employer. Miles has agreed that Captain Kendall should be transferred from your secure location to the house until you think his return to the world will no longer compromise your investigation. I also discovered that Tom Hammer was still alive. I served a warrant for his arrest for murder, and brought him here to the appropriate magistrate. Given the complexities of the local political situation I asked Mr. Baker to keep Hammer a prisoner on the estate.' Baker took up the explanation. 'I, in turn prevailed upon Captain Lloyd to build a temporary but secure stockade within your encampment to house the murderer.'

'But is he a murderer? I suspect he is a scapegoat for a far more important culprit,' Luke quietly stated.

Lady Cassandra made a noise that resembled a grunting pig and almost shouted at Luke, 'Piffle, Colonel. Tom Hammer may or may not have murdered Joe Muggs, but he certainly oversaw the despatch of the excise men, and a number of my husband's servants. He was my husband's henchman and at times seemed to control Sir Harcourt. On numerous occasions he countermanded Harcourt's orders, and twice pushed me against a wall when I remonstrated with him. Some of Sir Harcourt's clique, probably the Dales saw Muggs's murder as a way to rid themselves of a servant who had grown too big for his boots. Maybe Harcourt himself had had enough. Certainly since Rose Chidlow started helping with the estate's accounts, he, or somebody, seems to have gained a more decisive attitude to the management of the estate.'

'What has Hammer to say?' asked Luke. Baker answered, 'He refused to talk to me. Your captain has deprived Hammer of sleep since he arrived. That was two nights ago.' Luke had readily used sleep deprivation to obtain a confession from the barbaric Irish. He was never sure whether it was the simple desire to sleep that made the victim more amenable, or that the lack of sleep somehow weakened the resistance. Baker continued, 'Harry assures me that you are an experienced and effective interrogator. He will take you to the stockade. We will await the results of your gentle persuasion.'

Hammer who had received a thorough beating struggled to maintain his footing as he was bound to a central post by the arms, across the stomach, and at the ankles. Standing beside him was a trooper with a cane who kept admonishing Hammer at any sign that he had slipped into sleep. Hammer despite his broken teeth and bulging blackened eyes gave a faint smile when he recognised Luke.

'Come to save me a second time?' 'Quite the contrary. If you do not give me what I want, you go to The Tower to experience real torture. Parliament banned it a decade ago, but in a crisis the law must needs be suspended.' 'Can I have a drink?' 'You can have a drink, and a sleep—if you give me the answers I seek. You lied to me before, so I have little patience.'

'I never lied to you Colonel. I did not kill Captain Kendall.' 'But you killed the excise men, and probably several of your fellow servants.' Hammer remained silent for a time and then asked, 'What is going to happen to me?' 'Nothing can save you from the gallows. You will die for the murder of the government officials.' 'So what is the advantage of me confessing anything else?' 'If you did not kill Kendall, and I am inclined to believe you—don't you wish to seek revenge on those who blamed you, and then tried to kill you. Did Sir Harcourt order you to exterminate the excise men?'

'I will tell you what you want to know if you do something for me.' 'I don't make deals with murderers.' Hammer motioned Luke to come close and whispered to him. Luke was expressionless, but solemnly nodded his head in agreement to whatever Hammer had requested. He repeated his question, 'Did Sir Harcourt order you to exterminate the excise men?' 'Sir Harcourt is weak. He could not control his own wife, let alone run his estates, although Mistress Chidlow is getting his businesses back on their feet.' 'So you acted on your own initiative?' 'Yes, those excise men were trespassing, and spying on Sir Harcourt's gun powder operation.' 'Did you inform Sir Harcourt of your actions?' 'No.' 'So you were a free agent doing whatever you liked?' 'Not at all. Most of the landowners and businesses in the area paid a London entrepreneur to protect and enhance their enterprises. Mr. Grenville Reeves is his local representative and occasionally he gave me instructions to ensure that my actions did not annoy this powerful protector.' 'So Grenville Reeves is the local head of the Fox's network ?'

'Yes.' Luke then asked, 'Who tried to kill you?' 'I know who beat me, and left me to drown, but I do not know if they were prompted by any gentleman.' 'I originally suspected Mr. Grenville. Some of Sir Harcourt's wagoners, particularly the Hooker brothers had irritated him, and he blamed me for not keeping them under control. But I dealt with that problem. Both the Hooper brothers met with nasty accidents, especially after I heard that you were interested in questioning them. They had bad tempers and loose mouths. But I am not sure about Mr. Grenville. He visited me to let me know that I had been accused of murder, and that he would return the next day to take me to the constable. I took this as a hint that I should disappear before his return, an action which I tried to accomplish.'

22

'SO WHAT HAPPENED?' 'I gathered my few belongings and was leaving the Reeves' estate when five or six of my fellow servants, who had been drinking for hours, set upon me. They were mouthing sentiments of revenge for the way I had treated them, or their relatives, over my time at Reeves House. I had beaten many of them to an inch of their lives, and permanently removed several of their friends and relatives. But I had my reasons. Only recently the Hooker brothers stole a coffin from a wagon they were driving, and tried to sell its contents around the alehouses of St. Aiden. I put an end to their thieving. The men who beat me and tried to drown me were all wagoners. Some worked for Sir Harcourt, others for Mr. Grenville. They were avenging the Hooker brothers rather than taking orders from Mr. Grenville. I am convinced that he gave me a chance to escape, and that I was caught by my fellow servants bent on revenge.'

Luke turned to the trooper, 'Cut him down, get him a drink, and allow him to sleep.' During the early hours of the afternoon Hammer enjoyed a deep sleep. He never awoke. Someone entered the stockade and smothered him. Luke cursed the guards for their slackness. He ordered that the body be taken to Hammer's half brother once darkness had fallen.

Luke spent the night in camp, drinking with his officers and relaxing for the first time since his present assignment began. He told Harry and Andrew the details of his interrogation. Andrew was slightly appalled, 'For God sake Luke, what sort of a deal did you make with that monster Tom Hammer?' 'Well there lies another mystery. My part of the deal was to ensure that Tom died in his cell. He did not want to face public execution.' 'You didn't waste much time in keeping your part of the bargain,' commented Harry.

'No, gentlemen that's the problem. I did not kill Hammer nor order his killing. Someone else entered the stockade and smothered him. We have yet another murder to solve.'

After a hearty breakfast he reported to Miles and Matthew, who was staying at Baker Grange for a few days. He recounted that Hammer had confessed to a series of murders, including some that they were not aware of, but denied he had been responsible for the death of Muggs. His immediate local contact with regard to The Fox was Grenville Reeves. He did not believe that the Reeves nor the Dales had set him up to take the blame for Muggs's murder, or were behind the attempt to kill him. He blames the hatred of fellow servants. Grenville had apparently given him a chance to escape. Luke left the news of Hammer's death to the end. He hoped to shock them, and gauge their reactions. He lied, telling them that Hammer died during questioning.

Initially there was no great response from either Miles or Matthew. The latter had produced a pipe during Luke's account and began to suck noisily upon it. 'Colonel do you believe what you have been told?' 'Yes, Hammer was a hard and brutal man. He showed no remorse for his killings. I made clear that whatever he said he would hang. This was an ideal opportunity to get his own back on his enemies—yet he does not. He refuses to blame anyone for his predicament, and takes responsibility for a multitude of murders—almost as a badge of honour. To him the trespassing agents of a hated government deserved their fate—and his dogs a good feed.'

'Where is the body?' asked a concerned Miles. 'Given the circumstances it should be reported to the coroner.' Matthew was quick to intervene, 'No need Miles; Tom Hammer is already legally dead. Your own Quarter Sessions affirmed that only recently.' 'And the body will be buried miles from here,' added Luke. Miles was still unhappy, but acceded to the advice of his legal and military friends that the matter should be quietly forgotten. Matthew and Miles were not told that Tom Hammer had been murdered. Who had entered the stockade and killed him?

Luke instinctively knew who the murderer was, and he fully understood the motivation. Brian Kendall, who had been seen near the stockade at the time of the murder, had avenged the death of his friend and comrade Joe Muggs. Luke had more important matters to resolve. This death he would forget.

And then as if struck by lightning Luke experienced an epiphany. He understood who had really killed Muggs—and Meg had been lying to protect him. Just as Kendall had killed Hammer believing him to be the murderer of his deputy, Grenville Reeves had killed the man he thought was Kendall to avenge the murder of several of his men. Both Meg and Hammer were innocent.

As Luke was about to leave the room, a servant whom Luke knew to be Tamsin, Rose's personal maid, burst into the room and screamed, 'Mistress Chidlow has disappeared.' Miles and Matthew looked alarmed, and then at each other. Miles having obtained a nod from Matthew said, 'I know Colonel that you have been concerned with the fate of Rose Chidlow, and she speaks highly of your kindness to her. You followed her to her great uncle's premises, and he told you incorrectly that she had been sent back to France for her own protection. I know that your man followed Rose and her escorts to the river where he lost them.' 'We did assume she had continued down river and boarded a ship for France,' commented a peeved Luke.

'No, the barge slipped down stream, but the bargemen were only awaiting the change of tide to move upriver to the confluence of the Lea which they followed north for several miles. Rose was then brought here.'

'Matthew why did you take her from The Angel?' 'She told me that her husband Robert had become very worried about matters that he had unearthed in both the Dale and Reeves accounts. He was perplexed with what he should do, and especially whom he should confront. Before he could do anything he disappeared, believed murdered. As Rose assisted her husband in much of his work I feared that whoever had killed Robert might find it necessary to remove Rose. She had to be hidden for her own protection.'

'Robert Chidlow was a partner. Did he ever raise any of his concerns with you?' 'No, and he would never do so. Robert saw himself as a dedicated servant of the Dales and Reeves, living and working in a privileged position. He knew that I worked for people like Miles who could be considered a rival to their commercial empire and alliances. We both worked with Mr. Tournac, rather than with each other.'

Tamsin, who had remained in the room being comforted by other servants, slowly regained her composure. She smiled at Luke whom she knew from The Angel. He took advantage of the situation and asked, 'Did

Mistress Chidlow receive any visitors unbeknown to either Mr. Baker or Mr. Craven?' 'No, sir. No one has come to the house since we have been here.' 'Did she receive any messages?' asked a clearly agitated Matthew. 'We did meet old William, a fellow servant from The Angel this morning.' 'Where was this?' demanded a very intense Matthew. 'My mistress and I went for a walk along the long drive that leads from the house to the large ornamental gates. William was coming up the path and when he saw my mistress exclaimed that it was his lucky day, as he now did not need to walk to the house. He whispered something to my mistress who smiled and thanked him.' 'Do you know what William said to her?' 'No, but she seemed in a good mood as a result of that conversation. We returned to the house, and I have not seen her since.'

Luke excused himself. He would question William. On arriving at the inn Luke was devastated. William, Meg's personal servant, had left with his mistress for her regular long-term residence with Valentine Cole, 'You might catch them on the road, if you hurry,' advised Sam. 'Were Meg and William alone?' 'Yes.' Luke's spirits fell further. 'Have you seen Rose Chidlow?' 'Yes, she returned from Baker Grange after old William had taken her a message. She had a long chat with Meg and then asked me to gather up all her possessions and to send them to her.' 'Where are they to be sent?' 'No mystery there Luke. They are to go to Baker Grange—to the part of the manor occupied by Lady Cassandra. Rose and Cassandra Reeves have become close friends, and Rose is to become a lady companion to that volatile virago.' 'Very interesting. Both Miles Baker and Matthew Craven got themselves quite worked up, fearing that Rose had been abducted or worse. Cassandra could have put their minds at rest, but chose not to say a word. I wonder if Miles or Matthew have an interest in Rose beyond the obvious?'

Luke had a sudden thought. 'Are her possessions ready to go? I will take the wagon over to the Grange.' He drove it directly to his regiment's camp and ordered Harry and Andrew to personally search through every item for any evidence whatsoever. Harry was unhappy. 'Come on Luke, just because this woman is the ice maiden as far as you are concerned your suspicions are completely unwarranted. Do you suspect her of murdering her husband?' 'I do not suspect her of anything, but she is certainly central in the affairs of many people. And we know nothing about her, except unconfirmed gossip that she is highly placed in French circles, and has powerful friends. If such is the case what is she doing associated with minor country gentry, and married to an aging, far from wealthy Puritan lawyer?'

Luke's intuition was quickly rewarded. Harry found a courtly mask of pure gold encrusted with diamonds with a tiny engraving *"A mon precieux, le prince"*. To Luke this proved that Rose Chidlow had highly placed connections. There were a limited number of French princes. Andrew suggested that the mask should be inspected more closely through one of the new fangled lenses, one of which he had seen on Miles Baker's desk. Miles's steward, under orders to assist the military in every way, found the lens. Andrew's suggestion paid off. Under the lens, rows of decorative dots proved to be alternate letters H and A. Luke commented that, 'The number of Princes of the Blood with the initial H, presumably for Henri is limited. I know of none at the present.' 'But there was one until six or seven years ago, the greatest of all the French princes, Henri de Bourbon, Duke of Conde,' replied Andrew. Luke nodded, 'It's possible that our Rose could have been the late prince's mistress. She would have been in her teens and early twenties during the last few years of his life.'

The two men discussed their interpretation with Harry who immediately poured cold water on their speculations. 'What nonsense! Why would the alleged mistress of one of France's most powerful men finish up in England married to an English lawyer, an elderly nonentity? The French are less fussy than we English about matters of bastardy. The former mistress of a Conde would have been snapped up by the lesser nobility as a most appropriate marriage. You can solve your dilemma simply by asking Rose about the gold plate, without revealing your knowledge of the inscription and lettering. She probably stole the plate from a former employer, and had to escape to England in fear of her life. Consider that instead of having royal and aristocratic connections, Rose Chidlow is a common thief.'

23

THIS CONVERSATION WAS interrupted by a trooper, 'Colonel there is a drunken group at the main gate of Baker Grange refusing to leave until one of their number, a large buxom red headed wench speaks to you. According to his steward, Mr. Baker is not happy with this kind of disturbance.' Luke told the trooper to disperse the group, but hold the wench until he arrived. Luke walked from the camp to the main gate. Waiting for him, bedecked in her best clothes, was Jolly Joan. 'What brings you here Joan, upsetting your godly magistrate with raucous singing and lascivious utterances?'

'Since the coffin was found in Witches Deep my customers have argued about its original contents. Today we have been to a wedding up the road at St John On the Hill.' 'And celebrating most of the day,' added Luke. Joan ignored the interruption. 'On the way home a large covered wagon passed us, heading south towards the city. Some of the lads, a bit heavy in drink, abused the driver for splashing them as he drove past. As a bit of a lark Old Bill pulled off one of the covers. The wagon was loaded with coffins, exactly like the one recovered from the wetlands. The lads were a bit shaken, fearing they had disturbed the dead, but I jumped on board and lifted the lid of the nearest box. It was empty. Our group became very agitated, and insisted that the driver explain where he was taking so many empty coffins. Some of the women became hysterical, convinced that there had been an outbreak of plague nearby, and that the government was keeping it quiet by collecting the dead and burying them secretly. They started to pummel the driver demanding to know where he was collecting the plague victims. Old Bill rescued the driver, but threatened to throttle him, unless he told us where he was heading.' 'And where was he going?' asked a very interested Luke.

'He was going to meet a French ship that is to dock just east of London Bridge tomorrow morning.' Luke was ecstatic. 'How long ago was your meeting with this wagoner?' 'Given my delay in reaching you he would have an hour's start, but with the rain that was falling to the south his journey would be slow. You will recognise one of his horses. It is a large grey with a white heart on his forehead.' Luke gave Joan a big hug, and ordered the trooper to carry her on his horse until they caught up with the rest of the wedding revellers. Luke ran back to camp, alerted Andrew and Harry to the situation, and issued orders. Andrew and he would follow the wagon immediately. Harry would take a troop and wait for further orders at their old barracks in The Tower.

Luke caught up with the wagon sooner than anticipated. As they approached The Angel three wagons left its courtyard, heading south. A large grey horse helped pull the first. After an hour or more the three wagons pulled off the highway onto an extensive verge, and the wagoners slipped under the covers to sleep until morning. Luke and Andrew trotted past, convinced that the wagons would not move until dawn. They retired to The Tower for the night but were in place at first light to follow their quarry. The first wagon moved towards the river, but the other two wagoners appeared sound asleep. Luke followed the moving wagon. Andrew would wait and follow the others.

The wagon entered the gates of one of the areas along the docklands, and stopped parallel to the river, in a gap between a collier from Newcastle and a large Dutch merchantman disgorging sugar and tobacco from the Americas. The wagon was waiting for a ship that had yet to dock. Eventually the other wagons arrived and parked themselves behind the first. By their gesturing the wagoners appeared annoyed that the ship they were awaiting had not arrived. After some discussion one man remained with the wagons and the other two headed for the nearest alehouse, The Blue Anchor. Luke, rejoined by Andrew, followed them.

The room was surprisingly large and already full of porters who had been working since first light, and were taking a breakfast break. Apart from beer, bread and cheese the establishment sold steaming beef broth, which given the crisp morning, appealed to the two soldiers. The wagoners found an empty bench in the far corner of the room. Luke, with his hat pulled down, and his cape drawn around much of his face, sat with his back to them. Andrew sat at a parallel bench amidst a noisy group of disgruntled porters, who were more than happy to air their grievances to the stranger.

'There will be another riot on the docks if the tackle porters do not keep to their allotted tasks,' explained a small wiry, but well muscled dockworker. Andrew confessed his complete ignorance of the situation, explaining he had just recently been demobilised from the army, and was looking to find a position on one of the merchant ships, anchored along the Thames. 'Stay clear of the ships of the East India Company. The scurvy tackle porters have a monopoly of unloading and transporting all goods from that company's ships. Yesterday they moved in to unload a ship from Ireland which is in our jurisdiction.'

'You look like a bunch of sturdy fellows,' replied Andrew, 'Did you not challenge this intrusion?' 'We did, and were gaining the upper hand until the London Militia arrived to support the tackle turds. All appeared lost until the Red Ribbons arrived to help us. A major affray resulted and several of our friends were killed and dozens injured. There will be many teams short of workers today. Sadly, rumour has it that the military leader of the Red Ribbons is dead, murdered along the northern road.'

'Have faith,' replied a scar-faced porter. 'Rumour is that The Wolf has obtained the services of one of Cromwell's generals to lead the Red Ribbons.' Luke only heard part of the porters' conversation. He was listening intently to the two wagoners. They too were disgruntled. They were Grenville Reeves men who have been loaned to his father Sir Harcourt. Luke knew them well. He had seen them around the courtyard of The Angel. They were amongst the leading fire fighters when the inn was set alight; and they helped in the search and recovery of the bodies from the wetlands. Luke suspected they were also among the men who had beaten Tom Hammer, and tried to drown him in Witches Deep.

The wagoners were incensed that they would miss carrying expensive cargo to wealthy merchants and distant places, where there was always a chance of picking up additional rewards. This current enterprise had them visiting derelict priories and chapels, collecting empty coffins, and taking them to the docks. Apparently the empty coffins would be loaded onto a French barque. They were to wait and receive a load of occupied coffins in return, which were to taken to the destinations from which the empty coffins had come. Luke picked up a reference to Old Kate's semi derelict chapel, and a newly renovated priory in Sir Harcourt's woods. A third destination probably that of the missing wagoner was not mentioned.

Luke turned around, and faced the nearest wagoner who recognized him immediately. 'Don't be alarmed, Mr. Grenville has sent me and a few troopers to protect you on this important mission.' One wagoner who Luke recalled was Austin Perry, responded, 'I don't care how important it is, I do not like dealing with coffins. It sends a shiver up my spine. I have had nightmares about this even though I have been told the bodies we are to collect are those of good Protestant Englishmen who have been killed during the current disturbances in France.'

The second wagoner, William Fisher, intervened, 'They are always the copy cats, the French. We remove our King, now they want to do likewise.' Luke did not think a lesson in politics was called for. The French were not trying to remove their King, but control his policies. Perry was still uneasy about the full coffins they had to collect and return to various destinations. He confessed that Archdeacon Craven had threatened him with ecclesiastical sanctions if he opened any of the returning coffins. Fisher turned on his comrade, 'Why would you want to open such coffins, Austin? You won't get paid if you do. Sir Harcourt told me that these replacement coffins would be sealed, and if that seal was broken we would not be paid.'

Luke asked, 'Why would anyone want to keep the contents of a coffin a secret. What harm would be done if you had a quick look at the bodies?' Fisher nodded, 'I agree Mr. Tremayne. Something is not right. Why all these precautions, including your own presence here, for a few corpses? No, these coffins won't contain bodies. They will be filled with either gold and silver, or weapons and ammunition. Muskets would create an excellent arsenal for Sir Harcourt when added to all that gunpowder he has stored at Reeves House.'

Luke had played down the obvious. Coffins were an ideal container to import arms from overseas, and move them around the country. He turned to the wagoners, 'Why would Sir Harcourt want to import weapons?' Austin replied, 'Sir Harcourt Reeves has been manufacturing gunpowder for years. Perhaps he has become a trader in arms as well.' William Fisher was more direct, 'These are arms for our people to thwart the fanatics of a reforming army destroying England. They are probably for the London Militia, whose arsenal has been strictly limited by the demands and spite of the national army, and with whom Sir Harcourt has a brand new contract.'

Luke was about to follow up this revealing comment when two short followed by two long whistle blasts, emptied the alehouse. A new ship had arrived, and the allotted porters were immediately required. At the same time the third wagoner appeared at the door indicating that the ship in question was the one they were waiting for. Simultaneously Harry Lloyd arrived and immediately teased his colonel. 'Great life for some! Drinking warm beef broth, and eating freshly baked bread.' Luke ignored Harry's quip, and indicated by a raised hand that he wanted silence. Luke was listening to the two porters who had not left the alehouse. One was irritated, 'Hurry up, John! Shorty will cut us from the team if we arrive late.' 'The devil take Shorty,' replied John, 'I've paid for my pint, and I will finish it.'

Luke turned to Harry, 'Sorry for that but your arrival is perfectly timed. Arrest those two men, and hold them until dusk. Come on Andrew, you and I will report to Shorty as replacements for John and his friend.' The three soldiers left the alehouse. Harry summoned a couple of his troopers to arrest the two delinquent porters, while Luke and Andrew headed for the riverbank. Several teams of porters were already at work preparing the ship for loading and unloading. Another small group stood on the dockside being harangued by a man of small stature. Luke introduced himself and Andrew as replacements for John and his friend, who Luke claimed, had been turned over to the constables for not paying for their beer. Shorty turned to the rest of the team, seeking some assurance that these new recruits were genuine porters. A giant blond haired man explained that he had seen them in The Blue Anchor, and they had been fraternising with fellow porters.

Shorty was satisfied and revealed that his team's job was to unload the coffins from the three wagons that lay alongside the dock, and place them on the far side of the deck. One of the porters expressed surprise that they were loading before they had unloaded, and was told by Shorty that he too was surprised by the order to give the loading of the coffins priority. Andrew and Luke approached the third wagon, and the wagoner having removed the covers stared intently at them. 'What are you doing here? I have seen you two at The Angel in St. Michael. You are Mr. Dale's nephew, and a high-ranking army officer. Why are you pretending to be porters?'

24

'I'VE EXPLAINED IT all to your brother wagoners in the alehouse. I am Mr. Dale's nephew. He, with your master Grenville Reeves, and Grenville's father, Sir Harcourt. are engaged in a very dangerous operation. Mr. Dale sent us along to see that all went well. Pretending to be porters we can get aboard the ship without causing too much attention. We are also here to protect you, should the enemies of Mr. Dale attempt to thwart this mission.' The wagoner accepted Luke's story completely, and thanked him for being there to help if needed.

Due to congestion on the planks from the dock to the ship Luke and Andrew had to wait in line for several minutes. It gave them an opportunity to appraise the ship, *Le Lapin Noir*. Luke was intrigued. 'The ship has a French name but it is a Dutch galliot. I sailed on many when as a lad I fought for the Dutch against the Spaniards. They are shallow draft, flat bottomed cargo ships designed to move between the various islands of Zeeland and Holland.' He was even more interested when Andrew pointed out that it was not flying the flag of the French merchant navy, a blue cross on a white field. 'And it is even more curious,' continued Luke. 'Look to the quarterdeck! If I am not mistaken the officer there is a full captain in the French royal navy, but the ship is not flying the fleur de lis of the French King. What is that flag that it flies—a black cross on a white field?' Andrew had no idea but turning to the porter behind him was told that it was the flag flown by merchant ships out of the ports of Brittany.

As they walked back to the wagons to collect the next coffin Luke continued to think aloud, 'Why do we have a Royal naval officer in command of ship flying a flag of Breton merchants, who at the moment have all their ports under the control of the rebel princes? The provenance of this ship is remarkable. Its mission must be supported by the King, and by those in rebellion against him. And why would the rebels who are short of weapons allow a shipment of muskets, if that is what is in the coffins, to leave their ports for England? This is a major plot, sufficiently well supported, to unite the rival factions in France. Cromwell must be alerted.'

Further developments made Luke even more anxious. Immediately the last coffin was lined up on deck, armed men whom Luke recognised as French royal marines emerged, and having shepherded the porters off the ship, stood guard at both the dockside and shipboard extremities of the boarding planks. Nevertheless Luke felt that when they went aboard to unload the new set of coffins an opportunity might occur for him to break away. This was not to be. Shorty announced that *Le Lapin Noir* had a system of blocks and tackle that would unload the heavier occupied coffins onto the dockside. There would be no further opportunity to board the ship.

A junior officer organized a block and tackle that enabled the sailors, and not the porters, to manoeuvre each coffin directly onto the wagons that had been moved to the edge of the dock. Shorty was unhappy about this breach of jurisdiction, but was experienced enough not to cause trouble with a ship that had armed troops aboard. Once reloaded the wagons were surrounded by the porters, who appeared to prevent them from moving. Shorty climbed up the gangplank and a short, potbellied man with an exaggerated moustache met him with a fistful of documents. Shorty appeared happy, and waved to his men to release the wagons, but not before Luke had a close inspection of the new coffins. He was not sure if they were the same coffins that had been brought to the dock. There was now a large wax seal across the lid and body of each coffin. To Luke's surprise the seal appeared to the letter H or maybe an A. He must see inside.

While Shorty was talking to the potbellied man, and his porters surrounded the wagoners in a mixture of intimidation and good humour, Luke climbed aboard the third wagon, and hidden by the cover, and the frolicking porters, he raised a lid. The smell was enough. In the poor light there was clearly a body in the coffin. Luke quickly closed the lid. He gesticulated to Andrew that his search was negative. He was about to return to The Blue Anchor for midday refreshments, when Shorty indicated that although their work on *Le Lapin Noir* was finished, there was a small job awaiting them on the neighbouring ship the Dutch merchantman whose decks towered about that of the galliot.

Andrew wanted to follow the potbellied man whom he was certain did not reboard the ship, but who had disappeared into the melee of dockworkers and sailors that crowded the area. Luke over-ruled him. *Le Lapin Noir* needed closer inspection. You would get no better view than from the towering decks of *De Blauwe Tulip*. Their new job was to unload bags of sugar, which a previous team had overlooked, as they had been stored under cover on one of the decks, and not in the cargo hold. This was even more fortuitous for Luke. It placed him high above *Le Lapin Noir*, giving him a perfect view of the smaller ship's single deck.

His immediate impression was surprise. There was no more cargo to unload, and *Le Lapin Noir* was preparing to sail. Another amazing conundrum—a ship sails to London to unload a few bodies, and then leaves again on the next tide. The thirty odd empty coffins it took aboard and the same number it unloaded would hardly be a profitable exercise. Secondly as he watched the sailors go about their task he was more convinced that this was a royal ship, especially as the captain and the junior officer they had seen previously were joined by three more uniformed officers, and a platoon of some twenty marines were assembling in front of their own officers. The sailors were ready to release the hawsers as soon as the tide turned. The ship would drift out into the Thames, and then raising sail would head for the sea.

As Luke concentrated on the bag of sugar he was about to carry off the ship he was alerted by Andrew's unexpected oath, 'God's Blood, may the Devil take me!' Andrew was pointing to the captain of the *Le Lapin Noir* who had just been joined by a tall civilian—an elderly man with one hand missing. It was Robert Chidlow.

Luke dropped his bag. 'I will board *Le Lapin Noir* before it sails. The stern of *De Blauwe Tulip* overlooks the stern of the French ship. If I can get low enough on the *De Tulip* I can jump aboard *Le Lapin*.' 'Not without being seen,' replied Andrew. 'There are four French seamen at the stern with large poles to prevent a collision as *Le Lapin Noir* drifts out into the river, and there is a large body of marines that will not take your arrival lightly. You would need a convincing story to account for your illegal entry, which by the laws of the sea is an act of piracy.'

'I have General Cromwell's authorization to act in his name. This will be a good chance to use it. I will board the ship. You must ride post haste down river. Our warship *Providence* is docked several miles downstream. Its captain and I are old friends. Explain the situation, and ask him to stop *Le Lapin Noir* on the authority of the Lord General. If my story is accepted *Le Lapin* should be ready to allow Chidlow and myself to disembark at that point.' Andrew left the ship without his bag of sugar and could hear Shorty, screaming blasphemies after him, as he ran for his horse.

Luke looked over the stern of *De Blauwe Tulip* and was pleased to find there was a ladder built into it by which he descended to a point only six feet above *Le Lapin Noir*. He was also pleased to see that there was a roll of canvass near its stern that would cushion his fall. The French sailors had eyed his descent with interest, but were still taken by surprise when with one mighty leap Luke landed on their deck. In the best French he could muster, 'Portez moi a votre capitaine. Je represente le General Cromwell.' Before the sailors had a chance to react Luke realised he was confronted by six marines, who were carefully priming their muskets. Luke repeated his statement to the young marine officer who stared intently at him, and then responded in perfect English, 'We have met before Colonel Tremayne. Welcome aboard.'

Luke's only skirmish with French marines had occurred two years earlier in the Americas. The young officer, Andre de Paul, explained that he was part of the French expedition to establish a French colony on the Chesapeake, which Luke, with the help of the Governor of Virginia, had prevented. The French marine explained that he had accompanied his commanding officer to the ceasefire meeting, which had included Luke.

Luke was delighted. This fortuitous meeting would establish his credentials. And with Cromwell's authorization it would render the ship's captain more amenable to a civilised discussion. The Captain, who introduced himself as Claude, Comte de Sauvel, dismissed all but the marine lieutenant from his cabin, and signalled for Luke to take a seat.

'What brings a senior officer of the English army to board my ship illegally?' 'And what brings a senior officer of the French king's navy to enter English waters with a large detachment of marines, in a Dutch built galliot, flying a Breton flag, and discharging probable illegal contraband stacked in number of coffins?' retorted Luke. Even though he had found a body in the only coffin he opened, he was anxious to see how the captain responded to charges of smuggling. 'Well it appears we are at a standoff. I can charge you with piracy, and you hint I am guilty of smuggling—both serious offences. I am sure your government and the general are not concerned with the return of bodies of Englishmen killed in our current civil conflict, even though their coffins may contain additional items that strictly should pay customs. What did you think your dramatic entry would achieve? As you can tell by the movement of the ship we have ceased drifting into midstream, and have turned, with light sail hoisted, to voyage down river. Whatever you hoped for I cannot see how you can enforce it.'

'Wrong, captain. I can enforce my wishes absolutely. Anchored downstream is England's most powerful warship, *The Providence.* Its guns will be trained on you, and if you do not comply with my request it will blast you out of the water, or use its boats with chains to stop your progress. There are grounds to confiscate this ship as a prize. But it need not come to that. If you accept my proposal you will sail back to France with only the slightest delay, and without any enquiry as to the details of your mission.'

'What is your proposal that will put an end to this charade?' 'You have on board this ship a man wanted by the English authorities. When we reach *The Providence* I wish to go ashore with Mr. Robert Chidlow, and you can continue on your way.' 'Mr. Chidlow is not my prisoner. He is free to leave the ship at any time as far as I am concerned, but he has powerful reasons to stay out of your country, and it has nothing to do with threats from the English authorities. I would be glad to see him go. This mission is not to my liking, especially as I do not know what it is really about.' 'But you must know who ordered you to undertake it?' 'Not really! Both the King's chief minister, and the prince leading the rebellion against His Majesty signed my orders. I can only conclude that both sides in our current unrest wanted to please whoever is behind the enterprise. And your austere city lawyer does not have that sort of influence.'

Luke agreed.

25

LUKE PONDERED THE astute comment of Captain Sauvel, as that officer signalled the marine lieutenant to bring Chidlow to the cabin. Robert Chidlow, shocked to find Luke sitting next to Sauvel, began to shake. The captain offered the traumatised man a brandy. Luke appalled at the terror oozing from every pore of the lawyer tried to be relaxed and friendly. 'It is great to see you are alive, Robert. We all thought you were dead. Your blood was everywhere. But now your problems are over. I have arranged for you to leave the ship with me, and we will right the wrong that has been done to you.'

Robert who was still trembling, shook his head vigorously, 'No, Colonel you do not understand. I cannot go with you, and you must not interfere in my affairs.' 'Robert, I assume you were abducted, and that to ensure your compliance the kidnappers removed your left hand. Surely you want justice?' 'In normal circumstances I would, but I will not cause the death of my wife, Rose. Those that took me from The Angel made it clear that if I did not follow their orders Rose would be raped, tortured, and finally killed by the most painful means available. I made a valiant attempt to defend myself, and in raising my left hand, one of my assailants sliced it off. It was not premeditated, but a result of my clumsiness. I was blindfolded and taken in a wagon full of coffins into London where my wound was attended to, and the next day I was put aboard a small merchantman headed for what turned out to be St. Malo. There I was met by an English gentleman who kept me under house arrest in his spacious lodgings, but who refused to identify himself, or explain the situation. He eventually received orders and told me that I was to accompany a shipload of coffins back to England, and then return to await further orders. This I must do, or Rose will die.'

'If you don't come with me we may all die. Any minute the warship *The Providence* will loom into sight, and if it does not receive a signal from me it will blast *Le Lapin Noir* out of the water.' 'That might solve my problem Luke. If I am dead I cannot any longer be blackmailed into carrying out the orders of my mysterious captors.' 'Do you have any idea who they are, and why you in particular were abducted?' A now tearful Robert whispered, 'I fear it has something to do with my friend and employer, and your uncle, Adam Dale.'

The marine lieutenant re-entered the room. He spoke rapidly in French to the captain who could not conceal his smile as he broke into the discussion, 'Gentlemen, this conversation is at an end. Colonel Tremayne you are under arrest, and confined to quarters, which Mr. Chidlow will now share with you. Robert, lead the colonel to your cabin where no doubt you can continue your discussion until we reach St. Malo. *The Providence* is no longer at its anchorage. It sailed before it received your message Tremayne. My mission is complete as soon as I return Mr. Chidlow to his residence in St. Malo. Colonel, I shall not cause an international incident. My government wants to develop good relations with the English republic. You will be returned on the first ship available.'

Robert was obviously relieved that he was not forced into a position where he would place the life of his wife in danger. Luke would make the best of the situation. A relaxed discussion with Robert, as they crossed what hopefully was a calm Channel, might fill in many of the gaps that had troubled Luke since Robert's disappearance. The two Englishmen had no sooner settled into a tiny cabin that contained two hammocks—Luke preferred to lie on the floor—than a sailor arrived with cold meat pies, and a flagon of French red wine. Luke began to feel unwell almost as soon as they left the Thames estuary and turned southwest into a storm that was sweeping through the Straits of Dover. *Le Lapin Noir* with its flat bottom did not handle these conditions well. The captain decided to stay in-shore and follow the English coast west until he reached Plymouth, and then he would turn south and head for St. Malo, avoiding the hazards associated with the Channel Islands. Despite orders for his confinement Luke staggered out of the cabin, and made it to the ship's nearest railing. Meat pie was soon spewed into the mountainous waves that hammered the ship.

The storm ceased suddenly, and the sail westward along England's southern coast was a pleasant interlude as Luke and Robert, released from confinement, sat on deck on a couple of upturned wooden buckets. Luke was anxious to uncover more details of Chidlow's adventure, while Robert wanted to know the latest on his wife Rose. After painting Robert a bland non-eventful picture of Rose since Robert's disappearance Luke asked, 'Why do you think Adam is behind what happened?'

'I know nothing for certain, and cannot believe that Adam is engaged in any criminal, let alone national conspiracy. I am his steward responsible for the smooth running of his estates, The Angel, and numerous other enterprises. When I married, Adam suggested my wife and I take up residence at either the inn or at Dale Court. My bachelor room was a hardly a place for a newly wed. As a wedding present Adam made me a partner in several of his businesses.'

'Is there a particular incident that made you suspicious of Adam?' 'At the time I did not think much of it, but with hindsight the problems seen to have dated from the arrival of three government excise men. They took a particular interest in Grenville Reeves's transport enterprise. Knowing that Adam had no investment in that business I was surprised when he expressed the view that the presence of such men was not good for business. A few days later I was in the library at Dale Court discussing some business matters with Adam when the senior excise official requested an audience. Adam signalled for me to stay in the room. I retreated to the far end of the library where a protruding bookshelf hid me from the rest of the room. The excise man was agitated. He indicated that what he had to say involved criminal activity and that he was approaching Adam as the local constable.'

'Come on Robert! We will be in St. Malo before you tell me any thing significant.' Robert seemed oblivious to Luke's growing impatience. He was obsessed by his own story. 'The excise man told Adam that he had heard on many occasions in the alehouses of St. Aiden that the local gentry, in league with London criminals, were stockpiling weapons and ammunition, to prevent a military coup against the current government.' 'And who was to lead this military coup against which the local gentry were arming? asked

Luke. 'General Cromwell and General Harrison, aided by the religious fanatics of London.'

Luke was quiet for some time. He was saddened that rumours sweeping London attributed such a design to his leader. Oliver Cromwell was not a religious fanatic, but unfortunately the same could not be said for General Harrison and a few other high-ranking officers. Combined with the machinations of the religious sects Luke feared that the corruption and inactivity of the Parliament might force the hand of many officers like himself to participate in such a coup. He regained his composure and continued questioning Robert.

'How did Adam respond to this information?' 'He told the excise man not to tell anyone else, and he would inform the Government, and Cromwell.' 'These seem reasonable responses. How did they lead you to suspect Adam of being part of the anti-army conspiracy?' 'After the excise man left Adam swore me to secrecy. I know he informed General Cromwell.' 'Yes, my presence at The Angel, masquerading as Adam's nephew is a direct result of his visit to the general. I am not Adam's nephew. I am an agent of General Cromwell sent to investigate the stories of a plot, and also the murder of the three excise men.' 'In that case I may have misjudged Adam, but there are other pointers to something amiss in his behaviour.' 'Such as?' 'The excise men were murdered following their leader's discussion with Adam.' 'Nothing to do with Adam. We now know that they were the personal victims of Sir Harcourt's brutal servant, an errant rogue Tom Hammer. You need more compelling evidence even to make Adam appear a minor suspect in this alleged conspiracy.'

'I have more. My partner Matthew Craven confirmed my suspicions. He asked me whether I realised that my employer and friend, Adam Dale, was a close associate of London's leading criminal and political conspirator, The Fox. I immediately confronted Adam with the accusation. He just laughed. He said The Fox was an astute businessman who was a childhood friend, Valentine Cole, and that their various business interests coincided and that his friendship with Valentine continues to the present. In addition Valentine was his sister's childhood sweetheart, and although prevented from marrying by family complications, Meg and Valentine had continued their relationship over the decades. They now spend several months of the year living together. He specifically denied any part in an anti-army conspiracy.

He admitted that some changes of government might adversely affect their business interests, but that an army takeover would not necessarily be bad for business, although the current corrupt Rump was ideal. It did nothing to interfere in their activities.'

'It's all circumstantial, and none of it makes me think that Adam is an active member of an anti-army plot, or involved in your abduction and mutilation.' 'But what follows does. With my suspicions aroused I took a much more thorough look at Adam's accounts, and there was a striking change. Prior to the excise man's revelation of a conspiracy all of Adam's income related to expenditure was accounted for. After that incident, half of Adam's income disappeared. Part of it was transferred to his sister Meg, and the rest went to Grenville, neither of whose accounts I have access to. Both of these could be feeding funds into The Fox's conspiratorial activities—Meg because of her personal involvement; and Grenville because his business depends on the co-operation of numerous London working groups whom The Fox, until recently, completely controlled. Then my partner Matthew told me that a man he represented had been present in a London alehouse when a serving man approached a Major Nettle with the phrase, 'a present from Eve' and handed over a small bag. This Major Nettle, an exuberant individual, threw the bag into the air, but failed to catch it on its downward flight. It hit the ground and many, many gold coins rolled around the floor. Craven's informant recognised the deliveryman at The Angel a few weeks later. He was Grenville's leading wagoner Austin Perry. Of course Perry denied everything when I questioned him.'

'Robert, I note that you have been led into this negative attitude toward Adam by Matthew Craven. Maybe he has a vested interest in blackening Adam's name. Perhaps there is a conspiracy, but the real organizer is Matthew Craven using the Red Ribbons to achieve his ends.' Robert had not finished his catalogue of evidence against Adam. 'Except for one other telling coincidence, the I O U. Some weeks ago I wrote out an informal bill of credit for ten pounds on Adam's behalf. Just after the murder of the Levellers in St. Aiden, a well-dressed man arrived at The Angel wishing to speak to Adam. Adam was away. He presented me with the bill of credit. Normally such a bill would stay within the financial system for months if not years, until it was convenient to redeem it. I asked the man how he had come by it. He said that he was a London innkeeper who catered for the artisan classes. A week or so earlier a young man entered his establishment and chatted with a man who owned a large wood working business. After a while they approached the innkeeper and offered him the bill of credit if he would pay the woodworker several pounds, and be willing within the hour to dispense silver coins to anyone who approached him wearing a red ribbon and wielding a hefty piece of wood.'

'Another weakness in your argument. The Red Ribbons are the enemies of The Fox. They would not do the bidding of Mr. Dale. Matthew Craven has been feeding you lies.'

26

'NO, MATTHEW HAS already explained all that. The Fox had his thugs wear red to discredit the real Red Ribbons. The credit note is significant. The innkeeper said he knew of Mr. Dale, whose credit was good, and he accepted the proposition.' 'Again, not totally convincing. That bill of credit could have passed through many hands. You need to find the young man who approached the innkeeper and the woodworker, and link them with Adam, Meg or Grenville, and with the mob that killed the Levellers.'

French officers shouting orders as *Le Lapin Noir* approached the harbour of St. Malo brought their conversation to an end. To avoid any hostile reception from whichever party controlled the nearby fortress, Captain Sauvel ensured that flags featuring a black cross were displayed at every traditional part of the ship. In order not to provoke potential opposition, he kept his royal marines below deck.

After the ship had safely docked Sauvel summoned the two Englishmen to his cabin. Luke arrived first. The French captain was in a social mood as his table was full of food and drink. 'What are we celebrating captain?' asked Luke as a conversation ploy, rather than hoping for any meaningful answer. He was surprised when Sauvel raised his glass and declared, 'To the conclusion of a mission that never happened!' After Luke had finished his glass of red wine in almost one gulp, it was quickly refilled as he asked, 'What do you mean a mission that never happened?'

'Colonel, as you noted it is not normal for a French naval captain to sail a small merchant galliot into foreign waters. I am captain of France's newest and best-armed warship, *Le Soleil d'Or*. I was with the royal fleet off Le Havre, monitoring the movement of the rebels of the Fronde, when I received a strange order. I was to take a few of my men, including a unit of marines, and hire a small galliot at the rebel held port of St. Malo. I was to deliver unspecified cargo to London, and return on the first change of tide. The cargo was to be supervised by an Englishman who was not to leave the ship, assisted by a merchant, Alexandre Boucher, a potbellied man with an enormous moustache, who would handle the paperwork. On completion of the mission the Englishman was to be returned to house arrest in St. Malo.

My orders came from the Queen Regent herself, yet they were countersigned by one of the rebel leaders. The rebels would provide the ship, and its mysterious cargo. The period from when we left the Royal fleet off Le Havre, until we return there in a day or two is to be removed from our memory. My crew and I have been ordered never to refer to it. I am to take punitive action against any of my men who flout this command. What worries me, Colonel, is who, in a divided France, can call on both sides to mount this mission, which could have been carried out by any of the privateers that have made St. Malo their port. Someone wants to send a message to someone else that this mission has important backing. Who in these troubled times can call on such support? Who among the French aristocracy has a major interest in what happens in England?'

'I cannot think of any French aristocrat who has any real interest in England. The young lad who claims to be our King is in France, but I cannot see any French faction, given their own problems, wasting time and money on his hopeless cause.'

'Ah, you English, you miss the obvious! You forget your history. In France a quarter of a century ago the senior royal princess, Madame Royale, was King Louis XIII's younger sister, Henriette Marie. She then wed the King of England. For twenty-five years she was married to the man, Charles I, whom your army executed a few years ago. She remains the sister-in-law of our Queen Regent, and aunt of our young King Louis XIV. The murder of her husband may have slightly unhinged her. This desperate widow with high connections to both sides of our current conflict must be behind our mission.'

'Even if the person behind whatever is being planned is as exalted as the former Queen, it doesn't help me unravel her plans, and uncover the agents designated to execute them. On a more immediate matter, where is Robert?

He was summoned here with me, and has not arrived.' 'Sorry, Colonel a little ruse—while we have been having this interesting chat one of my officers has returned Mr. Chidlow to his residence. You will be put aboard a local fishing boat in a few minutes, which will take you to Jersey, from where unfortunately you will need to find your way home.'

Luke was cross with Sauvel, who had thwarted his plan to follow Chidlow, discover the location of his St. Malo residence, and identify his keeper. Before Luke could compose himself, he was bundled off *Le Lapin Noir*. An armed marine escorted him along the stone causeway to the inner harbour, where the local fishing fleet was preparing to put to sea. He had no conversation with his guard, who spoke no English. As they moved through a throng of fishermen and their farewelling families, Luke seized his opportunity. He gave his guard a mighty push which sent him crashing into the water. Luke sprinted into the crowd and headed towards the inner city, where he hid himself among the busy and bustling inhabitants.

He very quickly realised his stupidity. He was in a foreign town, had little money, and even less knowledge of the local language and geography. Luckily as a thriving seaport, the nearest tavern owner was ready to accept the English coins he offered for a drink, which was cider, and food—a well-developed and nauseous cheese with crisp freshly baked bread. While he contemplated his situation he drank and drank until he had spent all that he had. The alcohol and his situation combined to make him very sleepy. As an excess of cider clouded his consciousness he vaguely thought he saw someone he knew. He half rose to greet the familiar identity but passed out, and fell to the floor.

When he came to he was lying in a hammock. Blocking the door of the cabin on the inside was a French marine, who immediately on Luke's stirring left the room. Captain Sauvel entered. 'Colonel, I am surprised at your idiocy. What did you hope to achieve?' A somewhat contrite Luke replied, 'I hoped to find Chidlow and his residence, and identity his mysterious keeper. That information is vital to my enquiries into rumours of an armed conspiracy against General Cromwell.' 'No wonder my little mission was of interest to you, especially if those coffins contained weapons as well as bodies.'

'How did I get here?' 'I knew you would attempt some foolhardy gesture so when you left here with the marine, two of my officers followed you. One rescued the marine, who apart from a complete soaking, and swallowing a lot of water is back on duty. The other followed you to the tavern. He was very intrigued as he recognised two other Englishmen in the establishment. He initially thought it was a pre-arranged meeting between the three of you. He then realised that your journey to St. Malo was not planned. He was even more astonished when one of the men returning with replenished drinks passed your bench. The Englishman almost dropped the drinks as he tried to raise his cape over his face, obviously to conceal his identity.' 'I knew it,' shouted an elated Luke. 'Just before I passed out I saw somebody that looked familiar.' Sauvel nodded, 'They certainly recognised you, and your presence disconcerted them enough that they left immediately without finishing their drinks.'

'What happens now?' 'You may have heard the noise on the quay. The owners and rightful crew of the *Le Lapin Noir* are about to reclaim her. My men are assembled there ready to march to a fishing vessel that will rendez-vous with *Le Soleil d'Or* somewhere off Jersey. You will come with us, and we will put you ashore on Jersey. Give me your word as a gentleman that you will not try to escape again and you and I will walk together ahead of my men to the fishing boat. If you break your word my marines have orders to shoot.' 'Don't worry Captain, I am anxious to get back to England to pursue my enquiries. The two Englishmen in St. Malo who recognised me provide a new lead.'

On the quay Sauvel handed the real captain of the *Le Lapin Noir* a large purse—final payment for the hire of his ship. His unruly crew pushed their way through the orderly ranks of sailors and marines, making insulting remarks. Sauvel and Luke moved to the front of the officers and men, and to the beat of a sole drummer, marched along the quay. As they turned at right angles onto the quay which catered for the fishing fleet both men became alert. A large body of armed men barred their way, and others were gathering behind them. This was an ambush. As the mob ran at the sailors and marines brandishing swords, staves and cudgels, Sauvel ordered his men into a defensive square, and commanded his marines to fire at will. The leaders of the mob nevertheless reached Sauvel and Luke, who as professional swordsmen had little difficulty in dealing with them. As the second wave approached, the marines beside them unleashed another volley of well-aimed shots.

Luke was surprised that such a poorly armed mob continued to attack a royal company of armed sailors and marines. Their assailants were slow to realize the hopelessness of their situation. Then a single shot hit Luke.

Blood poured from his head. Sauvel inspected the wound and assured Luke that he was all right. The shot had nicked the lobe of his left ear. The marksmen at the back of the crowd was preparing for another shot at Luke. The marine commander ordered his men to concentrate their fire on the assailant and suggested that Luke move to the centre of the defensive square. Sauvel, noting that their designated fishing boat was still hundreds of yards along the quay, ordered his men to confiscate the boat that lay alongside them. They would hold off the attackers until all defenders were aboard this nearest boat, and it was under sail. The innocent crew of the unfortunate boat jumped overboard, making no attempt to resist the sailors and marines.

As Luke boarded the boat he recognised the two men who flanked the marksman. One was the person he had seen in the tavern who was vaguely familiar, and the other was Robert Chidlow.

The overloaded fishing boat was soon well out to sea, and coping reasonably well with the swell. Sauvel commented on their escape. 'You have certainly upset someone of importance. That was an attempt to stop you getting home and reporting their presence here.' 'How would they know that I would be there?' 'No problem. They saw that it was my men who rescued you and brought you back to *Le Lapin Noir*. They would have picked up from harbour-side gossip that the original crew would take over this morning, and that we were due to leave on a fishing boat at the same time It is not hard to raise a mob in any seaport.'

Safely aboard *Le Soleil d'Or*, Luke was given the freedom of the ship. Captain Sauvel was immensely proud of his vessel, as it was proof that the English and the Dutch were not the only builders of modern, heavily gunned warships. *Le Soleil,* in English terms was a first rate ship with at least three decks of guns totalling well over fifty cannon. Luke's inspection of the magnificent ship was suddenly cut short. Sauvel demanded his immediate presence.

27

SAUVEL'S NEWS WAS dramatic. 'Luke, I had orders awaiting me to sail directly to London, and I need your help.' 'I can foresee your problem. The English navy and shore batteries will not let a French warship sail up the Thames, unless you have permission from the English Government, and it will not have had time to inform all those that may come in contact with you.'

'Not the problem Luke. That has been taken care of. The French government, as a sign of goodwill towards your republic, has offered to show your shipbuilders and generals-at-sea, *Le Soleil d'Or*. This has become urgent for your government as you must increase your ship building program to counter the dozens of new ships that the Dutch launch every year.' 'You will be blown out of the water. You don't realise how slowly your government's request and the English government's approval takes to filter down to those in charge of England's defences.'

'Still not a problem. The necessary information was sent weeks ago. Apparently just after I left *Le Soleil* for *Le Lapin Noir*, I received orders to cancel my mission with *Le Lapin* and sail *Le Soleil* to England. Negotiations had been going on for months.' 'Why the sudden change of orders to revoke *Le Lapin* mission ?' 'The King's sensible advisers probably regained the upper hand and withdrew support from the harebrained scheme, whatever it might be. The same advisers want friendly relations with England, especially with the army and General Cromwell.'

'Given the chaos at the centre of the French government, who specifically is behind the move to create good relations with England?' asked Luke. 'Although he is in exile, the policy is in line with that advocated by Mazarin when he was chief minister. He still has great support on the Royal Council especially with the Queen Regent.' 'Then why do you need my help? If all the paper work is in order you should have a quiet passage up the Thames.'

'I have orders to deliver a set of documents to our envoy in London, which I believe is to help him negotiate a treaty with the present English government. A second set of documents is to be delivered secretly to General Cromwell. Neither our envoy, nor the English government is to know about that second set of papers.' 'Easily done, I can take the documents to the Lord General immediately I arrive in London.'

'That is the easy part. Getting the documents to our envoy is more difficult. Part of the agreement for my visit is that I am not to leave Greenwich, and our envoy has not yet received permission to leave London. Yet he will not accept the documents as genuine unless I present them in person. The envoy, Sieur Gentillot, and I know each other. I want you to get me to Gentillot, without my absence from Greenwich being noticed, nor any of Gentillot's entourage becoming aware of my visit. He has arranged for us to meet at the residence of a third party, which I will reveal once we are in London.'

Numerous small boats, whose crew and passengers were in awe of the magnificent warship, accompanied *Le Soleil* up the Thames. The reception at Greenwich was equally favourable as the English republic's leading admiral, still addressed as general-at-sea, Robert Blake, was there to welcome the French ship. Blake was very surprised to see Luke, whom he knew as one of Cromwell's confidantes, arrive on *Le Soleil*. Luke lied that he had boarded the ship down river to deliver Cromwell's personal greetings, as the Lord General did not want to interfere with the official naval reception.

Luke, armed with Cromwell's authorization, asked Blake to send a messenger to Baker Grange to order Harry, Andrew and large body of troopers to make haste to Greenwich. The next day Harry presented himself to the naval officer on duty and requested an interview with Colonel Tremayne whom he understood was aboard the French warship, *Le Soleil d'Or*. Half and hour later Luke and Harry left the ship, and rejoining Andrew, the troop trotted off towards London. Andrew rode up to Luke to explain what had happened after Luke had sent him to get assistance from *The Providence*. Luke suggested this was not the time, and that he too had much to report. Andrew, snubbed by his colonel, and in need of conversation drew alongside Harry who remained largely hidden behind a massive cape that protected him from the cold winds blowing along the Thames. Before Andrew could speak the man slightly moved his cape. It was not Harry. It was the French naval captain that Andrew had last seen aboard *Le Lapin Noir*. Luke motioned for Andrew to remain silent regarding his discovery.

When the cavalcade entered London Sauvel, reading from a hand drawn map, directed the group. Luke and Andrew recognised the area. Neither had a chance to comment before Sauvel indicated that the premises that lay in front of them was the rendezvous for the secret meeting. The soldiers had been there before. It was the work place and home of Emile Tournac.

Sauvel asked the Englishmen to wait outside, and entered the house alone. Luke whispered, 'We will come back and interview Mr. Tournac about this visit at a later date, after we have more information. After we return Captain Sauvel to *Le Soleil* I must report to the Lord General. Our troopers need not return to Greenwich with us. Instruct them to discreetly follow everyone who leaves these premises within two hours of our departure. They are to follow their quarry to their first destination, and report to us tomorrow at Baker Grange.'

The soldiers relaxed in The Book and Quill until Sauvel re-emerged. Luke lied that he had sent his troopers back to their barracks. He, and his sergeant, would escort the captain back to his ship. On arriving at Greenwich the group was halted at the gangplank of *Le Soleil d'Or* by the marine commander. 'I am sorry Colonel, but the Captain is ill and cannot see anybody today.' The man disguised as Harry pushed his face into that of the Lieutenant who was taken aback on recognising his commanding officer. The three men entered the captain's cabin and were greeted by Harry and two naval officers who were aware of the exchange.

Harry and Sauvel exchanged uniforms, and the group drank the health of the French navy, and the English army. Captain Sauvel handed Luke a satchel. Luke promised that it would be delivered within the hour. The senior officers saluted, and the three English soldiers left the ship.

Cromwell's stern secretary was very annoyed. The general had been unwell, and was not able to see anybody. Luke demanded that the general be informed that Colonel Tremayne needed to see him urgently on a matter of national security involving the French. Within minutes Cromwell, who had obviously dressed quickly, entered the room. 'You will try anything Luke to get an audience, but I am intrigued to discover how an agent assigned to north London becomes involved with the French.'

'I shall explain that shortly, but first I must ask you to send your secretary from the room,' said Luke glaring at Scroggs. Completely intimidated by Luke, the secretary left the room without waiting for Cromwell's direction. Luke tiptoed to the closed door, and opened it. A skulking secretary scuttled away. Luke left the door wide open, and motioned for a bemused Cromwell to move to the far corner of the room. 'Sorry for these precautions, sir, but I have been asked by agents claiming to represent the French government to hand you these documents, with the caveat that our government does not become aware of their existence. This is a confidential missive between France and yourself as the commanding general of the English republic. Do the French know more than we do? They seem to believe that a military coup is imminent.'

Cromwell took the satchel. He quickly skimmed the two documents it contained. 'Very useful and they do not require an answer. I will not reveal the contents. Summon back my terrified secretary and ask him to bring a lighted taper.' The sour faced secretary returned. Cromwell took the taper and moved to the chimney. He placed the documents he had just received into the grate and lit them. He did not move until they had been completely burnt, and he broke up the ash with his boot. He turned to his secretary and said, 'Please record in the day book that I received some useless information from Colonel Tremayne regarding France, the details of which do not need to be recorded.' 'Sir, if you could asked your secretary to leave again I can explain how I managed to get such useless information.'

'Not appropriate Tremayne, my secretary is not at your beck and call. Visit me in my private quarters this evening, and you can tell me all in a relaxed atmosphere. Bring young Harry Lloyd with you.'

That evening the commander of Cromwell's bodyguard, Luke's former sergeant, and newly promoted Captain, John Halliwell, admitted Luke and Harry to the general's living quarters. The general asked John to join them for what amounted, given Cromwell's frugal tastes, to a very light supper. Luke entertained the company with an account of his adventures from the time he boarded the Dutch merchantman to his reappearance on board *Le Soleil d'Or* as it docked at Greenwich. He did not mention escorting Sauvel to Emile Tournac, nor the documents he had delivered earlier that day to the general.

Harry was surprised that Robert Chidlow was alive, but perplexed by his part in the attempt to kill Luke in St. Malo. Luke defended Robert, 'He was not a willing participant. Robert is convinced that if he does not obey his abductors' every wish, they will kill Rose. I wish I could put a name to the man who was in the French tavern, and was with Chidlow at the back of the mob. I have seen him before. He has altered his appearance but I am sure I will remember. He knew me, and it worried him.'

The next day at the Baker Grange Luke recounted his adventures for the benefit of Andrew, and then asked his men to report their activities since he sailed down the Thames. Andrew was brief, 'I rode post haste to the berth of *The Providence* only to be told it had left on the morning tide for parts unknown. I galloped further down river and tried to get a barge across the river to Greenwich to see if any of the ships docked there could take action. As I waited for the bargemen, who were engaged in some sort of dispute, *Le Lapin Noir* sailed by.'

Harry's account was a little more detailed. 'After I released the two porters we followed the wagons back to The Angel where they rested for much longer than I thought necessary. I divided my men into three troops and each wagon was followed to their different destinations. My men had orders to demand that once the coffins reached their final destination that they be opened. One wagon went miles out into the countryside, crossing the county border into Hertfordshire. The local vicar was appalled at our alleged sacrilege, but all the coffins delivered there contained nothing but bodies, or in some cases parts of bodies. One of my men, who had worked previously with his father as a butcher, reported that not all the bones were human.' 'The coffins that went to Old Kate and Archdeacon Craven however contained complete human skeletons which the archdeacon identified from a list given to him by the wagoner.'

'Our third party, which I led myself, followed the wagon to Reeves House. I allowed the wagon to enter the estate and we followed it to that renovated chapel on the far side of the manor. A group of Reeves's men awaited its arrival. There was considerable jollity. Their leader asked the wagoner to open one of the coffins which he did very happily. He extracted a couple of muskets, and then handed his companion a pair of pistols. Both took mock aim at each other as the leader signalled for the men to take the coffins into the chapel. I decided not to forewarn Sir Harcourt that we had caught him dealing in illegal arms, and to leave further action to you.'

'That explains your animal bones,' commented Luke. 'Sometime during the transportation there were not enough human bones to cover whatever else was in the coffins.' He continued, 'And what about the troopers we left at Tournacs to follow anyone who left there within two hours of our departure ?'

Andrew produced a note he had scribbled earlier in the day after he had interviewed the men. 'Essentially most of Tournac's clients finished up in an alehouse. Three public houses were the destination of two or more of Emile's clients—The Falcon, The Golden Harp and The Book and Quill.'

The officers reviewed the situation and agreed that over the following weeks they would thoroughly investigate the leading suspects, and the three drinking venues mentioned. First on their list was Sir Harcourt Reeves— and in his case they would act immediately. Luke ignored the legal niceties. He would seek the necessary authorization from the civil authorities after the event.

Luke gave his orders, 'The whole regiment will be ready to ride within the hour. We will descend on Reeves House in great numbers and search every inch of the buildings and grounds. Andrew you will round up all persons on the estate. Place the workers under temporary arrest in one of the barns, and confine the superior sorts to the library. Harry you will organize a minute search of the house. I will command the remaining troops in searching the grounds.'

28

LUKE FURTHER DIVIDED his own group into two. The majority formed a long line along the western edge of the estate and moved slowly eastwards. Luke feared that if anyone had escaped Andrew's sweep, they might head to the chapel and remove the guns and ammunition. He led a dozen men directly there. They entered the building by its front door as stealthily as they could. There were candles burning on the altar, and above it a large crucifix—sufficient evidence in Luke's eyes that this was a Papist chapel. A thorough search revealed nothing. Luke knew the gun-laden coffins were there. The original building must have had a crypt, the entry to which had been cleverly concealed during the renovations. Luke and his men searched for over an hour without luck. They prised up every suspicious looking flagstone and did considerable damage to the walls as they sought hidden doorways. Luke paced over every inch of the building. The only part of the chapel that had not been probed was the altar itself. Although he had no time for superstitious worship, he was uneasy in dismantling the altar. His men removed the candlesticks and the altar cloths. One man tripped over a flagstone that had not been properly replaced. He fell, and in trying to save himself slumped heavily against the altar. To everybody's amazement the altar turned. It rested on a horizontal wheel. Luke's men pushed it until it was at right angles to its original position. It revealed a large trapdoor.

The smell of burning tapers that wafted up from below indicated that until very recently the crypt was well lit. As Luke led his men down the stairs a shot rang out, and Luke felt a pain in his left arm. The troopers threw themselves down the stairs landing on top of each other. They were in pitch darkness, except for the dim light coming through the trapdoor. Luke called up to the troopers still in the main chapel for light. In a few minutes several tapers were handed down to the men in the crypt.

What they saw amazed them. The crypt was twice the size in both width and length to the chapel above. There were rows and rows of boxes and trunks, and against one wall a row of coffins. As the troopers worked their way methodically through the crypt in search of the gunman Luke opened the coffins, and then several of the boxes. It was a veritable arsenal —muskets, pistols, pikes, carbines, and barrels of gunpowder and boxes of shot. On shelves in the far corner were breast and back plates and an array of helmets, and a hundred or so military saddles.

Luke and his men, perplexed by the disappearance of the assailant, heard noises coming from the far corner of the crypt. Luke signalled for his men to prime their weapons and to hide behind the various trunks and boxes. The tapers were placed in receptacles built for that purpose so that the room was now brightly lit. All focussed on the far corner of the crypt as the noise of incessant chatter increased. Suddenly what appeared to be a wall panel swung open, and a man entered followed by several others who were dragging a person who had obviously received some sort of beating—or had experienced a serious fall. Luke stepped forward and greeted the leader of the group, 'God's Teeth, Harry, what are doing here? You are supposed to be searching the house.'

'I am. I was in Sir Harcourt's bedroom when one of our men noticed handprints on one of the panels. This was suspicious because the rest of the room was obsessively spotless. His housekeeper must clean continually. After some pushing and prodding, the panel opened inward into what in Queen Elizabeth's day would be called a priest's hole. I was so delighted in discovering this hidden room I nearly missed that part of the far wall of this tiny room also pushed outwards. This led down some stairs into a passage way. After following it for some time I saw a faint light further down the tunnel. We extinguished our tapers and waited. A short fat man, with his taper flaring dangerously ran straight into the fist of one of my men, and just in case he still had some resistance, was coshed by another. I have not questioned him yet, but he is French.'

'And the varlet who shot me in the arm,' interjected Luke. Harry noticed that Luke's left arm was caked in blood and the wound was still bleeding steadily. Luke himself was beginning to feel faint. His men managed to get him back up into the chapel, and after confiscating a cart, drove him back to Baker Grange.

Harry took over the investigation and interviewed Sir Harcourt. Harry entered the library where Andrew had detained Sir Harcourt and another unknown man. The two prisoners refused to acknowledge him. During the silence Harry observed that Sir Harcourt was a small man, but well proportioned. He had a face that was almost square and his brown eyes were higher on the face than the norm, and separated by a flat broad nose. He had an exceptionally wide mouth. He wore his brown hair short in the Puritan fashion but he had a reddish brown beard similar to that worn by the late King Charles. He was dressed from head to toe in burgundy. His doublet was slashed, revealing a gold silk lining—and he wore on a short golden chain a large gold crucifix. He completely ignored Harry, and mumbling away in Latin, fingered his rosary. Somewhere, sometime Sir Harcourt Reeves had become a Papist.

Harry as a practicing Puritan had no time for such idolatrous nonsense. He pulled Sir Harcourt roughly from his chair, and set him down on a bench that ran along the end wall. 'Enough, Sir Harcourt, we have uncovered sufficient evidence to have you hanged. You are a practising Papist who has a veritable arsenal of arms and ammunition, and have probably harboured a Papist priest in your recently-built priest's hole.' 'My man you may have the power of the sword to effect this illegal search and detention, but you are woefully ignorant of the law. It is not illegal to be a Papist, and I have a licence to manufacture gunpowder and import arms.' 'Don't play games with me, Sir Harcourt. Since you became a Papist your licences to manufacture gunpowder and import arms would be rendered void. You must keep two sets of books—one outlining your legitimate manufacture and importation, and a second detailing your excessive stockpiling. I have not yet gone through the papers we have confiscated but I am sure they will prove your double dealing.'

Sir Harcourt suddenly seemed to become aware of his dire situation and asked almost plaintively, 'Am I now to meet an accidental death?' 'Not at all. You will be escorted to The Tower for proper interrogation.' 'And my arms and ammunition?' 'The legitimate part of your business can continue to operate. Maybe your son Grenville, or your wife Lady Cassandra can take over. The illegal excess will be confiscated.'

Meanwhile the fat Frenchman from the crypt was handed over to Andrew for interrogation. Andrew recognized him immediately. He was the man who left *Le Lapin Noir*, and disappeared into the crowd. His extensive moustache was caked in blood, and given the beating he had suffered, Andrew decided on a soft approach. He had the man's wounds tended to, and obtained food from the housekeeper. They then helped themselves to one of Sir Harcourt's bottles of fine red wine. The Frenchman revealed all. He was terrified that he would be mistaken for a Jesuit priest, and executed. He was a gun dealer, and had organized the most recent shipment of arms aboard *Le Lapin Noir*. Andrew asked, 'If you were the gun dealer supervising the transmission of weapons to England what was Robert Chidlow's role?'

'In reality he played no role at all. The trip was an opportunity to build up pressure on the poor man. He was desperate. The people, who paid me for the guns, and my services in ensuring their delivery, were blackmailing him. To keep the pressure on him for some future enterprise he was led to believe that he was responsible for the cargo from St. Malo to London. During the trip across I was just one of the passengers that happened to be on board.' 'How were the guns hidden? My colonel, the man you shot in the crypt, opened a casket and found only a corpse.'

'He did not look far enough. Every coffin contained a corpse, and under the body, weapons of various types. The three wagons met at The Angel. The weapons were removed from all the coffins and placed in empty coffins held in Grenville Reeves's barn. The coffins with the bodies were redistributed on two of the wagons, and those now containing weapons only, were placed on the third wagon and brought here.'

While Luke was recovering from his minor flesh wound at the barracks at Baker Grange he examined the accounts confiscated from Sir Harcourt. They revealed one simple fact. After Sir Harcourt's legal customers—the New Model Army in Ireland, the militias of London and its hamlets, and several garrisons throughout the country—had been supplied, he had enough over to arm a major uprising.

Within weeks lawyers employed by Sir Harcourt had secured his release. The magistrates decided that he had not harboured any Papist priest. He may have imported and manufactured more arms and ammunition than his clients needed, but this was a matter of supply and demand, and in no way proved he was equipping an insurrection. The army had failed to prove its case. Sir Harcourt's licence remained valid, if he handed the operation of his ammunition and gun dealing over to anyone who was not a Papist. Sir Harcourt could still receive the income, but not control the destination of the goods. Because evil intent had not been proved, the army was forbidden to confiscate the excess arms and ammunition in the crypt. But with an eye to national security the army was permitted to mount guard over the arsenal, and Harcourt's surrogate would have to obtain its permission to relocate any of it.

Everybody was surprised at Sir Harcourt's nominee to operate his licence. Luke expected Grenville Reeves to be named. Harcourt chose Sir Rowland Hille. On hearing the news Luke appeared to have been struck by lightning. Eventually he let out a cry of exultation, 'Cuds-me, I remember. The man in the tavern in St. Malo, and the one who stood beside Robert Chidlow during the attack on me, was Sir Rowland. When I met him at The Angel he was clean shaven with shortish hair, and the man in France was long haired with a beard, but it was Rowland.'

Luke's investigation was becoming more complex. Despite the views of the magistrates, Luke was convinced that Sir Harcourt's arsenal was to be the basis of a major uprising. But by whom? Was there more in the French connection than a source of the imported arms? Was this a French-driven coup on behalf of the exiled King? Or given Sir Harcourt's change of religion, was it a Catholic plot to overturn England's Protestant faith? Or was the excess of arms to be distributed to the various militias and garrisons as a counter to any activity by the New Model Army?—a program probably supported by the Rump, and the majority of old Parliamentarians.

Luke was sure of one thing. 'Whichever of these possibilities is true they all have the same aim—to destroy the Lord General and the national army, which we have served for over a decade.' Luke was depressed.

'Cheer up,' announced Andrew. 'Now that we are sure of the motives of our enemies it will be easier to discover and examine our suspects. We may find a clear pattern. Let's send our more able troopers, disguised as civilians, to follow everyone that we suspect. The men we left at Tournac's did a good job. This will save time. We can track several persons at once. Let our men loose for three days and then examine their reports. If there is any suspicious behaviour by any of the suspects we can follow up those discrepancies immediately. Meanwhile you and I can enjoy three days of heavy drinking.'

They got three hours. Having selected and briefed their men, and allocated the specific targets, they adjourned to The Angel where Sam joined in their projected drinking bout. They were interrupted almost immediately by the arrival of Miles Baker and Adam Dale. Adam could not contain himself, 'There has been another murder.' Miles, who appeared much calmer announced, 'Sir Harcourt Reeves is dead, and the popular rumour is that having failed to get him legally, the army murdered him. You will need to find the real killer, Luke, to clear you own name.'

29

'ARE YOU SURE he was murdered?' asked Luke. Miles retreated, 'Well no, I am going on the word of his housekeeper.' The group rode to Reeves House where they were met by Lady Cassandra who was engaged in a slanging match with the housekeeper. Miles was amazed to find his sister there, 'Cassie you were at home when I left an hour or so ago. What are you doing here?' 'Isn't it obvious brother. I am taking over as the Lady of this Manor. This is my lawful property, until the courts acting on Harcourt's will, determine otherwise. The legal proceedings will take years. I am leaving Baker Grange and Rose Chidlow is coming with me as my companion.' Miles was aghast at his sister's haste and insensitivity, and callous disregard for Sir Harcourt's longstanding housekeeper who was clearly distraught by the turn of events.

Harcourt's body still lay slumped over the dinner table. The doctor had been sent for, but the housekeeper had no hesitation in explaining her master's death. 'Sir Harcourt loved his wild mushrooms. He had them everyday as part of his midday meal.' She explained further, 'I gather them each morning from Priory Wood, and cook them myself, but they are served by his manservant. When Sir Harcourt collapsed I rushed in and immediately noticed his dinner plate. Amongst the mushrooms I had cooked were spoonfuls of a strange fungus that someone had added to his plate after it left the kitchen.' The male servant confirmed that the plate which had remained on a serving table for a few minutes had the strange mushrooms on it when he served it to his master. He assumed that the housekeeper had discovered a new variety of edible mushrooms. He too was distraught.

Luke had his suspicions. He remembered his first meeting with Miles who had mentioned his sister's knowledge of potions and poisons. He sought out Lady Cassandra. 'My lady, how long have you been here? Was Sir Harcourt alive when you arrived?' Cassandra was guarded. 'Why do you ask?' Luke had no time for games. 'You hated your husband. You would have a better claim over the arms licence, and everything else if you were a widow. Harcourt's death puts everything, at least initially into your hands. And you were in the house before he died.'

Cassandra suddenly realised the seriousness of her situation. 'Yes. I came to see Harcourt. As usual he made me wait in the antechamber until he had finished his meal—which I did. I heard the housekeeper scream and elicited from the servants what had happened. Harcourt's death is not to my advantage. By English law Grenville will inherit everything, except for my widow's dowry. My planned legal challenge will only delay the inevitable. As for the arms licence I was happy for Sir Rowland to operate it.'

Luke had had enough. While his instincts told him Cassandra was the murderer—she hated the victim, wanted his property and possessions, had knowledge of poisons, and was present just prior to his death—he would have difficulty proving it. The attempt to prosecute Meg as the murderer of Joe Muggs was a lesson Luke would not forget. His predicament was not improved when Cassandra whispered, 'I have a witness who can prove my innocence. Rose was with me.' Luke's anxiety increased. Rose's presence only added to the confusion. Her growing friendship with Lady Cassandra intrigued him.

Luke's depression intensified. His investigation was going nowhere, and everyday it became more complicated. Despite the rumours that Sir Harcourt's demise was the result of army intervention Luke was determined not to get involved. He left any further investigation of Harcourt's death to the civil authorities.

Luke took out his growing frustration on his regiment. He put it through its paces. There had been no drill for weeks, and since the Battle of Worcester the troopers had had a relatively easy life. Several days of intensive cavalry training, and mock battle manoeuvres would ready his unit for action given their ultimate return to Ireland. On the fourth day Luke, Harry and Andrew received the verbal reports of the fortunate troopers who had avoided these boring exercises as they followed the leading suspects.

The officers were delighted. Every report contained material that could be considered suspicious.

The report on Matthew Craven stood out. It raised two questions—why did he spend so much time in a tavern that appeared to be a church for religious extremists, and what was his interest in an incredibly wealthy looking, and recently built manor house on the south side of the Thames, which had Ketley Court emblazoned on the impressive front gate?

Harry remained at Baker Grange putting the regiment through its training program. Luke and Andrew dressed as London porters visited The Falcon in Cripplegate, the alehouse church frequented by Craven, and which had been mentioned in an earlier report. They were warmly welcomed with cries of brother as they all drank and listened to the testimony of one of the faithful who had turned his back on the temptations of the world. The Falcon was a church, but it had not relinquished its basic function of providing ale in limitless quantities to a multitude of chanting customers. Luke noticed a couple of brothers move a portable pulpit into a prominent position. At five o'clock a hush descended over the room. A man entered and strode to the lectern. After the rhythmic clapping and shouts of hallelujah had subsided, Matthew Craven began to preach. The soldiers well disguised, and now hidden behind a column, were appalled at what they heard. It was revolutionary, millenarian rubbish, aimed at the lowest elements in the community. Matthew was a charismatic, almost hypnotic speaker who had the ever-responsive audience in the palm of his hand.

'Brothers and sisters, you, the regenerate cannot sin. Sin and traditional religion are the inventions of the superior sorts to keep you oppressed. King and Parliament are both oppressors. You are free from the moral fictions of the past, and have a duty to bring about the downfall of established authority. The saints must rule the nation, and you, my brothers and sisters, must take steps to achieve this end. God's immediate design is to undo the mighty ones of the earth. And our weapon brethren, and God's weapon, is the army. The army has the call of the nation, and hears the common cry of the oppressed. And if the current Lord General does not heed God's summons the Lord God has in waiting a fiery and holy instrument in the person of Thomas Harrison. Rise up, throw off your shackles, seize power and prepare the earth for the coming of the Lord!'

Andrew muttered to himself about the wild and whirling words that spewed forth from this brainsick toad. Luke had heard enough, and given the enthusiasm and passion of the audience, the soldiers were able to leave unobserved. They could not believe that the quietly spoken conservative lawyer was a religious fanatic of the most extreme nature, calling for the destruction of traditional forms of authority, wealth and morality. They found a neighbouring tavern where they could see the entry to The Falcon. After an hour The Falcon began to empty, with many couples pawing each other and a few copulating in the street. Matthew eventually emerged with a much older woman. They stopped and had a long discussion with one of the congregation whom Luke immediately recognised. 'Zooks, I knew he could not be trusted. The man talking to Craven and the woman, is Zephaniah Scroggs, the General's secretary.'

After Scroggs left, Craven and his companion walked towards the river arm in arm. Luke and Andrew followed. Eventually they reached the site very familiar to them both—the building site where the bear baiting, and later skirmish had occurred. A barge was waiting for Matthew and his companion, and Luke and Andrew, unable to follow, watched as it was rowed upriver.

Next day Luke and Andrew set out for the new manor house on the river. Crossing London Bridge they turned west, winding their way up and down dead ends. The landward side of their targeted estate was finally reached. It consisted of one long high wall that ran for half a mile. There was no grand entrance nor even a large gate. There was one small yard-square door that was obviously securely locked from the inside. The street along which the wall ran was so narrow that Luke could not even get a glimpse of the house. Climbing the wall was impossible without siege equipment. If they wished to discover Matthew Craven's association with this lavish, very well secured estate, they would have to approach it by river.

Luke and Andrew hired a barge from steps near London Bridge. The wherrymen were not too happy that their passengers wanted to go a considerable distance upstream. As they approached their destination the wherry men pulled in their oars. 'We cannot take you to that new house. Only a small group of us have permission to land at that new quay.' Luke was incensed, 'How does anybody know which wherries can be rowed here, and which cannot?' 'Those who have access wear a red ribbon. You have a choice. We can take you back to London Bridge, and you can seek out a red ribboned wherryman, or as the tide is still well out we can drop you in the mud, and you can wade through the ooze until you reach what the river men have christened Ketley Quay.'

'The second wherryman suddenly interjected, 'Neither will be necessary. There is a small barge, manned by Red Ribbon men coming up riverside. We can signal them to take you aboard.' As Luke turned toward the approaching barge his mouth dropped. 'Andrew, that barge already has a passenger and we know him well.' The passenger was as surprised to see the soldiers. 'God's wounds! I thought I had just eluded your scrutiny after weeks of confinement, and I find you heading for Ketley Court.' Brian Kendall assisted Luke and Andrew aboard the barge.

Luke was not happy. 'Brian, you are under house arrest for your own protection. If the agents of The Fox knew you were still alive they might make another attempt on your life.' 'True, but I convinced Miles, supported by Matthew Craven, who needed me, that if I disappeared into the depths of London the agents of The Fox would be none the wiser.'

Luke changed the subject. 'Both Matthew and yourself have made your way to Ketley Court. Is this the home of the master criminal and commercial powerbroker, The Wolf?' 'I think so, but all my dealings with him have been through Matthew who asked me to come here.' The three men were amazed at the opulence of the house, and the grounds still being landscaped by hundreds of men, and the thousands of young trees still in pots arranged along the wide path that led from the river to the entrance portico. A liveried servant, a privilege legally limited to the high aristocracy, opened the door. They asked to speak to Mr. Matthew Craven, if he was currently in the house. The servant obtained their names, ushered them into a small antechamber, and disappeared. After a few minutes Matthew arrived accompanied by two servants with drinks and refreshments. 'So, Brian you failed to get away from your keepers. I trust none of The Fox's men saw you.' 'You misjudge me, Matthew. Luke and Andrew did not follow me here. They were already on the river and stalled just off your quay. I offered them a lift.'

Matthew was silent for some time as the men ate the array of sweetmeats provided. 'That raises some interesting questions. It suggests Luke that you have had me under surveillance.' 'True Matthew, but I have at least a dozen suspects under observation. But you are right, my men followed you here, so I thought a visit might assist my investigation. I would like to meet The Wolf.' Matthew smiled, 'That can be arranged very easily. The Wolf is in the process of moving into this house which he had built by those to whom he gave work and protection. Until now The Wolf kept his identity a secret, and has dealt with others through me. He now believes it is time to reveal himself to the world. I will leave you for a moment, and return with The Wolf.

Brian was quite excited. At last he would meet the man he had served loyally for several years. Even Luke could not escape the suspense. Would it be some one he already knew? Would it provide a breakthrough in his investigation? After a few minutes an elderly woman entered the room. Luke recognised her immediately. It was the woman that Matthew had escorted from the meeting of the religious fanatics. The woman signalled for men to resume their seats.

Was this The Wolf?—an elderly pale-faced woman.

30

THE WOMAN SPOKE so quietly that Luke had difficulty in hearing. 'Gentlemen I have the great honour to present to you my son, known to some as The Wolf but to me as…' The Wolf had a sense of the dramatic. Her introduction was cut short as the door was flung open, and The Wolf entered the room. Brian dropped his pork pie, Andrew spilt his drink and Luke's jaw dropped open in amazement. The dumbstruck trio stared at the most powerful man in London.

The Wolf was Matthew Craven.

'I asked mother to introduce me as my success is due to her. When I was nine she left my father, taking me with her. Father, the Venerable Dominic Craven made no attempt to get me back. He regretted his marriage to my mother who was a servant to his parents. Her family still live in St. Aiden. Mother's sister-in-law runs an alehouse there, and her younger sister was housekeeper to the late Sir Harcourt Reeves. She was a Ketley, therefore the name of this manor. My mother and I grew up within a radical religious group in the city, and as I matured an unknown benefactor provided funds to give me an education. My current legal partner Mr. Tournac, who over the years became my surrogate father, distributed these mysterious funds. He does not always approve of what I do, but it was his help that got me into the law. I trust that that answers most of the questions you had in mind?'

'Yes, as does this house and its location. You control the riverfront. The bargemen, wherry men, dock workers and porters seem to thrive under your protection.' Matthew could not help himself. He expanded on Luke's praise. 'As are the building workers. Soon nothing will be built in London without my approval. Most of the unskilled workers pouring into the city from the countryside, who are exploited not only by the wealthy, but also by the established artisans and tradesmen of the city, are seeking my help. Most reforming groups, such as the Levellers, have no time for these people and strive to increase the power of the skilled worker. I alone protect the underemployed, the unemployed and the poor. Soon The Fox and his dwindling followers, and all of London, will be at my mercy.'

Luke was unsettled. Matthew Craven was a very dangerous man, and somewhat demented. Luke was also disappointed. He had seen Matthew as an ally in his attempt to weaken The Fox, and in general to protect the interests of the army. Matthew on the surface remained a fanatical supporter of the army. It was an essential element in his vision of a better England. But scarcely hidden in this vision was the threat that if Oliver Cromwell did not behave as Matthew Craven desired, the saints would sweep him aside in favour of Thomas Harrison. This worried Luke. Harrison was the one senior officer who accepted the necessity of saintly rule, and he had considerable influence on Cromwell. The identification of Cromwell's secretary as a member of Craven's congregation increased Luke's anxiety. Perhaps Scroggs had talked to Craven, and Craven ordered the attempts on Luke's life?

Back at Baker Grange Andrew was even more direct. 'The man's a lunatic, and he has the wealth and influence to cause a lot of trouble. Warn the general! Craven and his supporters must be eliminated before they undermine established society—and before his wild ideas rage through the lower ranks of the army. The slowness of the Government in paying us our arrears in wages does not help. Unpaid soldiers are already among the most fervent supporters of Craven, who pays his men very well.'

'No point in telling Cromwell yet. Craven, on the surface, is a respectable lawyer who has shown his willingness to support the army. He may be closer to General Harrison than we know. I cannot see the Lord General agreeing to a pre-emptive strike against such a man on our say so.' 'Why not present the issue to Cromwell as the beginnings of a coup by the saints within the army and without, to replace him as commander-in-chief with Thomas Harrison,' suggested Andrew.

'Unfortunately if he thinks such a move is God's will, Oliver will simply resign. The providence of God has been his light on the hill, but it is also his Achilles heel. At the moment he sees the saints as the future of England.' 'Then report your concerns to the more secular of Cromwell's senior officers,' Andrew responded. Luke frowned, 'I have just realised another worrying aspect of a Craven organized coup in favour of Harrison. The government's and the army's major arsenal is located in the Tower of London. The man responsible for this arsenal is the Lieutenant of the Ordnance who happens to be Thomas Harrison.'

Luke remained silent for some time and then continued, 'Unfortunately the senior officers I could warn are either at sea, still in Scotland, on their way to Ireland or too old. Long distant communications with any of them would be dangerous, and I suspect we do not have time on our side.'

Andrew broke another long silence, 'There is one man you might tell— Cromwell's brother-in-law, John Desborough. He is in London as a Member of Parliament.' 'No, Andrew I will not go behind my general's back. I have loyally supported the Lord General for over a decade, and even more so now that he appears the only hope for a secure, safe, reformed and powerful England.' Harry was informed of the situation. He had no qualms. 'Luke, inform Cromwell immediately of Craven's potential threat to law and order, and to the general's position as head of the national army!'

The discussion was interrupted. A messenger entered the room and handed Luke a letter, indicating that he would wait for a response. Luke read the key parts of the epistle aloud. *The Lady Cassandra Reeves and Mistress Rose Chidlow invite Lieutenant Colonel Luke Tremayne to enjoy dinner with them at 12 noon next Friday.* Harry expressed the general response. 'Why have you been invited? Who else will be there?'

Luke presented himself at Reeves House at the appointed hour. Lady Cassandra had, in her brief time at the House, transformed it. New furnishings adorned every room and the staff seemed to have increased fourfold from the days of her late frugal husband. After drinks in an ante chamber a servant announced that dinner was being served and they were led into the hall, where a large dining table that had been neglected by Sir Harcourt, occupied the centre of the room. It was laden with food. Luke's fellow guests were predictable. Miles Baker and a woman Luke assumed to be his wife, Adam and Temperance Dale, Meg Dale and man Luke had never met, and two unattached males, Matthew Craven, and Rowland Hille.

As the group sat around the table and helped themselves to the food Cassandra welcomed her friends to Reeves House which she hoped under her care would become the centre of social activity for the neighbourhood. She then asked Rose to say a few words as she had received some very happy news. 'Friends some time ago I received some very good news, but until I could check its veracity I told no one except Sir Rowland. My husband Robert is alive and lives comfortably under house arrest in St. Malo. His kidnappers informed Sir Rowland who went to St. Malo on my behalf that he will not be harmed, but will be kept out of England until they achieve their ends.'

'And what Sir Rowland are their ends?' interjected Luke. Rowland looked at Rose who indicated that he might reply. 'I do not know Colonel. The kidnapper I met was English and a Royalist. Robert apparently discovered matters that would have aborted their mission in England. Consequently he was kidnapped.' 'But why did they have to remove his hand?' asked the naïve Temperance. It was Rose that answered, 'It was an accident. It was neither a punishment, nor a warning to others.'

Miles Baker asked if he could also address the gathering on an official and personal matter. 'Friends, as we sit around the table of our late friend Sir Harcourt, I can report on the investigation into his death. Some of you present here today suggested I look closely at the behaviour of his housekeeper, Mildred Makepiece, who happens to be the aunt of another guest here today, Mr. Craven.' Luke winced. Given what he now knew of Matthew the use of his aunt to remove a rival such as Sir Harcourt was quite conceivable.

Miles continued, 'I am happy to report that there was nothing suspicious about the death of our friend. A simpleton that Harcourt had employed was so grateful that she wished to do something nice for her master. She knew that he loved mushrooms so she gathered some of her own. Unaware that they were poisonous, she added them to the meal that the housekeeper had already prepared. Goody Makepiece confirmed, after examining the mushrooms that had been added, that they included several poisonous varieties. Given the child-like condition of the servant girl, no further action will be taken.'

After the meal Cassandra invited the guests to tour the house and garden—to show off her innovations and plans for the future. Luke found himself walking beside Rose as they moved from chamber to chamber. Luke was taken aback by her first words, 'Colonel I hope that my explanation of

Sir Rowland's visit to St. Malo is satisfactory. I know you recognised him. I am very disappointed that you did not tell me that Robert was alive. Surely a wife should be the first to hear good news?' 'I am sorry Mistress Chidlow but I was under strict orders from your husband not to tell you. I do not know what Sir Rowland has related, but Robert is not having a comfortable holiday. He is a frightened man, who cravenly obeys his kidnappers because he believes that if he does not, you will be punished. I hope Sir Rowland told him that you live under no such threat?'

An annoyed Rose flounced off. Luke fell back to Meg and her male companion. Meg was full of smiles and welcomed Luke warmly. 'Luke, I wish to introduce you to the man that has fascinated you since you came to St. Michael. This is my long time friend Valentine Cole, whom some call The Fox.' Meg had a mischievous grin on her face as she carefully observed the reaction of both men. Luke calmly acknowledged Valentine and announced, 'As Meg says, I have been seeking information about you, and above all hoping to have a discussion with you over the growing conflict in the city, especially regarding transportation, and the bearing of all this on the government and the army. This is not the place. May I call upon you at your convenience over the next day or two?' 'Certainly Colonel, I have heard a lot about you from my brother-in-law, Major Jasper Nettle. Why not dinner tomorrow, noon, at my inn, The Golden Harp?'

Luke recalled the earlier reference to The Golden Harp and wondered why clients of Emile Tournac were associated with the headquarters of The Fox?

Luke hastened ahead to join Temperance and Adam. Temperance was admiring some pottery from her childhood that Sir Harcourt had put away, and Cassandra had now resurrected as a main display in one of the chambers. 'It is very good news that Robert is alive,' said Temperance. Luke agreed and added, 'I am sure it will not be long before he is home with you all.' 'And what did you think of Meg's surprise? Valentine must have wanted to see you urgently, or he would not have come. He has protected his identity for decades,' said Adam.

'I will know more after I meet him tomorrow,' replied Luke.

Adam looked forlornly at his wife, 'Luke must be told, my sweet heart.' 'What should I be told?' Luke asked. Adam produced a letter from inside his doublet and handed it to Luke. There was no doubting its meaning.

'Mistress Dale, if you cannot persuade your husband to withdraw his support from the network of The Fox by the Sabbath after next, you will suffer personally. If your husband values your life, he will comply.'

It was not signed.

31

LUKE KEPT THE letter. It must be the work of The Wolf. Such a thought awakened him to an obvious fact. Where was Matthew Craven? He was not amongst the dinner guests ambulating through the house and gardens. Luke returned to the dining room. He asked a servant who was clearing the table whether he had seen Mr. Craven. 'Yes sir, he asked the way to the library.' Luke assumed that Matthew knew that the tunnel leading to the arsenal could be accessed from the library. Luke ran through the woods to the chapel, and down to the crypt where men from his own regiment were guarding the weapons and munitions. He pretended it was a routine inspection. He suggested they open the door to the tunnel and extinguish the tapers for a hundred yards down the tunnel and those within the crypt itself.

After some minutes in complete darkness they heard someone stumbling and crashing his way in the blackness down the tunnel. Luke then began to hear the hysterical murmurings of a man in fear of his life. Craven had a phobia. He could not cope with total darkness. As Matthew neared the end of the tunnel the tapers in the crypt were relit and Luke quietly left the chapel. Luke's childish attempt to irritate Matthew had revealed a surprising and unexpected fact. Matthew's fear of total darkness was a chink in his armour—a weakness Luke would not forget.

As he walked back through the woods Luke was determined to confront Sir Rowland Hille whom he considered both a liar, and a disgrace to the memory of his father. He found Hille in a walled garden which was under rehabilitation. He had a large drawing in his hands and was discussing the redesign with two of the gardeners. Rowland looked uneasy as Luke approached. He went ashen as Luke denounced him, 'It's fortunate for you Rowland that Parliament has banned duelling. Otherwise I would call you an unmitigated liar, and force you to defend your honour in a duel in which I would kill you.' Sir Rowland began to stammer as he struggled to say, 'I do not know what you are talking about.'

'The story you told Rose Chidlow is full of holes. What were you doing in that tavern in St. Malo? Why did you disappear when you saw me? Why didn't you help a fellow Englishmen, whom you knew, and who had drunk too much?' 'Colonel, there is nothing sinister or mysterious in anything that I did. Rose received a letter saying if she wanted to confirm that her husband was still alive she or her agent should meet a man carrying a burgundy book in a particular tavern in St. Malo on one of several dates. That is what I was doing. At that stage I had not established any evidence about whether Robert was alive or dead, and I certainly did not want your presence upsetting a delicate negotiation. You could have wrecked the whole enterprise.'

'Even if that is true why were you and Robert Chidlow on the quay at St. Malo participating in the attempt to kill me?' 'Robert's kidnapper made us stand there to witness what might happen to both of us if we did not follow his instructions to the letter.' 'This abductor; can you tell me anything about him?' 'Only that he is English, a former courtier who hates the current government, and especially its army. One unusual thing for a Royalist. He forced us to drink a toast, not to the King, but to Charles's mother our former Queen, Henriette Marie.'

Luke's visit to Reeves House had been very productive. He was still not sure whether to believe Rose and Sir Rowland's explanation of the latter's visit to St Malo, and their innocence in regard to Robert's abduction. He had enjoyed complicating Craven's inappropriate exploration of the tunnel leading to the arsenal. As he rode home his self-satisfaction was punctured by the sudden thought that Craven's tunnel adventure may have been a reconnaissance for a planned attempt to steal the arsenal. Craven's strength would be immensely increased, if his almost unlimited manpower were better armed. Above all meeting Valentine Cole, and his arranged visit to the powerful businessman could be the watershed in his investigation.

Next day as Luke sat across the table from Valentine Cole and enjoyed the food and drink proffered to him he assessed this powerful enigmatic figure. Valentine was a well built man, approaching fifty, with just a few streaks of grey in his light brown curly hair, which reached his shoulders. A flat squashed nose that Luke assumed had been broken more than once divided his large brown eyes. He was therefore surprised to see that when Valentine smiled he had a full set of teeth that were whiter than the norm. A bushy curly moustache that was more reddish than the hair of his head covered his upper lip. Dressed completely in olive green—from the hat that lay on his desk through his slashed doublet whose silk lining was simply a lighter shade, to his breeches and hose. He wore no jewellery and carried no visible weapons. Nor were the room and its approaches filled with servants and bodyguards. His warm and welcoming personality had already overcome Luke's instinctive suspicion.

After an hour of eating, drinking and exchanging comments about the weather Valentine ended the social activities. 'Colonel, down to business! I need your, or rather the army's help. The city and its trade are about to be brought to a standstill by a man who in imitation of my own popular sobriquet calls himself The Wolf. We both know his mouthpiece—that scheming lawyer, Matthew Craven.'

Luke raised his hand to stop Valentine continuing. 'Sir, why should I believe a man whose organizations seem determined to prevent the army forcing the current Parliament to reform the country, and may be in league with those elements gathering weapons and ammunition to forestall any anticipated army action.'

'I speak plainly Colonel. The situation until recently suited me fine. I controlled most of the areas that were vital to my business interests, and my power and influence enabled me to provide protection, or in more lofty terms, law and order to the expanding suburbs of London, where the authorities were unable, or unwilling to fulfil their duties. I reached an agreement with several alderman of the City to expand this role with the aid of their newly created militia. I know you have already had a confrontation with my brother-in-law, my sister's husband, Major Jasper Nettle—the city's ranking officer.'

'Jasper Nettle and I go back a long way. But I note your phrase "until recently." What has changed?' 'Come Luke! Don't take me for a fool. The Wolf has wrested control of river transport and much of the building trade from me. He is using labourers and demobilised unpaid troops to threaten apprentices and their employers to seek his protection rather than mine. Idiots wearing something red, go round terrorising the locals as they did to the Levellers in St Aiden.'

'So how can a simple soldier be of help?' interrupted Luke.

'Not so simple. I am aware of your true identity, and your current mission. I want you to explain the real situation to General Cromwell, and emphasize that any future role of the army will be greatly enhanced, if they have the city behind it.' 'Why should the General side with you against The Wolf?'

'Property, and the freedoms that the army claimed it was fighting for! There has been an immense upset to the landowning classes of England. The gentry, yeomen, merchants and tradesmen all have a stake in the country. Whether you are Royalist or Parliamentarian; Anglican, Presbyterian or Independent; or in favour of the current Rump of the House of Commons or a reforming Army there are clear limits to acceptable change. The Wolf goes too far. He will overturn established law and order and introduce a dictatorship of those who have nothing, except a crazy belief that they are the saints of an avenging God, whose earthly manifestation is indeed, The Wolf. I am sure if the army, under the moderate leadership of your General, supports the position I have outlined, the City is in a position to persuade even Royalists and Presbyterians to support the reforms he wishes to introduce.'

'I see a problem,' replied an increasingly impressed Luke. 'At the moment General Cromwell believes the future of the country would be better served by the saints than the corrupt members of the Rump or City.' 'That is precisely why I am meeting with you. For someone of your apparently lowly place in the army hierarchy I know you have unlimited access, and considerable influence on the general. If the stability of London, and therefore of the country is to be preserved you must convince him to support us—and suppress The Wolf.'

'The general would not be convinced by my unsubstantiated rhetoric. I need evidence that The Wolf is a dangerous man, and that The Fox is the responsible guardian of the values we all hold dear. Give me a day to consider your proposals, and to consult my officers. I will return tomorrow.'

'Agreed, but do not leave yet. Important decisions should be made on a full stomach. Let us continue dinner in the main dining room with a few of my friends and your acquaintances.' Luke mellowed by the drink, and impressed by his companion, readily followed Valentine through several rooms until they reached a large antechamber with a large table groaning with more food, a room buzzing with servants and diners who were crowded onto the benches that surrounded the table. His fellow guests were Adam and Temperance Dale, Meg Dale, Grenville Reeves, and his old antagonist Jasper Nettle and his wife, a couple of officers from the Tower Hamlet militia, and two pompous looking men whom Luke was told were Aldermen of the city, and their female companions. Luke was seated next to Temperance, and was surprised that she had dropped her ice maiden persona, and flirted outrageously with the increasingly relaxed colonel. Adam remained in deep and serious conversation with Valentine.

As Luke trotted home he tossed around the ideas and attitudes that Valentine had sown in his mind. After his meeting with Craven at Ketley Court Luke did not need to be convinced that The Wolf was a dangerous man, and potentially hostile to the Lord General—but was The Fox a reliable ally? When The Wolf was removed would Cole reassert his anti-army attitude, and oppose any genuine reforms that the army might want to introduce? Luke went straight to bed, informing his equerry that he wanted an urgent meeting with Harry and Andrew at first light.

Next morning Luke apprised them of his discussion with Valentine Cole, and in conjunction with his earlier meeting with Matthew Craven, had tentatively reached a major decision. 'You both know that I have spent a decade in the service of Oliver Cromwell as I believe he is the only man that can lead England out of its current crisis. But I believe if we do not act unilaterally to destroy Matthew Craven the general will not survive in a position to carry out his vision. He is currently misled by one aspect of that vision, which sees a great role for the religious extremists in the future of this nation. Clearly there are religious extremists who can improve the condition of the country, but not someone such as Matthew Craven who borders on a man possessed. I propose we assist The Fox to destroy Craven. I will explain our actions to the general, after this has been achieved.

The soldiers spent the morning developing a plan of action to assist The Fox, and at noon Luke and Andrew arrived at The Golden Harp. They were immediately taken to the dining antechamber where Cole, Nettle and one of Aldermen from the previous day were about to start their meal.

Cole introduced the Alderman as John Kendrick, Lord Mayor of London, and a member of one of the more moderate religious fringe groups. Luke opened the discussion simply, 'The Wolf must be destroyed. And I can tell you who he is and where he lives. Matthew Craven is The Wolf, not merely his spokesman. My troops will co-operate with you to achieve our mutual ends. I will not inform the Lord General in advance. This is what I propose.'

32

THE FOX WAS genuinely surprised at the extent of Luke's support. The Alderman present immediately issued the authorization to implement parts of the plan. Major Nettle was authorised to impress for naval service as many river boatmen that he could. Unspoken was the assumption that these would be the boatmen who remained loyal to The Wolf. Similarly building workers, and the unemployed associated with The Wolf would be conscripted for the imminent naval war with the Dutch. All English warships were desperately short of men. This action in which Luke's troops would assist could be depicted as a patriotic duty, given the recent decision of the Parliament to impress as a matter of urgency as many men as the fleet needed. This selective impressment would destroy much of The Wolf's popular support and force many workers back under the protection of The Fox as he could now offer exemption from conscription.

A more personal and provocative part of the attack on The Wolf was the impressment all the able-bodied male servants at Ketley Court. Nettle would use this weapon more generally against all known pockets of support for The Wolf. At five o'clock the next day the London militia surrounded the brethren conducting their service in The Falcon, and within the hour most of the male saints were aboard English men-of-war. Any male wearing a red ribbon was immediately conscripted. Recent migrants from the country who could not prove they had permission to leave their rural parishes were returned to their villages, cutting off any fresh supply of men for the Red Ribbons. These actions could be legally justified, and were unexceptional in terms of national security as the nation prepared for war.

Luke's next act defied a legal decision. Although he would use the rationale of national security his action exceeded his authority as a regimental commander. As such it could be accomplished in secret with his men disguised, or it could be done openly as if Luke had authorization from the top. Luke took the latter option. That evening with a full regiment of cavalry, and a large number of confiscated wagons and carts, Luke arrived at Reeves House. Luke hammered on the door and a frightened, lily-livered servant in a subservient crouch opened the door. 'Take me to Lady Cassandra!' demanded Luke, in his most imperious tone.

Cassandra and Rose were relieved to find that the commander of the troops and wagons that were pouring into the estate were under Luke's command. 'My lady and Mistress Chidlow, I am sorry to interrupt your evening. I have just received orders to immediately move the arsenal from your estate to the Tower of London. It is needed to provision our warships against the Dutch. The Ordnance requires all unallocated supplies available in the London area.' Cassandra was very amiable, and accepted the purported need for the transfer, adding that she was glad it would be gone. It was a temptation to all types of people to steal it, and put it to an evil purpose.

On the other hand Rose was visibly shaken, and did not hesitate to contradict her companion. 'You can't do it, Luke. The magistrates distinctly ordered that the arsenal must stay on this estate, although guarded by your men from any incident such as Cassandra fears. My new lawyer Mr. Matthew Craven re-iterated such a view only yesterday. It is private property and not subject to confiscation by the state.' Luke smiled and replied, 'Matthew may be correct in law. But in war, national security—in this case the need to supply our navy, and in so doing protect our commerce—overrides everything.'

Rose, flushed with anger, raised her voice, 'You cannot do this. I will go immediately to Mr. Craven and he will halt this act of theft.' 'Mistress Chidlow, you may go to Mr. Craven as soon as we finish here. You can accompany us with the arsenal as far as The Tower. From there I will personally escort you to Ketley Court.' Rose realised that it was too late. Once the arsenal was in The Tower Matthew could not get at it. She changed her mind. She would stay, but first thing in the morning she would get an urgent message to her lover.

Luke would have been alarmed if he had known of developments six weeks earlier.

SIX WEEKS EARLIER

Rose enjoyed her association with Cassandra, and her sojourn at Baker Grange. She was even more delighted when on the death of Sir Harcourt, Cassandra, as the not-very-grieving widow, invited her to share the expansive manor at Reeves House. The move suited her purposes, which with the death of Sir Harcourt had been seriously disrupted. Her mission on behalf of her patron would have to be curtailed, or at least modified. Yet she had her private agenda, the pursuit of which must be advanced. Her face must have exhibited signs of stress and despondency that was noticed by Cassandra. 'What ails you Rose?' 'With Robert's absence, and Sir Harcourt's death there are a few problems I need to sort out, and I have no male to confide in, and to help me execute what has to be done.' 'Stupid talk, my dear Rose! Women do not need men. I am a more reliable person to confide in, and assist you, than any male, and as effective when action is called for.' 'Dear Cassie I am well aware of that, but I do not wish to involve you in what may have to be done. You have been so generous towards me. I would not wish you to lose everything.'

Cassandra smiled, 'There is one man besotted with you and I know you and he have become close. He would do anything for you—young Rowland.' 'Yes, Rowland has already been useful, but he is a child. He does not have the stomach for what I may require of him. He is in quite a state over his St. Malo venture, and is terrified of any further interrogation by Colonel Tremayne.' Cassie did not comment, debating with herself what further advice she should offer her friend. Finally she suggested, 'There is one man who has the qualities you want—my lawyer, Matthew Craven.'

Rose had harboured a similar thought. Matthew, from casual observance, seemed to have the steel for what was required, but he was politically on the opposite side of the fence. She was French, Royalist and Catholic, whose answer to England's problems was very different, to that of a man known to belong to one of the more extreme Puritan sects. Matthew strongly supported the role of the army in reforming a republican England, and was a spokesman for the increasingly notorious Wolf. Matters were becoming urgent. Everyday she heard rumours of a potential army takeover. If only she and Matthew Craven had something in common that she could use to her advantage. She would invite him to dinner and explore possible areas of agreement.

Matthew was intrigued by Rose's invitation. He fully expected one from his client, the unpredictable Lady Cassandra. What did Rose Chidlow want? As she was carrying on some of Robert's activities she may have needed some legal advice. To seek it from his partner seemed appropriate. Besides, he might uncover more information about his enemies. He was surprised when he discovered that he was indeed the only guest, and Lady Cassandra and Sir Rowland Hille were not at home.

Matthew distrusted women.

The only woman in his life was his mother, who was determined that he should not become emotionally involved with any other female. Sexual encounters were another matter. God's saints could reflect their sanctity in sexual acts which brought them closer to God. Matthew was a confused character. Sexually he was experienced and confident in his ability to please women and God with the same act. Emotionally he was a child, under the powerful control of his mother.

Rose dressed to seduce. Matthew did not succumb. He was as ready to use Rose for his purposes, as she was to use him. After a long meal, in which quantities of wine were consumed, the couple found themselves on a padded bench. Rose gently took Matthew's hand and gave him a gentle kiss on the lips. Matthew was mellowing, and after returning her advances with increasing passion, he stood up and walked to the other side of the room.

'Mistress Chidlow, stop these silly games! Come straight to the point. You have not suddenly developed a desire for my body. My agents report that the boy Rowland has satisfied your frustration in that quarter since the disappearance of your husband. There is no need for this childish seduction. What do you want?'

Rose, a little annoyed by her lack of success, stared coldly at Matthew. 'Sir, I need your help. Although we support very different causes, I hope that there may be an area of common interest where we can help each other. I know you speak for The Wolf who opposes The Fox, whose supporters include the Dales, and the now Sir Grenville Reeves. I am sure The Wolf would be very pleased to obtain the arsenal stored on this estate.'

A delighted Matthew responded, 'Rose, I will help you achieve whatever mutual endeavour you have in mind, and I accept the arsenal as a token of your good faith.' Rose continued, 'There is one area that concerns me deeply, but I suspect you and I will not agree. I have a mission relating to the English army which tortured my first husband, but I am led to believe that you are a strong supporter of the army.' 'I support the army as a vehicle of reform, but I do not support particular officers. I have serious doubts about Oliver Cromwell. The army needs to be led by a more powerful advocate for reform such as Thomas Harrison.' Rose smiled. She could not believe her good fortune. The only area in which she and Matthew had a common interest was the one area she was concerned with —their antagonism towards Cromwell.

SIX WEEKS LATER

Matthew Craven was furious. His devoted boatmen had been pressed into the navy, while those that remained sought the protection of The Fox to escape a similar fate. The militia struck immediately and effectively against the Red Ribbons wherever they appeared. The army under Luke assisted the militia when needed. A shaken Rose Chidlow informed Matthew that the arsenal, which he had expected to seize that week, had been transferred to The Tower, by a cavalry regiment led by Tremayne.

Matthew was progressively stunned, infuriated and out for revenge. His enemies would pay for these outrages. And they would pay—now. He would implement his agreement with Rose Chidlow.

Two days later Luke, although initially unaware of its significance, was confronted by The Wolf's first victim. He was summoned to Reeves House where a distraught Lady Cassandra met him. She led him to the edge of a small lake where several of her servants had gathered. Lying on the broken reeds was the body of Sir Rowland Hille. A boat that was usually tied up to a small jetty was missing. One of servants suggested that Sir Rowland, who often went for a leisurely row on the lake had struck trouble, the boat overturned and he drowned.

Luke was not convinced. The death of Rowland was very convenient for Rose Chidlow. Rowland had been the weak link. Luke was convinced that on further interrogation he would have revealed all—to Rose's detriment. Now, the real details of the St. Malo enterprise would be difficult to uncover. Luke, joined by a company of his troops, searched the edge of the lake. After an hour one trooper waved frantically. On the far side of the lake from the jetty, there were keel marks of the missing boat. It had been dragged ashore and well up the embankment. Rowland had not been alone.

33

ROWLAND HAD GONE boating with another. His companion had rendered him unconscious and thrown him overboard to drown. The killer rowed to the other side of the lake, removed the boat from the water and had it taken away. This would fool people into believing the boat had sunk, drowning its only occupant. A more detailed examination of the body confirmed Rowland had been murdered. His skull had been crushed, and the fingers on both hands had been broken. Luke surmised that Rowland regained consciousness after he hit the water, and had tried to climb back into the boat. His assailant then smashed both hands forcing him to relinquish his hold.

Later Luke's men discovered wagon tracks leading from the edge of the lake to the highway. Andrew who was still with the body uttered a string of oaths. 'What's the problem ?' asked Luke. Andrew did not reply but extracted from Rowland's mouth a red ribbon. Luke exploded, 'His actual murderer might not be known, but the identity of the man who ordered this killing is clear—Matthew Craven. And he wants us to know that The Wolf is striking back.'

Luke was however slightly puzzled. Hille was not part of The Fox's network, and had done nothing to endanger Matthew Craven's interests. It did not take long for Luke to see a connection—and it alarmed him. Craven was assisting the one person who did have an interest in silencing Rowland, Rose Chidlow. Luke questioned the servants at Reeves House as to Rowland's movements before he went rowing. A drunken shepherd had seen him walking towards the lake with a man of dark appearance, leading a strange looking dog. The search for a dog proved fruitless, and the shepherd's story, giving his liking for hard drink and the tall tale, was discounted.

Luke had hardly completed the basic investigation at Reeves House when he was summoned to The Angel. The smell of gunpowder was overwhelming as he approached the inn. On entering the courtyard the devastation caused by a major explosion was apparent. The windows of the inn were shattered. The main door of the transport barn lay scattered across the yard, as did the remnants of one or more wagons. Several bodies or parts thereof were evident. Sam led Luke to something that he had covered with a cloth. It was the unmistakable head of Sir Grenville.

Witnesses to the event were plentiful. Three horsemen rode into the courtyard as Sir Grenville was inspecting a recently arrived wagon. One horseman incredibly somersaulted off the horse, did several cartwheels, and then placed, rather than threw, two grenades on the wagon. He completed a series of reverse somersaults and was back on his horse. His companions' accurate musket fire prevented any of the bystanders from removing the grenades from the wagon, or running away from the imminent explosion. A couple of men were shot trying to remove themselves from the danger zone. After the explosion the three horsemen wrapped a red ribbon around the only hitching rail that had not disintegrated, and rode away. They all wore masks and capes but Luke was certain that the somersaulting grenadier was Tommy Pitt the acrobat he had seen at the Bear Garden, and the accuracy of the marksmen suggested they were the same men who displayed their skills at the same venue—all servants of The Wolf.

Luke sent a trooper to apprise The Fox of The Wolf's murderous campaign of revenge, warning that everybody was at risk. He rode to Dale Court to inform Adam and Temperance. As he approached the house he met Adam who was returning from an inspection of his estate. He asked Luke, 'What has happened at the inn? One of my out-servants has just told me you sent a message for Temperance and I to go there immediately. Temperance left with your men, and I was just about to follow.' Luke's face fell.

'Heaven help us all. None of my men have been here.' Luke informed Adam of the deaths of Sir Rowland Hille and Sir Grenville Reeves by the hand of the Red Ribbons, and that they must assume that the same people had abducted Temperance. Adam shook uncontrollably.

After he regained his composure Adam rode into the city to report developments to his sister and Valentine. Harry challenged Luke's view that the same group of three or four men, on the orders from The Wolf, had carried out both murders, and the abduction of Temperance. 'Its too obvious. Others may be incriminating the innocent Red Ribbons. Anybody could push a red ribbon down a corpse's throat, or tie something red to a hitching post.'

Luke was unmoved, 'I am certain that Craven is responsible. The murderous campaign bears all the hallmarks of a wounded wolf. It is designed to force us to cease our campaign against him. I fear The Wolf has such a blood lust that he will continue his campaign of murder and mayhem, whatever we do. He will kill Temperance. We have provoked a monster. He feels no remorse for any of his actions, because, in his mind, he is doing God's will.'

Luke deployed the whole regiment to scour the countryside and to see if anyone had seen the victim and her abductors. He also alerted the militias around London. He did not believe that they would meet with any success. London was just too large. He then rode to Reeves House to ensure that Cassandra was taking the necessary precautions. A body of armed men met him. He was relieved. Cassandra had obviously taken steps to protect herself. Almost immediately he had second thoughts. Relief soured to apprehension. As he explained the purpose of his visit to the guards their commander appeared. He greeted Luke warmly. It was Brian Kendall. The Wolf's right hand man controlled Reeves House.

'What brings you here in force?' asked an alarmed Luke. 'To protect Mistress Chidlow and Lady Cassandra. Given the murder of Sir Rowland on this very estate, the massacre at The Angel, and the abduction of Mistress Dale, Matthew thought that the ladies of this household might be next. I am here to ensure their safety. But why are you here?' Luke sensed that he should be careful and not alarm the contingent of Red Ribbon soldiers. 'I am currently concentrating on the abduction of Temperance, and wished to question the women on what they know of her recent movements.'

Luke was admitted to a chamber where both women were busy working their embroidery. Rose was aloof and strangely smug. Cassie, usually buoyant and outgoing, seemed nervous and subdued, if not scared. Luke asked, 'Lady Cassandra I trust you have instructed Mr. Craven to represent you, should you be charged with Sir Grenville's murder.' Cassie went very pale, and looked as if she might faint. Luke did not hold back. 'After all, who is the only person who benefits from Sir Grenville's death?—yourself. As Harcourt's rightful heir he would have taken over Reeves House as soon as the legal formalities were completed, and probably evicted you immediately. You would have been forced to return to Baker Grange yet again.' Suddenly a smile appeared on Cassie's strained face. 'That Colonel is what I wish to do—immediately. Please escort me to Baker Grange this minute.' Rose inexplicably exploded, 'No, Cassie you will stay here. Matthew has sent his best men to protect us.'

Cassandra replied with passion bordering on hysteria, 'Matthew is only our lawyer, and has sent a dozen men. My brother Miles has a whole regiment of cavalry on his estate, and his house is full of my kinsmen. You are a great companion Rose, but in this crisis I need my family.' With that Cassie began to cry, and Rose alternated between cold fury, and clear indecision. Eventually she summoned Captain Kendall. She was determined to stop Cassie leaving.

Rose explained the situation to Brian, and emphasised that Matthew would not wish Cassie to leave. Brian diplomatically replied, 'Rose, I know you have Lady Cassandra's best interests at heart, as has Mr. Craven. But neither of you can restrain her. If I restrained Lady Cassandra, I would have to arrest Colonel Tremayne, as he appears willing to take her ladyship to her brother. If I detained Colonel Tremayne we would have a whole regiment of cavalry down on us. I am sure that Lady Cassandra will allow you to stay here during the present crisis, and my men and I will remain to protect you. Mr. Craven would see many advantages in you staying here alone.' He emphasised the word alone, which sent Luke's mind racing. What could Rose achieve at Reeves House more effectively without the presence of Cassandra? Rose was quietly seething.

Cassie did not farewell Rose. Cassie ran to the front door as Luke struggled to keep pace. There was a slight delay as she called for her favourite horse. For a mile or so she maintained a stony silence, despite Luke's attempts at conversation. Eventually she pulled into a small coppice and dismounted. She signalled for Luke to sit beside her on a fallen tree trunk. Slightly shaking and amid gentle sobs she thanked Luke for rescuing her. 'I took advantage of the turn in the conversation to make it very difficult for Kendall and Rose to detain me.' Luke replied, 'But, my Lady, I did not know you needed rescuing.'

'I wasn't sure myself until Rose made clear she would keep me there by force. That ungrateful French whore!' 'Why would Rose want to detain you in your own house?' 'Because over the last few weeks I have noticed things that are now beginning to make sense—and a horrible picture is beginning to emerge.'

Luke suggested, 'Let's detour to The Angel. Most of it is still standing, and you can tell me all you know in one of its warm and comfortable eating chambers.' After pork pies, mince tarts and several goblets of Bordeaux wine, colour returned to Cassie's cheeks. She began to display the aggressive buoyant personality for which she was notorious. 'Tell me what you would have done if Kendall had prevented me from leaving.' 'Absolutely nothing. One sword against Kendall's dozen men, who are all very efficient soldiers, would have achieved nothing. I would have waited. Kendall's only option was to kill us both, and I don't think that was part of his brief. It was lucky for us that Craven was not there. In his current mood that madman would have had no hesitation in executing both of us in the name of God.'

'I believe you. Matthew scares me. In the last week or so he has been at Reeves House most nights. He and Rose are lovers. I guessed as much and then one of my servants caught them together in bed. Then I remembered that Rose's bedroom was one which Harcourt had renovated in his last days to house a Catholic priest. There was a secret panel through which you then enter the tunnel that led to the chapel. I sent one of my servants to listen behind that panel whenever Rose and Matthew were together. It is only now that what he reported makes sense—and it is alarming.'

34

CASSIE CONTINUED, 'EVERYTHING did not fall into place until this morning. Matthew is obsessed with getting his revenge on The Fox and his supporters. Rose added four additional names to his list of victims—Rowland, her husband Robert, and yourself, although you had been targeted already by Matthew. Matthew readily accepted Rose's fourth nomination, someone they both referred to as The Deceiver. At first I thought that it was some sort of game. Then Rowland and Grenville died, and Temperance disappeared—names that the murderous couple had mentioned.'

'Why didn't you tell someone?' 'I had no opportunity and the events that convinced me that Rose and Matthew were behind the murders only dawned on me gradually. A few days ago Rose indicated that she was not to be disturbed. I was suspicious and sent my man to the tunnel to eavesdrop on her bedroom. He was lucky not to be caught. A man, who was not Craven used the tunnel to gain access to Rose's room, and the two discussed the imminent demise of their first victim. I now realise that their target was young Rowland. The strange man left with an even stranger dog. One of my shepherds, whose story was rubbished by Rose and ignored by you, reported he had seen Rowland with such a man and animal heading for the lake.

This morning after the troop had arrived under Kendall, my eavesdropping servant burst into my bedchamber unannounced, and told me the man whose voice he had heard in Rose's chamber was in the next room. It was Brian Kendall. This added to my state of terror. Your arrival at that very moment provided a window of opportunity that I had to take.' Luke hugged Cassie and explained, 'That strange dog was probably a monkey. Brian is a showman and he makes great military use of the acrobatic abilities, physical strength and expert marksmanship of his troupe.'

As Luke and Cassie approached Baker Grange four of his troopers led by Harry galloped to meet them. 'Thank God you are alive! I had men stationed along the road leading out of Reeves House as you ordered. Some time after you and Lady Cassandra left, three heavily armed and hooded horsemen, resembling the description of those that bombed the courtyard at The Angel, rode out in great haste. I imagine that they had orders to kill one, or both of you. Fortunately you took the diversion to The Angel of which they were ignorant. They continued at breakneck speed towards Baker Grange to stop you before you reached that destination. The sight of a large detachment of soldiers milling around the front gate of the manor sent them into reverse. Unfortunately they soon outran the troop I sent in pursuit of them.' Luke and Cassie were shaken. Cassie strongly proclaimed, 'That French bitch must have persuaded Kendall that Craven wanted us dead,' and with that she fainted, and would have fallen from her horse had Luke, riding close beside her, not held her upright.

Lady Cassandra quickly settled into her old apartments. She demanded that her brother as magistrate go to Reeves House in the morning with a troop of Luke's cavalry and free her servants, whom she believed Rose and Brian Kendall had confined to the estate.

Over supper Luke reviewed the day's futile search for Temperance. There was no way they could trace Temperance's movements and successfully mount a rescue. London was so large and Craven had so many contacts, she could be hidden anywhere. Andrew was more positive. 'I agree Luke; there is no way we can find Temperance by tracing her movements. But there is hope. Put yourself inside Matthew's mind. If you were a arrogant, God-driven, obsessed avenger where would you put Temperance, which would give you the most satisfaction, and be an affront to your enemies?' Harry answered with enthusiasm, 'A bawdy house. A blonde gentlewoman would bring a good price.'

'That doesn't help,' replied an annoyed Luke. 'There are hundreds, if not thousands of bawdy houses in London alone. We do not have the men nor the time to search a hundredth of them. Most keep a sharp lookout, and at any sign of approaching constables, or the military, Temperance would be moved on, or more likely killed. She might already be in the provinces, or on ship destined for the harems of the Ottoman Turk. We will never find her without striking a deal with Craven.'

Andrew continued in his optimistic vein, 'Luke, we can still raid the obvious—Matthew's chambers, Ketley Court, Reeves House and The Falcon. He is such a self-assured churl that he may even had Temperance imprisoned at Reeves House where Kendall and Mistress Chidlow could keep her confined. The very presence of Kendall there suggests something more is going on than simply protecting Rose Chidlow. If I were Matthew, I would lock her in that priest's hole.'

'This is so depressing. Let's have a drink!' The odd draught escalated rapidly into the many, and all three officers were drunk. This state accelerated Luke's depression, and in a slightly slurred manner he smashed his metallic tankard onto the table and uttered a plaintive oath. 'By the blood of Christ if I thought myself into the mind of that madman, and can justify anything in the name of Christ, I would have killed Temperance already. Even if her body is found, it would be impossible to trace her murder to Craven. He would be miles away from the scene. Given his ruthlessness in disposing of Rowland and Grenville another murder would cause him no concern.' After this drunken oration Luke slumped forward, and was sound asleep with his head resting on his arm. Andrew and Harry half dragged and half carried Luke to the room he now occupied at Baker Grange.

Within the hour the duty officer shook him awake. 'God's blood Captain, what is so important that you wake your commanding officer in the middle of the night. Has there been a revolution? Has the so-called King sailed up the Thames with a combined French, Spanish and Dutch fleet to overthrow our government?'

'No, sir but there is man here who has ridden through the night with an urgent message, from someone called The Fox.' 'Good God man, surely this could have waited until the morning?' 'The messenger is insistent that when you hear the reason for his night journey, you would understand the intrusion. Shall I bring him in?' Luke nodded, and a man wearing a long black cape, bearing a brace of pistols and carrying a heavy sword, with his large hat pulled down over his face, entered the room. 'My man what has led you to ride through the night on a highway infested with robbers and countless other criminal vermin?'

'My master pleads with you to accompany me immediately to The Golden Harp. Mistress Margaret Dale has disappeared.' Luke exploded into a cascade of oaths directed at Craven whom he immediately suspected of kidnapping Meg. The messenger continued, 'I have already informed her brother Mr. Adam Dale. He will wait at The Angel and the three of us can return to central London together.' 'Three men could still strike trouble. Seven of my troopers will accompany us,' added Luke.

It was well after midnight when the group reached Valentine Cole's inn. The Golden Harp was ablaze with every conceivable taper and candle. Cole led Adam and Luke into one of his antechambers, while the messenger and the troopers were offered tankards of freshly brewed ale in an adjoining room. Valentine immediately put Luke and Adam in the picture, 'I was out of town from very early this morning. Meg had dinner this afternoon with a friend who lives near Westminster Abbey. I returned just before dark and was alarmed to find she was not home. I sent a servant to the friend's place and he was informed that Meg had left at about three o'clock with every intention of returning directly here. I immediately had my men scour the area between the Abbey and The Golden Harp, and had them call on as many people that they could, seeking any sightings or news of her. Nothing was reported. At first light they will knock on every door in the liberty of Westminster. I have informed all the London based militias that I believe she is a victim of The Wolf.'

He then asked Adam if there was any news of Temperance. 'Luke has no leads but his men will raid the more obvious places where The Wolf could have hidden her, but none of us expect any great success. He feels that Temperance will only be found through a deal with The Wolf. It is not only Temperance that The Wolf has taken. My wife is with child.' The last phrase was blurted out and Adam began to sob.

Valentine put his arm around his distraught friend and quietly said, 'Gentlemen, thank you for riding through the night to be here. There is nothing we can do until first light. I have two of my most comfortable beds made up for you. You will only get a few hours of sleep, but you will be here to help me first thing in the morning.'

Next day Valentine alerted his whole network to the situation, and there was a buzz of activity as groups set out and returned on their expeditions of enquiry. As with Temperance, Meg had disappeared from the face of the earth. An air of negativity descended over the inn, and Adam and Valentine disappeared upstairs to Valentine's domestic quarters. After an hour both men returned, looking strained and edgy. Valentine approached Luke. 'You are right Colonel. Arrange a meeting with Craven! The Devil has won. Neither Adam nor I have any confidence in seeing our women folk again without some sort of deal with Craven. Let's hope he is willing to compromise, but from what you say he is more likely to screw every concession out of us.'

Luke solemnly agreed, 'The Wolf is so obsessed, that whatever concessions you make, he may still not return Meg and Temperance. You have to be realistic. Given his record they could already be dead. You must not surrender to this madman on the distant hope that he will spare your women folk. Meg would not want you to give into The Wolf just to save her life. The prime purpose of your meeting must be to bring The Wolf out into the open where we can take steps to eliminate him. Of course, if Meg and Temperance are still alive their rescue would become the first priority.'

Valentine felt like punching Luke. He did not know what Meg would have wanted. It was not the love of Luke's life that was being considered. He would surrender all to The Wolf, if it meant the return of Meg. He controlled his anger. 'Our mind is made up. We must talk to Craven immediately. Hopefully you have completely misinterpreted him. We may be able to divide London into spheres of influence. A monopoly in certain areas rather than competition may appeal to him,' concluded a naively optimistic Valentine.

Luke remained pessimistic but he would arrange a meeting between The Fox and The Wolf—if The Wolf could be found.

35

LUKE WAS JUST about to leave when Valentine was informed that there was a legal looking gentleman at the door who had news of Mistress Dale. Valentine tripped in his haste to welcome a small man carrying a large case, who immediately sought confirmation of Valentine's identity. The stranger handed him a sheet of paper while announcing, 'I am a lawyer for the keeper of Gatehouse Prison. He has a prisoner, Margaret Dale, who will starve to death unless her friends and relatives pay for the cost of her food and lodgings. Will you sign to that effect sir?'

Valentine was lost for words. His joy to find that Meg was still alive, and relatively safe, was countered by the fact that she was in prison. Luke spoke for the dumbstruck Valentine, 'Mr. Cole will sign the paper, but why is Mistress Dale a prisoner? With what is she charged?' The little man replied with some pomposity, 'With witchcraft, sir.' Luke could not hold back an involuntary laugh, 'That is ridiculous. Meg does not believe in that rubbish.'

'Nevertheless sir, the High Bailiff signed a warrant for her arrest on the basis of depositions presented by a reputable London lawyer. I suggest that you or your lawyers visit the High Constable of Westminster who will be dealing with the case before it goes before the magistrates. Witchcraft is a capital offence, punishable in England by public hanging. And from what I have read the evidence against her is overwhelming.'

Valentine regained his composure, signed the papers, farewelled the prison's lawyer, and instructed a servant to go immediately to Mr. Tournac's chambers and ask him to meet them within the hour at the rooms of the High Constable. Luke uttered a mild oath of surprise, 'I am amazed Valentine that your lawyer is a man who is a partner of, and mentor and

patron of our villainous enemy.' 'Emile and I go back a long way—much
further back than any association he might have developed with Matthew.
When I started out on my own, Emile was the only lawyer who would
accept me as a client. Both of us were new to the London environment.
He was a foreigner and I did not have the right gentry background for the
established attorneys of the day. He is a very fair and trusting man. I am
sure he is completely unaware of Craven's recent activities—but we will soon
put an end to his ignorance.'

As they waited in an out chamber of the High Constable, Valentine
brought Emile up to date. The aged lawyer appeared surprised, and
challenged the account he had been given. 'I am sorry Valentine, but I
cannot believe that young Matthew would behave in this manner. There
must be a more favourable explanation for his actions than that which
you have advanced. I have been as a father to him, and have never seen
signs of a violent disposition, although I am aware of his extreme religious
views. His domineering, simple minded and slightly unhinged mother
has unfortunately encouraged these obsessions. If the boy has fallen from
the paths of the rational, blame his mother, who feeds him with ideas of
grandeur, and his special role as God's chosen agent.'

The discourse was interrupted by the entry of the High Constable's
assistant who announced that his master would now speak with Mr.
Tournac. After a short meeting with the High Constable Emile returned
to Luke and Valentine. 'I have good and bad news. The good news is that
Meg will be bailed, as long as she remains located at The Golden Harp,
Dale Court or at The Angel, and that you sign sureties for several hundred
pounds that she will appear before the Westminster magistrates at their
summer session. The bad news is that evidence against her is compelling.
Matthew has brilliantly compiled the case. I know the boy's style and there
are a dozen depositions to support the charges.'

'What precisely are they?' asked Luke. Emile produced a paper on
which he had made a few notes, 'Matthew has cleverly turned the events
that you attribute to him onto Meg. She is accused of bewitching her
sister-in-law Temperance Dale to wander off to the detriment of her own
safety, and that of her unborn child, because Meg did not want the child
to inherit her brother's vast fortune; she used diabolical means to persuade
unnamed persons to place poisons in the drink of Colonel Luke Tremayne

as she believed he would inherit Adam's fortune, if no child was born to Temperance; that she so confused the mind of Sir Rowland Hille that he believed he could walk on water, and as a result of his befuddled thinking he drowned. This was to prevent him reclaiming the property that was now Adam's, but which had been unjustly sequestrated from his father by the government. Sir Rowland's appeal, with new support from General Cromwell was on the brink of success.'

'Surely most of this can be dismissed outright. The magistrates would need evidence.' 'That is the problem Luke. There are a dozen depositions from servants at The Angel and Dale Court, and labourers within St. Aiden, especially those that frequent Widow Ketley's alehouse that support these claims. Matthew had spent his money very effectively.' Luke turned to Valentine, 'Surely a man of your power can convince the magistrates that this is nonsense.' 'If the case was being heard by the magistrates of Middlesex, or those of the City of London, I could have it thrown out within the hour, but the law officers of Westminster are above reproach. I would find myself in prison if I tried to influence them. No, if needs be, I will assist Meg to disappear, forfeit my sureties, and join her outside of England. In the meantime I hope to reach an agreement with Matthew Craven. Have you arranged the meeting?'

Emile interrupted, 'Valentine, let me arrange the meeting. Colonel Tremayne is now too much an antagonist to persuade Matthew to attend. I am equally committed to both parties, and therefore suggest we should meet on neutral ground—in my chambers. There I will reveal information I have kept secret for three decades that may assist you all in finding reconciliation, and put an end to this destructive conflict.'

Luke and Valentine made their way back to The Golden Harp and as they entered the main door Luke was accosted by an agitated trooper. 'Colonel, I have an urgent message from Captain Halliwell.' Luke read the note with increasing alarm. 'What is it Luke? You look as if you have seen a ghost,' commented Valentine.' 'Worse than that. Our enemy has arranged a meeting with the Lord General himself. The day after next Major-General Harrison, Matthew Craven, and Brian Kendall will meet with him. We have provoked a resourceful enemy.'

'Jesu! Craven might use the meeting to assassinate the Lord General?' said a distressed Valentine. 'No, given the General's bodyguard and intensive searching for weapons on any visitor, only an assassin who is willing to die in the attempt would have any chance of success. I do not see God's agent on earth willing to make that extreme sacrifice, nor the ever practical Brian Kendall.'

Luke immediately sought an interview with Cromwell which took place the next day. Luke outlined the developments that attributed much of the unrest, malaise and murders to Matthew Craven. Cromwell raised his hand to stop Luke's impassioned diatribe.

'Tremayne, the last time you were here you were convinced that the cause of all our troubles was Major Nettle and the London militia. Now you accuse a radical sectarian lawyer of orchestrating a series of murders and abductions— the very lawyer who is meeting with me and General Harrison tomorrow to discuss the desires of the religious sectarians. Given the current failure of Parliament to reform they want the army to intervene. I understand that Mr. Matthew Craven is the leader of, and preacher to, one of the best attended congregations of like-minded saints.'

'That he is. I have heard him preach, and his message is revolutionary. He would overthrow not only the established political order, but would redistribute property from those that have it, to those he would call the saints. This man is a threat to the security of the government, and the established order. You cannot lend your name to any schemes of this madman.' 'Enough Luke, if you have evidence for these wild charges, what would you have me do?' 'Cancel the meeting and place Craven in The Tower.' Cromwell waved his hands in despair. 'Luke you are not in Ireland. The army cannot go around arresting English citizens on the flimsiest of evidence.' 'In that case let me attend the meeting as your aide.' 'No you are so clearly biased against Craven that your presence would give him the impression that I am not receptive to his views. Frankly I find your claims hard to believe. My own secretary has given me a very favourable picture of the man to that which you advance. It was Scroggs who arranged the meeting.'

'That sir is another serious problem. Zephaniah Scroggs is a member of Craven's extremist congregation and the man who passed on information that I believe led to the two attempts on my life. You might be his next victim.'

Cromwell was initially stunned but recovered immediately. 'Your assumption that Scroggs is a threat to me rests on the yet to be proved premises that Matthew Craven is a danger to law and order, and the security of the state; and that Scroggs's information led to the attack on you.' The general paced up and down the chamber as he carefully weighed his options. Eventually he came to a decision.

'Luke you have never let me down. You are an able agent. I will compromise. You shall command my bodyguard for that meeting, and after the visitors have been admitted to my chamber you can stand outside the door where every word that is said in here can be overheard. That is why the door is wide open now, and no one is within hearing distance. I will send Scroggs on an immediate mission to Scotland that should keep him out of the way until the situation clarifies.'

Luke was still unhappy, but the next morning after the visitors had entered Cromwell's room he took up his position. He listened intently to the conversation emanating from behind the closed doors. Craven outlined the needs of the religious sectarians. He advocated the abolition of the compulsory tithe and the national church, and demanded law reform that would give the lesser sort equal access to the system. He railed against corrupt lawyers and a corrupt Parliament. He demanded that the army act immediately to rectify the situation. Luke smiled. The passion with which Matthew expressed his views would not impress the cold, sober and logical Lord General. Craven was overplaying his hand.

Cromwell' s response was cautious, 'Thank you Mr. Craven. I concur with many of those views, and my record over a decade is proof of my commitment to them. But what is it precisely that you wish the army to do?' Matthew seized the opportunity to continue his diatribe. 'The public is uneasy, and unless the army acts to remove the parliament, people may take it into their own hands. Or they may turn back to the King.' 'Mr. Craven, if the army were to dismiss the Parliament would not a new election return the same sort of people? And we would have done the nation no service.'

General Harrison intervened, 'As you know Mr. Craven there are many religious groups such as yours and mine, who see that the only hope for the country, and in preparation for the return of our Lord and saviour, is in an electorate restricted to the saints. I support army intervention to create a new government that will abide by Christ's law—a government that would take immediate steps to bring about Christ's kingdom on earth by dealing with those who falsely assume dominance over God's chosen.'

'I could not have put it better myself,' commented a jubilant Matthew. Cromwell, who was privately alarmed by Harrison's statement, added a note of caution. 'Thomas, you and Mr. Craven are aware that in the real world, while many of your views have wide support, many do not. Most of the officers of the army, on whom my power depends, are gentlemen or landowning yeomen. They will not readily support major changes to the structure of society. A New England, a New Jerusalem must be built around property not sainthood, but that is not to say that the saints can be denied whatever God has in mind for them. Gentlemen, I rest on God's providence. If it be God's will that there is a major role for the saints in the future of this country, it will happen.'

36

LUKE HAD TO smile. Cromwell had a reputation for combining contradictory ideas in the one sentence. Was he supporting a takeover by the saints or was he not? The speech clearly angered Matthew. The man's arrogance, and self-opinionated persona came to the fore as he launched into a direct attack on the Lord General. 'General Cromwell, at the moment the majority of saints see you as God's agent, destined to lead us into the New Jerusalem. But if you falter, if you fail to grasp God's intentions, then the saints would look for a new leader to steer the army on the path of reform. You, General Harrison seem much more aware of God's will than your leader.'

Harrison who had no personal desire to replace Oliver quickly retorted, 'General Cromwell has led the saints very skilfully. Any attempt to precipitate reform before either the people are ready for it, or the army is in a position to implement it successfully, will only alienate vast numbers of people. As Oliver says if it is God's will that we should take the lead in reforming this nation, it will be so.' Cromwell turned to Matthew Craven, 'And now sir on a practical level if we were to take the lead in reforming the nation what can you contribute to the cause? My agents tell me you control a large private army that could assist the national force achieve its ends.'

'Yes, general, I can rally large numbers of saints, and an efficient force of fighting men, mainly retired soldiers whose lack of pay make them willing participants. At the moment they maintain law and order in those parts of the city where the authority of the existing rulers has collapsed. Captain Kendall is the commander of these men, and an experienced officer who served under your former commander-in-chief, Sir Thomas

Fairfax.' Cromwell relieved the growing tension by chatting about Fairfax's achievements with Brian after which he brought the discussion to a rapid close.

Matthew, as he was leaving whispered to Cromwell, 'Remember if you falter, the Lord God will replace you.' Cromwell was still seething when ten minutes later Luke entered the room. 'That insidious prating puffed-up toad. The arrogance of the man to threaten the Lord General! He told me in essence that if I did not use the army to speed the pace of reform, God, in the form of his agent Craven, would replace me with Tom Harrison. I was almost convinced by the man until his own ego exposed his true colours. I see God's will very clearly. We must expunge those who would bring the true saints into disrepute. I want a meeting here tomorrow with the so-called Fox, Major Nettle and yourself.'

'Sir, I strongly advise against such a meeting. Craven is a dangerous and clever man. The normal procedures of the law, and even the extra-legal actions of the army may not contain him. Let me meet with The Fox and Major Nettle and deal with the problem. You must remain ignorant of our plans. Your reputation, and that of the army must be preserved. I will act, if necessary as a private individual.' Cromwell, after a long silence nodded his approval. Luke saluted and withdrew.

He returned to barracks clear as to what must be done. Craven must be attacked with every means available and Luke would act as a private avenger. Harry and Andrew insisted on joining him. Luke was reluctant to act outside the law and in ways that his General might not approve, but it was for the greater good—the protection of the Lord General, and the reform of the nation along sensible moderate lines. He would not tell Adam or Valentine of his precise intentions. Adam's concern for Temperance might lead him to oppose the extreme measures that Luke proposed to take.

A messenger arrived at the Baker Grange from Greenwich with an urgent dispatch for Colonel Tremayne. It read,

> *Dear Luke, I am still in English waters but with the escalation of hostilities between you and the Dutch I have received orders to sail to the Mediterranean. Before I leave I have information regarding your national security, and the issues that you are investigating. Meet me on board ship tomorrow at noon? One*

*of my boats will await you at Greenwater Stairs at eleven.
It will be quicker to use the receding tide than ride. Yours
Claude, Comte de Sauvel.*

After a quick trip down the Thames due to a very fast tide, Luke boarded
Le Soleil D'Or. A jovial Claude greeted him. 'Glad you could come.' He then
turned to a small man standing beside him. 'This is Monsieur Gentillot, the
French envoy in England. He now has permission to move about England
but he is having difficulty gaining access to your government, but hopes
that in return for the information he is about to impart, that you can at least
obtain an audience for him with General Cromwell.' Luke and the French
envoy nodded to each other, and then both sat on the quilted bench that
ran along the back of the cabin.

Gentillot spoke, 'Last week Captain Sauvel held a reception for the
French community of London. Among the guests were two persons well
known to you, an elderly lawyer Emile Tournac, and a woman who claims
to be his great niece, and who married a Robert Chidlow.' 'Mistress Chidlow
has indeed become even more important in my investigations than when I
last spoke to Captain Sauvel,' said Luke in anticipation.

'Colonel, your Mistress Chidlow is no such person. She is an obsessed
agent for certain interests in France that the government is not keen to
encourage. She is one of countless illegitimate children of Henri, Prince
of Conde, the father of the current prince. Her mother, to conceal her
pregnancy, was sent to the court of your Queen Henriette Marie where she
gave birth to Angelique.'

'Her father's high status far outweighed her illegitimacy and she was
married as a young teenager to a wealthy courtier and courageous soldier
Gabriel, Comte de Neuville. I saw her at court on a number of occasions
before my duties sent me to the provinces. During your civil war the Count
went to Ireland to assist the Royalists, was captured and cruelly tortured by
the English, and reduced to the status of a vegetable.'

Luke was astonished, 'By St George! I know the Comte de Neuville.
I fought against him in Ireland. The story that the English tortured him
is a lie put about by the Irish. He was a very effective soldier, and brought
order to the rabble that were the Irish Royalists. It was vital to English
interests to remove him. Rumours were sown amongst the Irish that the

Comte de Neuville was an agent for the English Parliament. It was the Irish who tortured him. It was I who organised his return to France, assisted by captured Royalist officers who obtained their freedom from us by taking part in this act of charity. It was a very sad story. I had no idea that Rose was the wife of that brave man.'

'Whatever the truth of the torture, Angelique believes it was done on the orders of Oliver Cromwell, and swore on the blessed milk of the Virgin that she would extract her revenge.' 'How did she get support from persons in high places to facilitate her mission?' 'When your Queen Henriette Marie arrived in France she set up her own court. Angelique's mother who had served the Queen a quarter of a century earlier, recommended her daughter as a lady-in-waiting to the exiled Queen. The Queen also harboured an obsessive hatred of Cromwell, whom she blamed personally for the execution of her husband. Angelique offered to come to England to assist French agents prevent Cromwell assuming power, by fomenting a French financed and equipped Royalist uprising. Sir Harcourt Reeves who had been converted to Catholicism, met the Queen in France, and became the centre of the plot. Henriette, despite her hatred of Cromwell knows nothing of Angelique's personal agenda to assassinate him.'

'What role does Emile Tournac play in this conspiracy? Why did he pass her off as a great niece?' 'Emile Tournac is an interesting figure. He too has royal connections. He was one of Henry IV's hundreds of illegitimate children. When his father became King many of these offspring fled the country fearing they might be eliminated as a threat to the stability of the Crown. However once a legitimate heir was sired the threat disappeared, and Tournac became a conduit for the French government. He was particularly close to Henriette Marie, his half sister, and to Louis XIII, his half brother. Tournac's intimate relationship with Henriette was used by her husband, your late King Charles, to transmit delicate material to France that he did not want to go astray through the formal channels.'

'Did Tournac know of Angelique's personal mission?' 'I don't know. He probably received a request from his half sister Henriette Marie to help out a fellow countrywoman who needed to find a home among the local power brokers in an area where a French funded insurrection was being launched. Ask Tournac how much he knew.'

Luke was delighted, 'This information is invaluable.' 'There is more colonel.' Gentillot continued, 'Knowing that the French government did not want any operations in England endangering its attempt to conduct cordial relations with your republic, I put a couple of men onto following Angelique to uncover any French nationals who might be involved. Simultaneously I sent a messenger to persuade the French government to curtail Henriette's activities, and to free Chidlow from his confinement in St. Malo. My agents reported to me that Angelique spends much time with a lawyer who has just built a large manor house on the south bank of the Thames, a Matthew Craven, Emile Tournac's new partner.'

Gentillot kept his best information until last. 'I almost forget one item of trivia which now appears crucial. At the reception, Angelique was overhead to say that she would be returning to France on the 5th of the month. And Sauvel has this morning been ordered to delay his departure until she is safely aboard *Le Soleil D'Or.*' 'So her powerful friends are protecting her to the end.' Gentillot simply smiled and turned away.

Luke returned to his barracks on a horse borrowed from the troops guarding Greenwich. Emile Tournac now appeared central to his investigation. Could he be the mastermind behind everything that had been happening? Maybe Matthew Craven and Rose, or rather Angelique, were simply his stooges. Was Tournac the puppet master, orchestrating a French inspired insurrection, and the assassination of Oliver Cromwell? He would look forward to the meeting arranged by Tournac between The Fox and The Wolf. It would be the time to confront the elderly lawyer.

Luke brought Andrew and Harry up to date and set out his plan of action to deal with Matthew Craven. They would implement it immediately following the meeting at Tournac's at which Luke, Adam, Valentine, Matthew and Brian Kendall would attend. If Luke emerged from that meeting wearing his hat they must act immediately. Disguised as porters wearing red ribbons and carrying long leather bags they took a second floor room at The Book and Quill. Their window overlooked the entrance to Tournac's chambers. They carefully uncovered their muskets and readied themselves to assassinate Matthew as soon as he left the meeting. If Luke emerged bare headed this action was to be suspended.

On his arrival for the meeting Luke noticed numerous barely concealed armed men surrounding the Tournac chambers. He hoped that Andrew and

Harry had noticed their enemies, and were adjusting their plans accordingly. He also hoped that Adam and Valentine had taken precautions to protect their own safety. Matthew would not behave like a gentleman. They could all be entering a fatal ambush. Luke himself was heavily armed both overtly, and with additional concealed weapons.

37

THE GATHERING SAT on the benches that lined three of the four sides of Tournac's room. They sat in silence until Emile spoke, 'Valentine asked for this meeting with you Matthew. He has a proposition. Although I do not believe all the stories about your activities I have enough concern to break a silence I have kept for over three decades. I hope it will change your attitude to the situation.'

Luke was immediately alert. What secret could possibly change Matthew's attitude to the current conflict?

Tournac continued, 'Margaret Dale, as a thirteen year old schoolgirl was raped by Harcourt Reeves. He could not marry her, because he had just married, and his new wife was pregnant.' Matthew was irritated, 'Old man, events of decades past have no bearing on my life and attitudes now. Being raped at thirteen does not excuse Mistress Margaret Dale of her current satanic practices.'

Luke put his arm on Valentine's shoulders to restrain him from attacking Matthew. Tournac was not flustered by Matthew's uncompromising position. 'Unfortunately lad the past has everything to do with you. As a result of the rape, Meg delivered twin boys. At the same time Harcourt's child by his wife was stillborn. Harcourt's father had agreed with the local landholders to maintain both children in return for no charges being laid against his son. When the heir to the Reeves estates was stillborn, the agreement was slightly altered; one of the boys would be accepted in place of the stillborn child. Grenville Reeves was the child of Harcourt and Meg Dale. Not knowing this— she never saw her babies—when Harcourt found it difficult to bring up the child a few years later, Meg offered to take him in.'

Tournac now had Matthew's attention. For the first time, other than in the darkness of the tunnel, Luke sensed his adversary was vulnerable. Emile continued. 'The other child was adopted out. Never knowing the real identity of the baby, it was taken in by Dominic Craven and his wife, formerly Mary Ketley.' Tournac rose from his chair, knelt in front of Matthew and took his hand, 'Matthew, your real mother is Meg Dale, the woman you accuse of witchcraft; Grenville Reeves whom Valentine claims you had murdered was your twin brother, Harcourt Reeves who you may or may not have killed was your real father, and Temperance who you are accused of abducting is your half-sister.'

Matthew's reaction surprised everybody. He was consumed by rage. He rose to his feet, pushed the kneeling old man away with such force that Tournac lay motionless on his back for several minutes. Matthew spat at the old man as he lay immobile and shouted, 'Lies, lies, lies. You have known me all my life. Why do you turn on me now? I looked on you as my father. How do you know these things?'

Assisted to his feet by Luke, Tournac answered, 'I was lawyer to the landowners who were party to the agreement. I received the regular payment from Harcourt's father, and later Harcourt himself which I transferred to your adoptive mother. That money paid for your education, and particularly your time at the Inns of Court. I took a special interest in your situation, as like you Matthew, I am a bastard, and I know the difficulties that situation can bring.'

This was Luke's chance to push Tournac on his background and affiliations, but he like everybody in the room was speechless. The old lawyer may have expected his revelations to shock Matthew into a spirit of reconciliation, or at least compromise. He had not thought that it was equally disconcerting to Adam and Valentine. They had known of the rape, and of the twins, but they had no idea of what had happened to the babies.

Valentine was distraught. The man he wanted to kill was his partner's child. Valentine had tears in his eyes, as he relived the events of three decades earlier when betrothed to young Meg Dale, he was told that he would never marry her. She had disgraced her family and was pregnant, and he was sent to London to make his own way in the world. Despite the veto of both families on a marriage between the two, the young lovers had remained in contact, and in recent times had lived for much of the year as man and wife.

It was Adam who spoke. 'Emile, given what you have just revealed Valentine needs to reconsider the proposition he was to put to Matthew. We should meet at another time.' Matthew had already stormed from the room catching Luke off guard. Luke quickly followed him out of the room but was delayed by a crowd of people jamming the stairwell. With his hat firmly on his head Luke finally reached the street but it was too late for Harry and Andrew to implement their plan. Matthew had faded into another group of supporters.

Luke joined his men in The Book and Quill and commented, 'I will explain what happened at the meeting as we ride to the General's apartment. I must speak with John Halliwell. Information I sent him yesterday suggests that an attempt will be made on Cromwell's life in the next few days. Given Matthew Craven's current mood, it will be sooner rather than later.'

Luke had alerted John Halliwell to the possibility of an imminent attempt on the general's life. Rose was to leave the country on the 5th, and it was currently the 2nd. An attempt could be made on any of the four days. Halliwell reported, 'Your information confirms evidence from my men. In addition to the formal bodyguard that group tightly around the general, we have outriders, front, back, left and right of the main cohort, who are often in civilian clothes. On two occasions last week when the general walked through St. James Park to the Parliament, the outriders well back from the main group reported that the same two men followed the general from his apartments to the Parliament.' 'When does the general walk to Parliament again?' 'Parliament meets on the 4th and 5th.' 'Then that narrows the possibilities; we can expect an attack on the general on one of those dates. Inform the general, and take steps to ensure his safety! I will act independently to achieve the same end.'

Luke's independent plan was simple. Eliminate Matthew before he could do more harm. The next few days were an absolute disaster. Matthew Craven could not be killed because he could not be found.

A raid on Ketley Court under the authority of the local magistrates on the off chance that they may find Temperance proved a complete failure. The manor house was deserted, apart from a couple of elderly servants, Mary Craven, and a dozen or so saints who were holding a prayer meeting for the safety of God's servant Matthew Craven. As this raid was a legal act, Luke did not proceed with his planned act of retaliation. Later he would fire the mansion, and if need be abduct Mary Craven.

His plan to stop Angelique also failed. She too had disappeared. Captain Kendall and she had left Reeves House on the 2nd. To Luke, this implied a major activity involving Angelique, Matthew and Brian. It must be the assassination of Oliver Cromwell.

Mid morning on the 4th, a troop of cavalry left Cromwell's apartments with the general walking in the centre of a close phalanx of troopers. All the outriders were in full uniform, and clearly visible to the public. As the group approached the centre of the park their attention was diverted by an incident in which a gentlewoman was being assaulted by a group of thugs. The woman fell to the ground, and the thugs began kicking her. Part of the general's cohort rode off after the now fleeing assailants. The main body, even more alert to trouble, eventually reached the woman, lying as dead on the edge of the pathway. Cromwell, being the only person not on horseback, bent over the woman to assess her condition, and to offer comfort, if she was still conscious. As he bent over the woman she pulled him towards her with one arm and with the other rammed a dagger into his chest. He rolled over and lay motionless.

At the same time a shot was fired which just missed the prone body of the general. Almost immediately it was followed by several shots. The spectators that had gathered to witness the commotion saw a man fall from a tree. Two men with smoking muskets rode up to the prone body of Oliver Cromwell. The newcomers were Luke and Andrew, who had just shot Brian Kendall out of the tree. Luke dismounted and went to comfort the stricken general. Luke was pleasantly surprised. A voice whispered, 'I am all right,' and the voice was not that of Oliver Cromwell. John Halliwell anticipated the next question, 'The general is still in his apartment. He will go to Parliament later.' Luke bent over the body of the impersonator, 'Remain dead. I will have you carried back to the general's apartment. Andrew, ride immediately to the general's rooms! Cromwell must not leave his apartment. The rumour that Cromwell is dead, or lies close to death, will bring his enemies out of the woodwork.' Luke congratulated John, and explained that it was imperative that everybody knew that an attempt had been made on Cromwell's life, and that it may have been successful.

He then approached the gentlewoman who thought she had fatally stabbed Oliver Cromwell. It was Rose, or rather Angelique, Comtesse de Neuville. Luke could not stomach the gloating grin and glow of satisfaction that emanated from this angelic assassin. He remained silent. Then he slapped her across the face, and ordered her taken to The Tower. Her whereabouts would remain a secret, and she would be dealt with permanently without bothering the legal system.

Luke reached Cromwell's private apartments. He outlined what had happened and that he would like the general to stay hidden for a day or so, and pretend that he was near death. The bodyguard would shortly return to the apartment with the body of his impersonator, who was not injured, as he wore considerable padding, and under it, rather than on top, a metal breastplate. The woman did not have the strength to press the dagger very far, and the impersonator had been briefed to collapse onto the ground, and feign death at the first contact.

Luke expressed his concern that some officers, encouraged by Matthew, would take advantage of the situation to replace Cromwell with Harrison. This fear was immediately justified. An emergency meeting of the Council of Officers was called for the next day to consider the situation. The Council of Officers was the body of the senior officers of the army who advised the government's Committee of the Army on all matters related to the army, including appointments. In reality it was only attended by officers serving in and around London. Luke acted quickly. He sent troopers to those garrisons that were within a day of London, requesting that their senior officers attend the meeting, as he believed there would be an attempted coup against General Cromwell. He sent others to the ships still in port, where many of the senior officers still held their military rank. He had to ensure that Cromwell's supporters were in the majority.

38

THE COUNCIL OF Officers met in the parish church of St Clement Dane. General Harrison chaired the meeting, although a group of recalcitrants, encouraged by Luke suggested that the meeting be postponed until General Lambert who was moving from Scotland to become commander-in-chief in Ireland, and who would be passing through London, could take the chair. Lambert had been informed, and Luke hoped that he would receive a reply that he could table demanding that the meeting be suspended until Lambert's arrival. As Luke had no letter, and Lambert was not present, Harrison was confirmed as chairman, and opened proceedings.

He asked Luke, as colonel of the regiment providing Cromwell's bodyguard, to report on the general's condition. As previously planned, Luke gave the impression that Cromwell's life was in the balance, but that a clearer picture would emerge shortly, as any change in the general's condition would be conveyed immediately to St Clement Dane. At once an officer who Luke knew belonged to one of the extreme religious groups, jumped to his feet. 'General Harrison, in this critical time when the Parliament increasingly refuses to listen to our voice, we cannot risk having a Lord General who is at best, incapacitated. The army must show decisive leadership now. As General Cromwell is unable to do this, I move that the Council recommend to the Committee for the Army that General Harrison be immediately appointed Lord General.'

There was uproar encouraged and led by Luke who then addressed the meeting. 'Gentlemen, I am surprised that my brother officer is so keen to dispense with the services of General Cromwell. Surely it would be more appropriate for us to recommend as a matter of urgency that General Cromwell's position be re-affirmed. That will recreate an atmosphere of stability that the rumours of his death have undermined. I propose that after confirming General Cromwell as the Lord General we appoint as his deputy a man who can act for Cromwell both personally and professionally, a man who is the Lord General's brother-in-law, and an officer who played a distinguished part in the Battle of Worcester, John Desborough.'

Luke's speech divided the meeting. A small group of sectarian officers were determined to use the opportunity to have Cromwell, whom they increasingly saw as lukewarm to their cause, replaced by a man who would introduce the rule of the saints, General Harrison. After a long rowdy debate the original motion to replace Cromwell with Harrison was finally put to the meeting.

The vote was overwhelming.

Luke breathed a sigh of relief. There were only seven ayes and over sixty nays. Luke then moved that John Desborough be empowered to act for Cromwell until he had recovered. Before the motion was put, as arranged, a messenger purporting to have come from Cromwell's sickbed arrived, and informed the gathering that the general had made a surprising recovery. He could carry out his duties as Lord General without the need of assistance. Luke withdrew the motion. Harrison closed the meeting.

The seven officers who had voted for Cromwell's removal would be dealt with over the following months during which time Luke would try to establish a connection between them and Matthew Craven.

But the urgent task was to find Matthew. Later that night three men rowed silently to Ketley Manor, dealt with the odd elderly servant who got in their way, abducted Mary Craven, and set the manor house alight. The blaze was seen across the river, and for many miles around. Sightseers packed the Thames in little boats or watched from the opposite shore. Three men, carrying a woman, who appeared to have fainted, explained they had rescued her from the flames. They rowed away without any interference.

Next day Luke explained to Valentine and Adam that the arson was designed to provoke Matthew, and bring him out into the open. The abduction of his adoptive mother was designed to prevent him harming Temperance, and to be a bargaining point in a mutual exchange. Luke suggested, 'Get the word around the grapevine. If Matthew wants to see his adoptive mother again, he should inform Emile Tournac where he is willing to meet Colonel Tremayne to discuss an exchange of the two women.'

Adam was delighted that Luke's abduction of Matthew's adoptive mother offered a promise of the return of Temperance and her unborn child—heir to Adam's vast empire. Luke and Valentine, aided by the London Militia and additional troops under Cromwell's command, as well as the civil authorities throughout the various London and Middlesex jurisdictions, combined to search for and arrest Matthew Craven on the charge of conspiracy to assassinate the Lord General.

Luke had his men placed, as unobtrusively as possible, around Emile's chambers, the charred Ketley Court, and The Falcon. There were others rowing casually around the southern bank of Thames in case Matthew should approach his destroyed home by boat. Luke was almost immediately distracted from these endeavours by news from The Tower. Angelique, Comtesse de Neuville had escaped.

Luke could not believe what he was told by one of his own men who had been seconded to The Tower, specifically to see that Angelique did not cause any trouble. The officer explained that while he was away having his meal, the officer deputising for him allowed an old man, who claimed to be the woman's father, and a younger woman who said she was her sister, to enter the prison cell with a meal for the prisoner. 'Not the old rope or implement hidden in the pie,' exclaimed an incredulous Luke. 'No sir, the food was thoroughly prodded and poked. There was nothing hidden in the food. The cell was securely locked after the relatives had entered it. I am afraid they employed an even simpler ploy. All three partook of the meal in the privacy and security of the locked cell. After the meal, the doors of the cell were unlocked, and the couple left. When I returned to duty I checked the cell, and immediately saw that the woman who remained there was not Angelique but a wench who later confessed to being her servant.'

Luke knew that Angelique was scheduled to leave England that day on *Le Soleil D'Or*. Unfortunately given the tides that he had noticed in riding to The Tower the ship had probably left. Nevertheless it was the only clue he had. He arrived at Greenwich, and to his delight *Le Soleil D'Or* was still in dock. Luke approached the local military guard and asked that they get a message urgently to the Captain enquiring if Angelique de Neuville was aboard. After a few minutes he received his reply in the person of Captain

Sauvel. The two men adjourned to the nearest tavern. Sauvel with a twinkle in his eye said, 'So you failed, my dear Colonel. Even with my help, and all the information you had, I thought you would have had Angelique locked away.' 'I did Claude—until this morning. She escaped from the Tower of London, using the most simple of devices. Is she on board?'

'Yes.' 'Can I see her?' 'To what end my friend? I have orders that as soon as the ship leaves English waters I am to arrest her, and hand her over to French authorities in Toulon. She will disappear. The French Government does not want her intrigues in England being made public, and your Charles II does not want any embarrassment associated with his mother's indiscretions.'

'Come on Claude; let me take her back to The Tower. She will be charged with the attempted murder of Lord General Oliver Cromwell.' ' So the general lives,' exclaimed Claude. 'Oliver Cromwell is hale and hearty,' replied Luke.

'Poor Angelique! She does not know this. By her demeanour she believes her assassination attempt was successful. She floats on a cloud of self-satisfaction. I will permit you to come on board and tell her the truth.' Claude had Luke surrender his arms before he boarded *Le Soleil D'Or*. Both men went to the captain's cabin, and Claude asked an officer to bring Angelique to his quarters. When she entered the cabin and saw Luke, she immediately shouted at the Captain in French, demanding that he protect her from the lies of English soldiers. Luke waited until the diatribe had finished, 'I must commend you and your accomplices in arranging your escape from the Tower, from which you would have been tried for the murder of ...' Angelique joyfully interrupted, 'Enough Colonel. Stop babbling! I don't care what happens to me. I have achieved my mission and sent that murdering deceiver to everlasting hell. My beloved husband, Gabriel, is avenged.'

Luke had no pity for this embittered woman. He enjoyed delivering what must have been an immense emotional blow, 'Unfortunately my lady Angelique your role as an angelic assassin has failed. Cromwell is alive and well. Even the man you attempted to stab to death, a man impersonating the general, is also unharmed.'

Rose fell to her knees, crossed herself several times and fainted—or feigned as much.

Sauvel had her placed on one of quilted benches that lined his cabin. Rose eventually revived. Luke did not relent, 'Countess I ask that you accompany me ashore, and stand trial. As Cromwell was never attacked, and the man you did stab was uninjured the charges against you would be reduced.' Angelique laughed, 'Why should I be so silly. I am safe here on French territory, and will soon to home.'

'You are naïve, countess,' pontificated Luke. 'You will never be safe on French soil. Do you think the French government or that of the English Royalists in exile will want you alive? You are now an embarrassment to them both.'

'That is enough Luke', announced a slightly annoyed Claude. 'You have told the countess that her mission failed. She is a French citizen, on French territory, and the French authorities will determine her future as they see fit. They do not need advice from an English republican officer. Take the woman away!' Angelique, Comtesse of Neuville left the cabin a broken woman. Luke thanked Claude, and disembarked.

On his way back to Baker Grange Luke considered the identity of Angelique's accomplices. Matthew was not in the habit of disguising himself, although he could probably call on dozens of older men to act for him. Luke arrived back at barracks hoping to receive reports from the dozens of men deployed at strategic sites where Matthew had been seen. One report caught his eye. There was considerable movement in and out of Tournac's chambers, and one soldier who had been deployed at both Tournacs and at Ketley Court recognised that some of the men he observed had been at both sites.

39

LUKE OBTAINED A warrant to search Tournac's chambers. He would do so with the utmost overkill possible. He took double the men he needed. Perhaps Emile Tournac had helped Angelique escape. But more important, Luke had reasoned that he was probably hiding Matthew Craven. With his mother abducted, his organization in tatters and his right hand man Brian Kendall dead, whom else could Matthew turn to? Luke's hunch paid off. Despite protests from Emile every inch of his premises was searched and in a concealed section of the cellar the soldiers discovered a quivering Matthew whose prolonged experience in the dark seemed to have unhinged him even further. Whether it was the news of his real identity, the abduction of his adoptive mother, the overall weight of his killings, the destruction of his empire or the failure of his aims in regard to the English army and its leadership, Matthew had turned into a whimpering idiot.

Luke was both furious and disappointed. He had looked forward to a final confrontation with the evil genius during which he would extract the maximum of revenge, and then finally dismiss the creature to hell. There was no satisfaction in confronting the quivering cretin who crouched in front of him. But Luke had to make one last attempt to find Temperance. He spoke quietly to a Matthew whose eyes were darting everywhere, and who had developed an annoying twitch, 'Matthew, your adoptive mother is safe, and I will return her to you in exchange for Temperance Dale and her unborn child.'

Matthew regained a moment of lucidity. 'Colonel your threat against the woman I have known all my life as my mother, does not worry me. You won't kill an innocent old lady. Even if you did, I would rejoice that mother has joined our Lord Jesus Christ, and awaits me in Paradise.' Luke asked again about Temperance, but Matthew had reverted to inane babbling. Luke walked behind him and fired his carbine into the back of The Wolf's head. He ordered his men to dump the almost headless body into the Thames. Luke thought this a fitting end for a man who at one stage controlled the river.

He then turned his attention to Emile. He excluded all his men from the room, except Andrew. The three men sat around the Emile's small table. Luke made the position clear from the beginning, 'Emile, when you leave this room you will do so as our prisoner, charged with conspiracy to murder the Lord General Cromwell, and to overthrow the government of this country in favour of the King. You had me fooled, old man. I was very slow in uncovering your role in this conspiracy.'

'I had the opposite view of you Colonel. From the very beginning your involvement was my major worry. Scroggs told Matthew of your planned intervention based at The Angel so I had the Red Ribbons place gunpowder at The Green Bottle. When that failed I ordered Angelique to get rid of you before you had begun your enquiries. Her servant, who couldn't tell damp hay from dry straw, lit the fire in The Angel's courtyard, and while you were dealing with it, Angelique poisoned your ale.'

'Your role Emile only became clear to me by logical deduction rather than evidence itself. As this case developed I seemed to be involved in several different conspiracies—the plot by landlords to support the Rump against the army, Harcourt Reeves's Royalist conspiracy backed by the French, Matthew Craven's desire to bring about the rule of the saints, and Rose Chidlow's vendetta against Cromwell. Then I asked myself the simple question, what if they were all linked? And then a second question came to me. Who would benefit from the destruction of London trade and the nation's economy by the destructive conflict between The Fox and The Wolf? It came to me slowly. I did not see it clearly until I was riding back from Greenwich yesterday as I pondered on the identity of the old man that had rescued Angelique. That common factor is you. And now we find The Wolf sheltering in your cellar.'

'Even though you are a republican churl I always liked you, Luke. I wish we had more of your sort on our side. I confess. I was not only the common factor in these adventures, dare I say it, I was the mastermind. Matthew didn't have the brains, was obsessed by his religious views and over controlled by his mother. He was a big disappointment to me. He thought increasingly he was God's agent with a mission to reform the world. As such he carried out unauthorised adventures which endangered the main mission. His beating up of a troop of cavalry, the murder of the innocent Levellers and the viciousness of his campaign against The Fox, did not have my approval. Finally offering you command of his private army when he thought Brian Kendall was dead was stupid. I hoped that by revealing his real identity I might have brought him back to earth, but sadly as you have seen, it reduced him to a babbling idiot.

You already know my background. I am of royal blood and I lived happily in England until a few years ago acting as an agent between the French government of my half brother, Louis XIII and more recently my nephew, Louis XIV: and my half sister, Henriette, Queen of England. Over the years I came to admire and respect her husband. Charles Stuart was a saintly man, generous, kind, and compassionate. He grieved nightly that his evil Parliament had brought England into a bloody civil war.'

'Enough of the history, why and when did you embark on this campaign? 'The murder of Charles due to the intense pressure from Oliver Cromwell convinced me that Cromwell must pay for his crimes, and if possible I should do everything to assist the return of young Charles to the throne. I organized the supply of arms to Sir Harcourt Reeves. I placed my partner Robert Chidlow in the employ of Oliver Cromwell, and had him recommend Zephaniah Scroggs as the general's secretary. When Henriette told me of the hatred Angelique had for Cromwell I brought her to the country. I suggested she go through a form of marriage with Chidlow to get her closer to Cromwell, and to be better placed to assist Sir Harcourt.'

'Your arrival should have made her access to the general even easier. You were a known confidante and personal agent of the general. One of Angelique's great failures was her lack of success in seducing you, and her subsequent inability to turn you into an unsuspecting agent of her mission. Given your reputation as a notorious womanizer I could never understand your reluctance to bed her. She was never quite able to use your connection to further her ends. Recently she confessed to me that she had never attempted to seduce you because she just did not like you. You represented everything she detested. Nevertheless you did seem to disconcert her, so I had to get Matthew to bring her to me so that I could help her refocus on her mission. I did not want her to confront you so soon after our talk. That is why I lied to you that she had returned to France.'

'She wasted her allure on boys like Sir Rowland and later the disturbed mother-boy who could not love. Poor Matthew, I blame myself for the battle to control London, and the almost laughable conflict between The Fox and The Wolf. As Valentine Cole was my client, I showed Matthew, as my legal partner, the network that The Fox had built up, and indicated how I thought Matthew could dismantle it. He could then take over a vast part of London's trade and crime. I hoped to use The Wolf's empire for my ends when the time was right. If I could have had Matthew and his religious extremists, with the help from the army, rise against the Rump at the same time that Sir Harcourt Reeves led a Royalist uprising on the edge of London, the republic would fall, and the young King return.'

'Unfortunately I underestimated Mary Craven's ability to keep Matthew devoted to his religious beliefs. In the end he put the aggrandisement of his criminal and business empire second to leading God's preparation for the New Jerusalem. Secondly I underestimated Robert Chidlow's ability to read returns and accounts. He was convinced that something was amiss in the accounts of Sir Harcourt. I could not risk exposure of the double accounting which hid the vast arsenal he was assembling. I fed Robert a lot of false information regarding The Fox and his network to make them appear corrupt. But unlike Matthew, I could never justify unnecessary killing.'

'I suggested that Harcourt invite Robert to Reeves House for a meeting. The French agents who were supposed to abduct him from there failed, and had to follow him back to The Angel and they grabbed him just before he visited Angelique. Robert was to be kept a prisoner in France until our enterprise was complete. I used a former English royalist client of mine, who was in exile in St. Malo, to take care of him. He believed he was acting on the direct orders of Henriette Marie.'

'I must also confess that I asked Angelique to remove young Hille. He knew too much, and could have revealed a lot about the planned Royalist uprising, especially given your reputation as an interrogator. He was getting cold feet and I felt that once you knew he was the man in St. Malo it was only a matter of time before he told you everything, which could have jeopardised our operation. The major blows to my plans for a Royalist insurrection was your discovery of the arsenal, and then the death of Sir Harcourt, who I understand was poisoned accidently by a loyal, but demented servant. It is sad that a plate of mushrooms, and Angelique and Matthew's personal agendas, will condemn England to years of republican rule, or even worse to a military dictatorship by Satan' s own agent Oliver Cromwell.'

Luke finally responded to Emile's confession. 'I share your concern about the future of England under a republic, and the current corrupt nature of the administration of law. Therefore I do not believe those killed as a result of your activities will get justice from the legal system. You will be spared the tediousness of a trial and the terror of a public execution.' Luke nodded to Andrew who moved behind the old Frenchman with the intention of breaking his neck with one extreme twist. They would then throw the body down the cellar stairs and announce to the outside world that Emile had slipped, and in the resultant fall had fatally broken his neck.

Such was not to be.

A dozen armed men bounded up the cellar stairs and flooded the room. Their leader directed his two pistols at Andrew while others targeted Luke. The commander of the intruders whom Luke recognised declared, 'Touch that old man and you are both dead. Colonel Tremayne, we do not want to harm you or your sergeant. You will come with us!' The English soldiers had their arms tied behind their backs and they were quickly and professionally disarmed. The grey cloaks that the intruders wore did not completely cover their unique uniforms—this was a unit of French marines.

Bundled down the stairs to the cellar Luke was surprised to find that the far end of it opened into a tunnel whose walls seeped a continuous stream of water. Luke feared that being so close to the river the roof and sides might collapse at any moment. Two marines aided the aging Emile while Luke and Andrew were placed in the middle of the group surrounded on all sides by their well-armed opponents. In no time they emerged from one of the many drains that led into the Thames. Anchored next to the drain's outlet were two boats which took them to *Le Soleil D'Or*. The marines led Emile Tournac away, while Luke and Andrew were taken to the captain.

Sauvel was apologetic. 'I am sorry Luke for my intrusion. I was just about to set sail with the Comtesse de Neuville aboard when I received direct orders from the King of France himself. Given Emile Tournac's lifetime of service to France, and his blood relationship to the King he is to end his days under house arrest somewhere in France, and not suffer the humiliation of what purports to be English justice— although my marine commander informs me that you were about to save him from that fate.'

EPILOGUE

LUKE AND ANDREW were put ashore just before *Le Soleil D'Or* left English waters. Three weeks later Luke delivered his final report to Cromwell. Plots against the army had been foiled. Intensive interrogation of former Red Ribbon adherents had substantiated that two of the officers that had moved against Cromwell at the meeting, had direct links with The Wolf and had augmented Brian Kendall's men with regular troops under their command. They were now languishing in The Tower. Matthew Craven's adoptive mother was released into the care of her religious brethren. Robert Chidlow returned to take over a large legal practice left leaderless by the death of Matthew and the flight of Emile. The Fox re-established his network, but in co-operation with the army, whose moderate reforms he was willing to accept and help implement. He and Meg Dale finally married. They purchased what was left of Ketley Court, and rebuilt themselves an even bigger manor house, which was mischievously named Fox House.

Temperance and her unborn child were never found.

After a year of grieving Adam married the widow, Lady Cassandra, ending the traditional feud between Adam, and Cassandra's brother, Miles Baker, whom Luke had cleared of any anti-army or subversive activity.

The Rump continued to resist reform. In April 1653 the politicians doublecrossed the army leadership regarding plans to call a new election. Cromwell used troops to close it down, and listening to General Harrison, replaced it with a body of saintly men nominated by the religious sects.

Within the year Cromwell dismissed this saintly assembly, as an unmitigated failure.